Commentaries on Bible book[s] [...] errors. They are either wonde[...] tively little contemporary app[...] and interesting, but sit fairly [...] Derek Tidball's book on Colossians helpfully avoids both these traps. Derek's clear, thoughtful and sensitive scholarship makes sure that we genuinely understand what Paul really meant to say to those early Christians in Colosse. Our understanding of the first century times and of this small church will be greatly enhanced by this book. However, Derek is unwilling to leave us in the first century. The book provides helpful illustration and application to real life today. I thoroughly recommend this book to all those who have a passion for God's Word, and an equal passion to see it lived out and applied in personal lives and churches everywhere.

Stephen Gaukroger, Gold Hill Baptist Church

Derek Tidball is Principal of London Bible College. Previously he has pastored Northchurch Baptist Church, Hertfordshire and Mutley Baptist Church, Plymouth. For Christian Focus he has also written *That's Just The Way It Is*, a study of the Old Testament book of Ecclesiastes. He is also the author of *Skilful Shepherds* (Apollos), *Discovering Leviticus* (Crossway) and *Introduction to the Sociology of the New Testament* (Paternoster).

The reality is Christ

The message of Colossians for today

Derek J. Tidball

Christian Focus

Christian Focus Publications publishes biblically-accurate books for adults and children. The books in the adult range are published in three imprints.

Christian Heritage contains classic writings from the past.

Christian Focus contains popular works including biographies, commentaries, doctrine, and Christian living.

Mentor focuses on books written at a level suitable for Bible College and seminary students, pastors, and others; the imprint includes commentaries, doctrinal studies, examination of current issues, and church history.

For a free catalogue of all our titles, please write to
Christian Focus Publications,
Geanies House, Fearn,
Ross-shire, IV20 1TW, Great Britain

For details of our titles visit us on our web site
http://www.christianfocus.com

ISBN 1 85792 491 6

© Derek Tidball
First published in 1999
by
Christian Focus Publications
Geanies House, Fearn,
Ross-shire, IV20 1TW, Great Britain

Cover design by Owen Daily

Printed and bound in Great Britain by
The Guernsey Press Co. Ltd., Guernsey, Channel Islands

Contents

Preface 7

Christ and the Christian Gospel

1. The church of Christ (Colossians 1:1-14) 11

2. The person of Christ (1:15-20) 35

3. The gospel of Christ (1:21-2:5) 57

Christ and Christian Experience

4. Fulness in Christ (2:6-15) 81

5. Falling from Christ (2:16-23) 105

6. Focused on Christ (3:1-11) 129

7. Living for Christ (3:12-17) 153

Christ and Christian Relationships

8. In the Family (3:18-21) 177

9. In the Community (3:22-4:6) 201

10. In the Church (4:7-18) 225

References 248

Preface

The message of Colossians is true for all time, but it is particularly apt for our time. Its three major themes make it so.

It speaks, first, of who Jesus is. The primary problem facing the church at Colosse was that their understanding of Jesus was muddled. Alternative religious options were being offered them which left a place for him but no longer worshipped him as God himself, born as a human and sufficient for all our needs. His majesty was being dethroned, his power questioned and his salvation challenged. The folk religion of the day was a kind of pick-and-mix religion which stressed religious experience and seekership. A little bit of this and a little bit of that type of religion led to Jesus being downgraded. Paul writes to set the record straight about Jesus and to remind them that he was pre-eminent. As God's unique Son he is the one in whom God's fulness dwells, who is supreme over every other power in the universe and who is an adequate and sufficient Saviour and Lord. In our own day, when religious pluralism is not just an observable fact but has been exalted to the status of a creed itself, we need the message of Colossians. Whether the challenge comes from inter-faith dialogue, from the religious seekership of New Agers or from the plain old-fashioned folk religion, we too live in a time when the person and status of Jesus is being devalued. So we need to be clear on what the apostolic faith taught about him.

The letter, secondly, speaks to the widespread quest for religious experience which we encounter both outside and within the church. People have become impatient with the institution of the church and yet still long to believe in something and to experience something beyond themselves which they can feel deep within themselves. It manifests itself in ways too numerous to mention. Within the church there is a yearning for intimacy with God and to know him in a 'felt' way. The quest is good but we need ways of knowing whether our search is in the right direction and an ability to tell when we have reached our destination. At Colosse all sorts of religious experiences were being offered, many of which seemed to promise satisfying solutions in the short term but many of which were fundamentally flawed. In the central section of his letter Paul spells out what it will mean to be those who have the fulness of Christ living within us.

The third area to which the letter turns is that of relationships. Modernity, and even more postmodernity, has created a culture of lonely and isolated individuals. We long for relationships, but don't understand how to form them and haven't been brought up to have the emotional equipment to sustain them satisfactorily when we do. The issues at Colosse were different. But still the message of the later part of the letter has much to teach us about how to form and nourish relationships and the difference Christ makes to our doing so.

The agenda of Colossians, then, is our contemporary agenda. In view of society's failure to find contemporary solutions to the questions posed and the churches' uncertainty in proclaiming its message, it is wise to go back and listen again to the original apostolic faith. We will find some true solutions here.

I have enjoyed teaching Colossians over the years in numerous situations, including the churches I have pastored at Northchurch and Mutley, Plymouth, as well as, most recently, Spring Harvest at Skegness. I was due to expound this letter to the Christian Pastors' Convention in Pakistan earlier this year, but sadly the visit was cancelled at the last moment because permission to use the venue was withdrawn by the Government. It was a vivid reminder of the difficulties under which much of the church worldwide lives and of the situation in which Paul was writing when he wrote to the Colossians.

My thanks are due to numerous people including my colleagues at London Bible College for their stimulus. Several of them would have a greater expertise to write a book on Colossians than I. As always, I am grateful to my loving and understanding wife and son. On this occasion I am particularly grateful to my friend Andy Partington. Andy read the whole manuscript, correcting my grammar and challenging my theology. I am grateful to God for him, especially in connection with this book, where the student at times corrected his teacher! He was right more often than I. Using words of Paul from the end of Colossians, I pray that he who is already a dear friend and faithful servant may go on to fulfil his ministry.

May this book above all lead to a firmer grasp of Christ; a deeper reverence for his person, a swifter obedience to his will, a greater experience of his fulness and a surer hold on his salvation. For he alone is the supreme one.

Derek J. Tidball

1

The Church of Christ

Colossians 1:1-14

[1]Paul, an apostle of Christ Jesus by the will of God, and Timothy our brother,

[2]To the holy and faithful brothers and sisters in Christ at Colosse:

Grace and peace to you from God our Father.

[3]We always thank God, the Father of our Lord Jesus Christ, when we pray for you, [4]because we have heard of your faith in Christ Jesus and of the love you have for all the saints – [5]the faith and love that spring from the hope that is stored up for you in heaven and that you have already heard about in the word of truth, the gospel [6]that has come to you. All over the world this gospel is bearing fruit and growing, just as it has been doing among you since the day you heard it and understood God's grace in all its truth. [7]You learned it from Epaphras, our dear fellow servant, who is a faithful minister of Christ on our behalf, [8]and who also told us of your love in the Spirit.

[9]For this reason, since the day we heard about you, we have not stopped praying for you and asking God to fill you with the knowledge of his will through all spiritual wisdom and under-standing. [10]And we pray this in order that you may live a life worthy of the Lord and may please him in every way: bearing fruit in every good work, growing in the knowledge of God, [11]being strengthened with all power according to his glorious might so that you may have great endurance and patience, and joyfully [12]giving thanks to the Father, who has qualified you to share in the inheritance of the saints in the kingdom of light. [13]For he has rescued us from the dominion of darkness and brought us into the kingdom of the Son he loves, [14]in whom we have redemption, the forgiveness of sins.

1. The greeting he sends (verses 1-2)

How Paul speaks of himself (v. 1)
How he speaks of the Colossians (v. 2)
How he greets them (v. 3)

2. The thanksgiving he offers (verses 3-8)

The fruitfulness of the gospel in Colosse (vv. 3-8)
The fruitfulness of the gospel in the world (v. 6)

3. The prayer he voices (verses 9-14)

That they might have knowledge (v. 9)
That they might be holy (v. 10)
That they might experience power (vv. 11-14)

On 18th November 1978, 913 people committed suicide in Jonestown, Guyana. Four years previously, Jim Jones, a boy preacher who became the pastor of the San Francisco People's Temple, had led his followers to Guyana with the vision of a new society, free from poverty and racial division; a society based on a new religion. It ended in tragedy. They felt threatened by the visit of a U. S. Congressman on an investigative mission and decided to end it all. 'If we can't live in peace,' they cried, 'then, let us die in peace.' Since then we have witnessed the equally tragic happenings of the Branch Davidian, the Solar Temple and the Heaven's Gate Cult of Los Angeles. The warning bells, rung so fiercely by many new religions, have gone unheeded. They have not served to quench the thirst for new religious movements, which seems as insatiable as ever. Around the world some ninety-six million people are estimated to adhere to new religions, many offering a new, improved version of Christianity.

And that's only the religions which people join. On top of these there are the religions people don't join – like New Age Religion. Not many people would claim to be fully committed New Agers, yet some ten million followers can be identified in the United States. It's a religion without a cult, without a priesthood and without a clear set of doctrines. At its heart lies a belief in the self and a conviction that people can be transformed by their own inner resources. As Shirley MacLaine puts it, 'If everyone was taught one basic spiritual law, your world would be a happier, healthier place, And that law is this: Everyone is God. Everyone.' Elsewhere she says, 'It all starts with self.'[1] New Age religion is a pick'n'mix religion. Without a coherent framework anything goes. A little bit of this and a little bit of that, mixed with a little bit of something else, and you can invent your own religious potion. A 1993 Gallup Survey found that while many retained some beliefs in traditional Christianity, 25% believed in reincarnation; 25% in the influence of astrology; 40% believed in a 'life force' and 13% in channelling. Some, no doubt, held on to these whilst trying to hold on to the historic Christian faith at the same time. This confusing picture is captured, for me, by the young man who said to Pastor Leith Anderson that he believed in the inerrancy of Scripture, Reformed theology and reincarnation. He liked the Bible, John Calvin and Shirley MacLaine. Any inconsistencies didn't bother him.[2]

Not too much has changed since the days when Paul wrote his letter to the Colossians. That little church faced the threat of the genuine Christian faith being supplanted by a new version of the faith: a version which was a syncretistic, mix'n'match religion with overtones of the astrological and the angelic. It was to combat this error that Paul wrote.

Reading the New Testament is often like listening to a telephone conversation. We only hear one side of what is being said. We can often guess fairly accurately what's being said on the other end from the comments we can hear at our end, especially if we know who the caller is. But we can never be 100% sure. In reading the book of Colossians we have to piece together the situation Paul is addressing and especially the heresy, that is, false teaching, he is countering. Though many things are clear, we cannot afford to be dogmatic about it. Scholars have pieced it together in all sorts of ways.[3] But from what Paul writes in chapter 2 (from 2:8, where the problem is first directly mentioned, to 2:23) some features of this new heretical religion emerges. I believe the best explanation, given recently by Clinton Arnold,[4] is that the danger was that the pure gospel of Jesus Christ was being contaminated by the local folk religion, much of it Jewish in origin, which was seeping into the Christian church.

It had these features to it:

■ It dealt with the fear which characterised people's lives. Their lives were precarious and uncertain and they believed that the power of magic would give them some security and control over the supernatural powers which were hostile to them.

■ The worship of angels was central to this folk religion. People believed that venerating these supernatural beings would afford them protection from harm. Angels were thought to be intermediaries between mankind and God.

- The citizens of Colosse had a special place in their popular religion for the Archangel Michael. He was believed to have once saved the city from destruction by diverting a torrential flood of water from their city.

- They boasted they had a spring where people could find healing if they called on God's name, using the Archangel as a mediator.

- Many of these features found expression among the Jews who lived in Colosse who were also concerned, in typical Jewish fashion, with observing special holy days and practising other ascetic habits.

Add all this to a belief in Jesus, and the faith of the Colossians was in danger of becoming a mishmash of inconsistencies. The resulting spirituality was one which devalued Jesus Christ. In effect, they were saying that he was not adequate to meet their needs, deal with their enemies or provide them with the security they needed. Jesus needed to be supported by the help of other intermediate beings and faith in him had to be supplemented by other religious practices.

Paul sees that such a view is not an improvement on the original gospel but a perversion of it. It is, in reality, no gospel at all because it belittles Christ and renders him an inadequate saviour. Paul wants them to understand their faith to the full and profit from all the benefits they could find in Jesus. So, he sets about explaining to the Colossians who Jesus is and what Jesus has done for them. It is a Christ-intoxicated letter. It claims that he is the supreme one (1:15); that the fulness of God himself is found in him (2:9); that he has triumphed over all principalities and powers (2:15); that reality is to be found in him and nowhere else (2:17); that he is seated on the throne at the right hand of God; and, that one day he will appear again in glory (3:1,4). Christ is woven closely into the fabric of the whole letter which was written so that believers might become mature in him (1:28).

But that's to jump ahead. Before he rhapsodises on who Jesus is (in 1:15-20), Paul has some other things to say, by way of introduction, to the church at Colosse. These follow the conventional patterns of letter writing in Paul's day, but they are far from ordinary. The opening verses introduce us to the church of Christ and underline for us how important the church is in the purposes and plan of God.

1. The greeting he sends (verses 1-2)

How he speaks of himself (v. 1)

It's important to realise that Paul had never visited the church at Colosse. It had probably been brought into being by the ministry of Epaphras (v. 7), possibly as an offshoot of Paul's missionary activity in nearby Ephesus. Acts 19:10 tells us that as a result of Paul's daily addresses in the lecture hall of Tyrannus 'all the Jews and Greeks who lived in the province of Asia heard the word of the Lord'. So that might well explain how the gospel reached Colosse.

The believers in Colosse would certainly have known of Paul even if they had not met him personally. But, since he is going to correct their false understanding of the gospel, it was reasonable that he should remind them of his authority for doing so. He doesn't write to them as a private individual to share his own opinion but as *an apostle of Christ Jesus by the will of God* to state the truth that God had made known. An apostle, in the original and limited sense being used here, was one who had seen the risen Lord, as Paul had done on the road to Damascus and who had received a commission from Jesus Christ himself to plant and establish the church.[5] Paul underlines his authority by saying that he was in this role *by the will of God*. It was not a human committee that put him forward as a spokesman, nor a church council that elected him to the position. His was a divine appointment. When he writes to the Galatians[6] he makes the same point even more forcefully, since they are in even greater danger of selling out to a false gospel and require even more urgent correction.

Postmodern days like our own find talk of truth and authority very uncomfortable. We prefer opinions, different viewpoints, alternative perspectives, individual experiences, and we dethrone authorities, in case they should exercise some power over us which oppresses and imprisons. Common sense suggests, however, that there is such a thing as truth and, when handled by competent authorities, that the truth sets people free. Christianity, as a revealed religion, is certainly not a matter of opinion. It is a faith where truth can be distinguished from falsehood and where true teachers need to be distinguished from false ones.

Paul sends this letter from prison (4:3, 18). Fortunately he is not alone. Later he will tell us more about those who are there with him, but right at the start he includes Timothy in his greeting. Timothy was Paul's son in the faith,[7] but here he is referred to as *our brother*. Although not an apostle, Timothy still has a significant role to play. His inclusion in this opening greeting has suggested to some that the letter was actually penned by him since Paul, in chains, may well not have been able to do so. If so, it would explain why although all the teaching in this letter is thoroughly characteristic of Paul, some of the vocabulary differs from his normal range of words. Maybe Paul did not so much dictate the letter to Timothy as talk it through with him and then Timothy wrote it using his own words. It's yet one more illustration of the importance of the body of Christ at work, to which the letter will allude later. Whichever way the letter was written, its truth is inspired and its message trustworthy.

How he speaks of the Colossians (v. 2)

For a church that's about to stray off course, he addresses them with remarkable respect. Criticising the church is common sport today. It is easy to be impatient with it and speak of nothing but its faults. The church at Colosse was far from perfect. Indeed, it was in great danger, but Paul still speaks to them with astonishing spiritual courtesy. He speaks first of their spiritual character. They are *holy* and *faithful*. In spite of all their imperfections and failings, from God's viewpoint they are set apart for him, which is what holiness means. It doesn't mean that they have achieved a certain level of saintliness, but that they are God's own people, dedicated to him and his service. They are marked men and women; marked out as his. Furthermore, they are *faithful*. That is, they are firmly committed believers and seeking to be loyal even if they are misguided about many things and not as secure in the understanding of their faith as they might think.

Next, Paul comments on their location: both spiritual and geographical. They live in two locations at once. Geographically they live *at Colosse* but spiritually they live *in Christ*. They are influenced and conditioned by so much that they pick up from their surroundings in Colosse. It is through living there and being exposed to the local folk religion that they have a problem. But their real environment, the one which should exercise the most formative influence on them, is Christ. He should encompass them. Living in him should be the most significant influence in their lives.

As Christians we are called to live in two locations at the same time. It's not so difficult to understand how this can be. It's not like some wealthy people who have a house in town during the week for business and a house in the country at the weekends. They don't live in the two places simultaneously; they're either living in the one or the other. Sadly, that's how many Christians seem to live. In the church, on Sundays, they're in Christ. But in the week, when they are in other company, they're very much in the world. That's not how it should be. We are called to live in Christ while we are living out our lives in the world. The better picture, to help us understand what it means to be *in Christ*, is to think of flying on an aeroplane. I've just come back from South Africa and spent a whole night 35,000 feet up in the air. That was my physical location. But, thankfully, whilst being 35,000 feet in the air I was also inside an aircraft. It was only because I was in the aircraft that I could be in the air. The aircraft was the more significant reality for me, enabling me to get off the ground and stay in the air, free from the effects the cold temperature and air pressure would have had on me if I had been outside it and not protected by it.

So Christ should be the sphere in which we live, even while

we live out our very ordinary lives in the towns and cities which we occupy on earth. It's obvious from this that being *in Christ* is no shallow catch-phrase referring merely to a cerebral belief in him. To be *in Christ* is to be in a living and real relationship with him, to enjoy an intimate companionship with him. It is to allow him to shape and sustain our lives in every way. So crucial is this phrase that Paul uses it eleven times in this letter,[8] not only in reference to Christians but also, as we shall see, in reference to creation itself.

Their earthly location was the little town of Colosse. Situated one hundred miles east of Ephesus in the Lycus Valley, it was in a mountainous and beautiful area. But, truth to tell, it had seen better days. The main trade artery which used to run through it had been diverted elsewhere, causing Colosse to decline in wealth and significance. It had been overtaken in importance by the nearby cities of Laodicea and Hierapolis. The people who lived there were a cosmopolitan bunch, made up of Gentiles and Jews. They mostly earned their living by growing crops, farming sheep and selling and dying wool. The members of the church, then, were ordinary believers, not budding Oxbridge theologians. We need to bear that in mind as we look at some of the great theological ideas which Paul expounds for them. These were doctrines that mattered to them as they dug their fields, tended their sheep and went to market. Here is teaching which was of spiritual and practical value for ordinary men and women and which was to have a life-changing effect on their daily lives.

How he greets them (v. 2)

He wishes them *grace* and *peace*. *Grace* is where he both begins and ends the letter (4:18). It speaks of God's favour towards men and women when they don't deserve it and takes us to the heart of the gospel. It is the word which captures what God has done for us in Christ. We who fall short of God's glory 'are justified freely by his grace through the redemption that came by Jesus Christ'.[9] And now we live moment by moment by God's grace. Philip Yancey points out how hard it is to find grace in our world:

From nursery school onwards we are taught how to succeed in the world of ungrace. The early bird gets the worm. No pain, no gain. There is no such thing as a free lunch. Demand your rights. Get what you pay for. I know these rules well because I live by them, I work for what I earn; I like to win; I insist on my rights; I want people to get what they deserve – nothing more, nothing less.[10]

He's right in his assessment. But the church is a community where grace should flow back and forth freely, for it is a community called into existence by grace. So Paul rightly makes it his first word of greeting to his fellow believers. How much we are tempted to put other things first and assume the answers lie elsewhere. But grace is all we really have to offer. Gordon MacDonald puts his finger on it when he says, 'The world can do almost anything as well or better than the church. You don't need to be a Christian to build houses, feed the hungry or heal the sick. There is only one thing the world cannot do. It cannot offer grace.'[11] So, let's boast about grace and live by grace.

Peace is equally one of the big and deep words of the faith and even more so when you understand its Jewish background. In using the word, Paul is not merely wishing them to know freedom from conflict, like that negotiated by a temporary but fragile peace treaty which leads to a neutral, limbo sort of existence. He's praying that they might experience positive well-being in their lives – a deep harmony between themselves and God, between themselves and others, and, between themselves and the world God has made.

Although he begins all his letters with this greeting,[12] this is no empty formality. Christian experience begins with grace, continues in grace and will climax in grace. Peace with God and his creation, including his human creation, is the great objective of grace. At Colosse they lack the full measure of both these qualities, as he will point out to them. They need both more grace and more peace than they have yet been capable of receiving and they would get them by trusting more fully in Jesus.

2. The thanksgiving he offers (verses 3-8)

After the opening greeting it was also usual for Paul to set out
some reasons why he is thankful for those to whom he is writing.
He is quite happy to omit any thanksgiving when the occasion
doesn't demand it, as in his letter to the Galatians. But here, though
he has never met the Colossian believers, he has heard enough to
offer thanks to God for them. He highlights two causes of
thanksgiving: the fruitfulness of the gospel among them and the
fruitfulness of the gospel in the world.

The fruitfulness of the gospel in Colosse (vv. 3-8)

How does Paul know that these people are genuinely Christian?
By the fruit of the gospel which is evident in their lives. 'Each
tree is recognised by its own fruit.'[13] The fruit of the gospel is
summed up in a familiar trio of virtues – faith, love and hope.
These are the hallmarks of the work of God in their lives.

Faith is not the woolly idea of wishful thinking which many
believe it to be. 'It's my faith that got me through that illness,'
people say to the minister visiting in hospital when they have no
active Christian belief. They mean they drew on their own inner
reserves and summoned up their own courage and believed that
something would bring them through. Such an attitude reminds
one of President Eisenhower's statement about America. 'Our
government,' he famously once said, 'makes no sense unless it is
founded on a deeply felt religious faith.' But then he added, 'And
I don't care what it is.' Genuine Christian faith is faith of a different
kind. It is *faith in Christ Jesus*, not in self, fate, religion or the
stars. The Colossians have looked to him for their salvation and
trusted in him to overcome their sin and defeat their enemies.

Faith speaks of the upward dimension of their belief. Love
speaks of the outward dimension of their belief. They demonstrate
a *love...for all the saints*. Paul is not thinking of an ordinary kind
of love when he writes of their love, but love of an extraordinary
kind. The word he uses for it is 'agape' love. Love that gives itself
beyond reason and calculation. It's not natural. It's faith in Jesus
that enables people to love like Jesus.[14] It frees them from being

preoccupied with their own concerns and problems and releases them to be concerned for others; to give themselves in the service of others instead of self. Paul seems to recognise how counter-cultural, how unnatural, such love is, since, in verse 8, he returns to it and says they have a *love in the Spirit*. It's evident he's saying that naturally they don't have the ability or the reason to love others in the way they do. Their love must have come from outside of themselves, from beyond their own resources, and to have been generated and sustained by the Holy Spirit, as all such agape love must.

The third aspect of the fruit of the gospel in their lives has a forward dimension to it. The faith and love which they have arises from *the hope that is stored up for you in heaven*. Paul frequently uses the trio of faith, hope and love in his writings, but he feels free to alter the order so that the one he really wants to emphasise comes last. It serves as the crown of the trio. Here the stress is on hope. The Colossian Christians must not give up or be side-tracked. They need to keep persevering in the faith they have learned.

Hope is often essential if we are to keep going. It differs from faith, as Jurgen Moltmann explains:

> ... faith believes God to be true, hope awaits the time when his truth shall be manifest; faith believes that he is our Father, hope anticipates that he will ever show himself to be a Father towards us; faith believes that eternal life has been given to us, hope anticipates that it will someday be revealed; faith is the foundation on which hope rests, hope nourishes and sustains faith. ... Without hope faith falls to pieces, becomes faint-hearted and ultimately a dead faith. It is through faith that man finds the path of true life, but it is only hope that keeps him on the path.[15]

Without the hope of graduating one day the student might throw in the towel and give up her studies. Without the hope of wearing a particular wedding dress one day, the bride might throw in the towel and give up her diet! Future goals, held out to us in the present as a promise to be realised in the future, often determine how we live. So it was with the Colossians. Their hope of heaven would keep them believing and keep them loving. Eugene Peterson

captures it so well, as he often does, in *The Message*.[16] Paul thanks
God for them because 'the lines of purpose in your lives never
grow slack, tightly tied as they are by your future in heaven, kept
taut by hope'.

To these three virtues, Paul adds two other great words of the
gospel. In verse 5 he talks of them hearing about the *word of truth*
and in verse 6 he talks about the Colossians understanding *God's
grace in all its truth*. Grace and truth characterised Jesus Christ,
and equally they characterise the good news preached about him.[17]
The gospel is about a grace to be received and a truth to be understood.

Paul tells them that they have understood it, and for that he is
thankful. But clearly they had not understood it perfectly. That's
why he needs to go over it more thoroughly for them again. Those
of us who are not very conversant with computers will understand
what's going on here. When some new programme arrives or I
want to do some new trick on my word processor, I call in our IT
manager and he shows me in his expert manner just what to do. A
few quick movements with his fingers and there it is. The goal is
accomplished. 'Did you follow me?' he asks. 'Yes,' I confidently
reply. 'You did this and then that and then this again and there it
is.' But when he's left and I try it on my own, it never seems to
work. I do exactly what I think he taught me, but there's usually
some vital step in the process I miss and it never seems to work. I
have to call him in again and get him to teach me, more slowly
this time, all over again. So it was with the Colossians. They had
learned and understood the gospel but they needed someone to go
over it again lest they should misunderstand it and fail to live by it.

The fruitfulness of the gospel in the world (v. 6)

What was happening in Colosse was no isolated incident. The
gospel was bearing fruit all over the world. If the Colossians were
ever tempted to think of themselves as a tiny and isolated
community or were ever tempted to give up because of the seeming
lack of success, then they should stand back and view things in a
much wider perspective. The story of the growth of the early church

is one of the most remarkable stories of all time. From being a movement associated with a handful of backwoods boys in Galilee, within decades it was being spoken of as a movement which turned the world upside down. Within centuries it brought about a radical transformation of the Roman Empire, leading to the abolition of slavery and the eradication of many other social evils. All that was in addition to the fruit it bore in the lives of countless individuals who found healing, peace, forgiveness, reconciled relationships and personal transformation through it. It would seem that the claim Paul was to make in 3:11 was justified. This gospel embraced people of all cultures and ethnic groups in one great international movement in which Christ was all and in all.

The statement that all over the world the gospel is bearing fruit and growing, remains as true now as when Paul first made it. Two things flow from it. First, the claim comes as an encouragement. In days when the western church is experiencing massive decline we need to look and see that the gospel is still making triumphant progress elsewhere. Currently, 53,000 people are being added to the church every day.[18] In Africa and Asia the church is growing by four per cent a year. 2,000 new churches are being opened every week.[19] Patrick Johnstone is right when he claims: *The Church is Bigger than You Think*.[20] Secondly, the claim comes as an incentive. If this is true, as it is, then surely we'll want to get involved in world mission and to participate as near to first hand as we can in the progress of the gospel. We won't want to be mere spectators. When Paul writes like this, it's obvious that he's sharing a passion with us, and not merely making a statistical observation. Here is a cause of excitement and of praise. Let's give thanks to God for its truth. Equally, here is a reason for action. Church growth matters. The spread of the church matters. So let's get involved.

He concludes his thanksgiving by turning his attention back to the Colossians (vv. 7, 8) and underlining, as we have seen, the supernatural origin of their love for one another. As he does so, he mentions Epaphras who was almost certainly one of their own number and had first brought the gospel to them. Paul will speak of him again at the end of the letter (4:12-13). But note what a commendation Paul gives him here. He is our *dear fellow-servant* and *a faithful minister of Christ*. Praise indeed. Epaphras serves as an example for all ministers of the gospel to imitate. All ministry should be marked by slavery (a total commitment to Jesus as Master), by teamwork (a total commitment to one another as disciples) and by faithfulness (a total commitment to the gospel as the answer).

3. The prayer he voices (verses 9-14)

The good for which Paul gives thanks is not the conclusion of the matter. Reflecting on how much good there is in the church at Colosse and how much growth there is in the church worldwide simply drives Paul to pray for yet more. His prayer for them, like all the prayers for the churches of the New Testament, is fascinating simply because it is so different from what we tend to pray. The concerns we voice in prayer are often very short-sighted and self-indulgent. In some churches, they don't know how to pray unless some are in hospital and then they'll put them on the prayer list. What we pray reveals a lot about us. The Spice Girls asked, 'Tell me what you want, what you really, really want?' We would have to admit that it's what we pray that often betrays what we really, really want. So, what was on Paul's agenda for the church? He prays for an increase in their knowledge, their holiness and their power.

He prays that they might have knowledge (v. 9)

As a school teacher, many years ago, I felt the urge to write on a number of end of year reports, 'If ignorance is bliss, your son is going to live a very happy life.' I could never understand why my headteacher was so reluctant to let me do so. Instead I had to write in that special code that all school reports adopt in the hope that parents would have the gift of interpretation! Spiritual ignorance is certainly not bliss. It is misery and disaster. It should never be a matter for pride or boasting, as some have made it in recent years. To do so is to think in an unbiblical way.

Knowledge is a vital ingredient of our spiritual development.

As John Stott puts it, 'The repetition of these words "knowledge," "wisdom", "discernment", and "understanding" (in Paul's prayers) is surely very striking. There can be no doubt that the apostle regarded these as the very foundation of the Christian life.'[21] But what sort of knowledge is it that Paul prays the Colossians might be filled with?

The focus of our knowledge is to be *his will*. We frequently think of the will of God as a question of finding out whether God wants us to buy a new car, move to a new district, find a new job, or marry a wife. But Don Carson is right in saying that often that's just another form of self-centredness, no matter how piously we dress it up.[22] It's really not about God's will but ours. When the Bible speaks about the will of God it has a much grander idea in mind. It is talking about what God has revealed to us about his plan of salvation as well as how he wants us to behave. The stress on his will places us in the inferior position and calls forth both our worship and our obedience to him as Lord. Psalm 143:10 picks up the moral and ethical dimensions of this: 'Teach me to do your will for you are my God.' As Carson so aptly warns, 'It is folly to pretend to seek God's will for your life, in terms of a marriage partner or some form of Christian vocation, where there is no deep desire to pursue God's will as he has already revealed it.'[23] How many try to do just that. They desperately want to know God's will about some purchase they want to make or some question of personal relationship while ignoring altogether what God has already said about covetousness, sexual purity, being unequally yoked, or a host of other things. So, for example, a believer prays as to whether it is right to marry a particular unbeliever when the Bible has already made it clear that this is not God's will. Or another believer prays whether it is God's will for them to divorce their partner who is also a Christian when God's hatred of divorce has already been made clear in Scripture. Guidance might come a little easier to some if we worked according to the agenda of God's revealed will rather than forcing our agenda on to him.

When Paul tells us more about the kind of knowledge he has in mind he shows that he thinks about it in a typically Jewish way.

Christians, he prays, will be filled with this knowledge *through all spiritual wisdom and understanding*. The knowledge he is concerned about is not the speculative, abstract and academic knowledge which characterises so much of the Western educational system, but a practical ability to think soundly with the result that we live wisely. How many clever people today live foolishly because they apply themselves to the wrong kind of knowledge. Paul's concern is for the kind of knowledge which Joshua was encouraged to pursue in Joshua 1:8. He was instructed to meditate on God's law 'so that you may be careful to do everything written in it', not so that he could go and tie the priests up in knots with esoteric intellectual discussion. It's the kind of knowledge demonstrated in the spirituality of the Psalms and in the everyday wisdom of the Proverbs.

One more detail about this knowledge deserves our attention. Twice Paul indicates that he is not praying for an increase merely in our natural capacity to know and to think. The knowledge he is concerned about is supplied by God. He asks God to *fill you* with this knowledge. Shortly afterwards, he speaks of wisdom and understanding as *spiritual*. We have great natural capacities which God placed within human beings at creation. But the capacities are marred and distorted by sin and as a result are not sufficient or trustworthy in and of themselves. Relying on human knowledge alone might well lead us to address the wrong question, start on the wrong premise and arrive at the wrong conclusion. That's why the source of our knowledge must be God himself, with the Holy Spirit as our teacher instructing us through minds which are both renewed by him and dedicated to him.

He prays that they might be holy (v. 10)

1 Thessalonians 4:3 says bluntly, 'It is God's will that you should be sanctified.' That's exactly what Paul has in mind here as he moves from praying that the Colossians might be filled with knowledge to praying that they might live lives which are *worthy of the Lord*. The society in which Paul lived was acutely conscious of questions of honour and shame. It was the basic value system

of virtually all societies in Paul's day. People would do all they could to avoid bringing shame on their families and would fight to defend their family's honour. If a member brought disgrace on the family they would merit punishment, disowning or worse. They were expected to live in a way which was worthy of the family name and which would augment its honour and reputation rather than cast any shadow or slur on it.

Given the rampant individualism of western society we find it hard to grasp how vital the connection is between the wider family or social unit and any individual member of it. Those from the Far East have no problems in understanding it. They still live, to a large extent, by this value system. This is why if, say, a student from Korea fails his examinations in a British University, it is extremely hard for him to return home without having recovered his honour in some way, for he has proved unworthy of the family name. For many Westerners, any such idea is just a vague memory from the past. We can recall headmasters berating their pupils in school assemblies because they had committed the heinous crime of eating fish and chips in the street, or some other such offence, while wearing their school uniform. In doing so, they were thought, in some unfathomable way, to have brought disgrace on the name of the school and been unworthy of its uniform.

So what Paul prays for is a very straightforward thing. He wants Christians to bring honour to the name of Jesus by the way they live; to be worthy of wearing the Christian uniform. Negatively, it meant they would avoid bringing shame on the name of Jesus. But Paul's concern is more positive than negative. He desires that they *please [God] in every way*. Note how comprehensive that desire is. There is no room for pleasing Jesus on some occasions but not others or in some ways but not others. The goal must be to please him *in every way*. It is a reminder of how comprehensively our lives will be affected if we pursue holiness. J. I. Packer has given one of the best summaries of what holiness is that I know. It picks up the inclusive nature of Paul's phrase *in every way*:

Holiness is a matter of both action and motivation, conduct and character, divine grace and human effort, obedience and creativity, submission and initiative, consecration to God and commitment to

people, self-discipline and self-giving, righteousness and love. It is
a matter of Spirit-led law-keeping, a walk, or course of life, in the
Spirit that displays the fruit of the Spirit. It is a matter of seeking to
imitate Jesus' way of behaving, through depending on Jesus for
deliverance from carnal self-absorption and for discernment of
spiritual needs and possibilities.

It is a matter of patient, persistent uprightness; of taking God's
side against sin in our own lives... and of single-minded,
wholehearted, free and glad concentration on the business of pleasing
God.[25]

How does holiness manifest itself? The New Testament plan
of holiness is anything but a scheme for precious piety which
demands withdrawal from the world. It is a practical, world-
engaging, other-directed, servant-hearted vision of action. The
holiness for which Paul prays will result in the Colossians *bearing
fruit in every good work*. Christians are called to good works,
even if they are not saved by them. As a Jew, Paul might primarily
have been thinking of the good works of alms-giving and offering
hospitality. As a follower of Jesus he might well have been thinking
on a broader scale of doing all that Jesus taught his disciples to do
in the Sermon on the Mount:[26] of being salt and light; of loving
our enemies; of not judging others and so on. His words echo
God's creation command to humanity to 'be fruitful and increase
in number; fill the earth and subdue it.'[27] The Christian is to hear
the re-creation command to be fruitful and fill the world with
good deeds.

Where does holiness lead? Holiness leads to believers *growing in the knowledge of God*. Obedience is the key. Obedience, of
a practical kind, will lead to a greater and greater knowledge of
God. He cannot be known where obedience does not exist.

Paul has already spoken, in verse 9, of the knowledge of God.
So why does he repeat himself so soon? Is he engaged in a circular
argument? No. This second mention of *the knowledge of God* is
far more comprehensive than the first. In verse 9 he was concerned
about the knowledge of God's will. Now he is concerned about a
knowledge of God himself; of his person, being, character and
ways as well as his wishes and his will. This is not a circular

argument but a spiral argument, for as he orbits back over the territory about the knowledge of God he does so on a higher plain altogether, encouraging his readers ever onwards and upwards. They are always to be making progress. They are never to be content with the status quo.

He prays that they might experience power (vv. 11-14)

It is a demanding vision which Paul sets before them, so it is no wonder that the third part of his prayer requests that they might be *strengthened with all power according to his glorious might*. None of this desired spiritual progress and spiritual impact is possible unless God gives the strength for it. It is beyond our own resources. It is, just as Jesus said. 'If you remain in me and I in you, you will bear much fruit; apart from me you can do nothing.'[28]

But his might is *glorious*. His might is the might of a Sovereign Creator, who brought the world into being out of nothing; of a miraculous Saviour, who brought his oppressed people out of Egypt; of a majestic deity, who showed himself in thunder and lightening at Sinai; of a triumphant life-giver, who brought Jesus back from the dead through the resurrection. We need have no fear that his resources will be inadequate. He can more than strengthen us for the task. We may be feeble and inadequate. But, no matter. He is not.

With such a bold assertion of the power of God, we expect Paul to go on to say that the Colossians should use this strength to conquer the world with the gospel or to live perpetually in the realm of the miraculous. But he doesn't. The purpose Paul has in mind seems at first sight to be something of an anti-climax. This glorious might is needed to enable the Colossians to *have great endurance and patience*. As Don Carson remarks, these 'are less than stellar qualities'.[29] Maybe. But Paul is realistic. What the Colossians need more than anything, given their situation, and what many of us need given our situation, is an ability to carry on. If there is a difference between the two words, endurance and patience, it is this: endurance is what we need in response to circumstances; patience is what we need in response to people.

These are active and affirmative qualities. Paul does not say 'grin and bear your situation'. He is not advocating weak resignation. That would be the message the Stoic philosophers preached, not the one the Christians would preach. He prays that they might have the stamina of a long-distance runner and keep racing towards the finishing tape. So much of what we do today is short-term. Our desire, which fits our instant world where MacDonaldization[30] with its emphasis on speed, simplicity and efficiency has triumphed, is often for immediate success. And when it doesn't come we give up. Paul's prayer is as relevant for the church today as it was for the Colossians.

This endurance and patience is to be accompanied by joy and thankfulness. He looks for attitude and gratitude. The attitude of joy underlines the fact that Paul is not inviting the Colossians to stoical resignation, but to active endeavour. The gratitude which is directed *to the Father* saves us from thinking the power which we experience is our own. It keeps us humble. If we succeed in persevering, gratitude will remind us that we endure because God has enabled us to do so.

As soon as Paul mentions joy and thankfulness his horizons begin to widen. The real cause of joy and of thanks is not their perseverance but God's salvation, which he spells out in verses 12-14. The real good news is about the inheritance God has prepared; the darkness he has defeated; the rule he has inaugurated; the redemption he has worked. The real good news is about *the Son he loves*. Despite his concern for their perseverance, these verses exude a confidence in the Colossians, but not a confidence based on their abilities or qualities but one based on the Son of God who loved them.

Eugene Peterson translates these words brilliantly, once again: 'We pray that you will have strength to stick it out over the long haul – not the grim strength of gritting your teeth but the glory-strength God gives. It is strength that endures the unendurable and spills over into joy, thanking the Father who makes us strong enough to take part in everything bright and beautiful that he has for us.'

So, Paul has introduced us to the church at Colosse, a church much like our own.

- He's told us about its character – holy, faithful and in Christ.
- He's told us about its strengths – faith, love and hope.
- He's told us about its needs – knowledge, holiness and power.

It is a church that has come into being because of the gospel. That's what has constituted it. It is a church he cares for deeply, though he has never met them. It is a church he writes about respectfully, even though it is far from perfect. If we love the gospel, we too should love the church. In days when it is so much subject to criticism, both on the inside and the out, we should learn to imitate Paul. Don't criticise! Be thankful. Be prayerful. Be confident, not because of the church's members but because of the church's gospel. Never lose sight of the big picture. Behind a feeble collection of fallible human beings there lies a mighty God who has rescued them from the dominion of darkness.

2

The Person of Christ
Colossians 1:15-20

[15]He is the image of the invisible God, the firstborn over all creation. [16]For by him all things were created: things in heaven and on earth, visible and invisible, whether thrones or powers or rulers or authorities; all things were created by him and for him. [17]He is before all things, and in him all things hold together. [18]And he is the head of the body, the church; he is the beginning and the firstborn from among the dead, so that in everything he might have the supremacy. [19]For God was pleased to have all his fullness dwell in him, [20]and through him to reconcile to himself all things, whether things on earth or things in heaven, by making peace through his blood, shed on the cross.

1. Christ and the God of creation (verse 15)

    The image of the invisible God
    The firstborn over all creation

2. Christ and the original creation (verses 16-17)

    He is its agent (v. 16)
    He is its goal (v. 16)
    He is its sustainer (v. 17)

3. Christ and the new creation (verse 18)

    He is its head
    He is its beginning
    He is its firstborn

4. Christ and the ultimate creation (verses 19-20)

    The person he is (v. 19)
    The plan he has (v. 20)
    The peace he achieves (v. 20)

We all have our heroes. They seem to grow larger with distance. They often don't seem that great while they are alive, even though we can acknowledge that they have achieved some great things. But after their death, the warts begin to disappear, the failures are forgotten, their ordinariness recedes and the criticisms diminish. They visibly grow in stature. That's certainly true of a man like Winston Churchill. Remembered, now, as the great victor of the Second World War, his many fiascoes, political, military and personal, are all but buried in a conspiracy of silence.

None of our hero-making, however, compares to the claims made by the early Christians about Jesus Christ. They began during his lifetime and continued apace after his death. Before long, without the benefit of any distance at all, the most fantastic claims were being made about the carpenter's son from Nazareth. Colossians 1:15-20 provides us with a concentrated statement of who the early Christians believed this Jesus to be. As they looked at him, they could not rest content until they had given him the highest status in the universe and attributed to him the greatest significance in the cosmos, past, present and future. The claims are such that some say they could not possibly be attached in any literal sense to the man from Nazareth. The New Testament scholar, James Dunn, for example, says that to do so would be 'to read imaginative metaphor in a pedantically literal way'.[1] Perhaps you find it so. But the language gives every indication of defying imagination and stretching faith as it attaches itself directly to the one who had lived among them as a human being some thirty odd years before. This is the Christ who is at the heart of Christianity. This is the one in whom Christians, then and now, believe.

The style and structure of these verses is poetic, suggesting that Paul may be using one of the hymns sung in the early church. Paul was probably quoting something with which they would have been familiar. Some say he added to it a bit to serve his own ends. A few even say that Paul himself composed it for the purpose of this letter or just got so caught up with his subject that his writing reaches great poetic heights, but that is doubtful. More likely, we have here an insight into a song which was already in existence in which the early Christians affirmed what they believed about

Christ. Note how full of doctrine it is, particularly in comparison with some of our more recent songs which concentrate so much on our own feelings. It is more like what we know as a creed. But it is doctrine on fire. It is a ringing declaration of the greatness of Christ. In Dermot McDonald's words, 'it is dogmatics born of doxology.'[2] This is not something to be recited matter-of-factly but something to be sung triumphantly. For, 'in a burst of confessional praise, it arches from the dawn of creation to the restoration of all things, and Jesus as the Son of God is dominant throughout.'[3]

What, then, does it state about Jesus? There are several ways in which the hymn may be analysed. We do so by looking at what is says about Christ and the God of creation (v. 15), the original creation (vv. 16-17), the renewed creation (v. 18) and the ultimate creation (vv. 19-20).

1. Christ and the God of Creation (verse 15)

The song begins, in the original, with the word *who*, and immediately tells us two remarkable characteristics about who Christ is before telling us anything about what Christ does.

He is the image of the invisible God

How can we know a God who cannot be seen? Where do we start looking? How do we know when we have found him? The claim here, as throughout the New Testament, is that he can be seen in Jesus Christ. What was invisible became visible in him. The God who cannot be seen in himself can be seen in his Son. As John's Gospel puts it, 'No-one has ever seen God but the only Son, he has made him known.'[4]

Men and women are made in the image of God,[5] but Jesus Christ *is the image of the invisible God*. We need to be careful using the word *image* for it tends to mean something looser to us than it does here. To us an image resembles something else. It is a representation of something, like a son resembling his father or a rubber stamp leaving its inked impression on a piece of paper. We are aware that the image is different from the real thing. Often it is a poor reproduction of the original. The likeness is not too exact. 'We can just make out the image,' we say. Idols were images of this kind. They were very poor, smudged images of the one who really existed. In fact, their representation of God was usually so distorted that it was difficult to recognise him in them.

The Greek word that is translated 'image' is 'icon' and means an exact representation. It is like some of the new superb photocopiers that pick up every mark of your original, including those which you did not know were there because they were invisible to the naked eye! Except, even that illustration falls short, since this image is a living, dynamic one, not a static reproduction of something flat. Jesus is the exact reflection or representation of God. He is the perfect likeness of God. There is nothing of God that we need to know that we cannot see in him.

The firstborn over all creation

The second characteristic to which the hymn draws attention in describing Jesus Christ is that he is the *firstborn over all creation*. Again, the English translation is likely to mislead us unless we are careful. We are likely to think that *firstborn* means the first in time, the first in a line which many others will join. If this were so, then Paul would be talking of Jesus as one who was created by God, prior to the rest of us; that he's at the head of the queue which we joined when we were born. But nothing could be further from his intention.

The NIV hints that such an understanding would be wrong. Christ is not the firstborn in all creation but *over all creation*. The claim is not that he is the first created being. Indeed, he stands over against creation for, as we shall shortly learn, he is the one who existed prior to it all and brought it into existence. Verse 17 makes that clear: *He is before all things*. He is the pre-existent one who had no origin in time and did not come into being when born in Bethlehem. To put it the way John does, 'In the beginning was the Word. ... He was with God in the beginning.'[6]

So what does the word *firstborn* mean? It is being used here in the sense of talking about the firstborn in a family who has the place of honour, enjoys a very special relationship with the father and assumes the right of inheritance.[7] To talk of Jesus as *the firstborn* is to credit him with the highest rank within the family and the place of special affection. Psalm 89:26-28 captures what it means when it speaks of David's relationship with God. 'He will call out to me, "You are my Father, my God, the Rock my Saviour." I will also appoint him my firstborn, the most exalted of the kings of the earth. I will maintain my love to him for ever, and my covenant with him will never fail.' Jesus, then, has the primacy over all creation.

The words *image* and *firstborn*, used here, have not been plucked out of the air. They were special words in the wisdom literature of Judaism. In this literature 'wisdom' is personified, called 'the image of God's goodness' and given a significant role in the creation of the world. Something of the flavour of this teaching can be found in the Bible, in Proverbs 8. There, in verses 22-23, wisdom speaks of being brought forth 'as the first of his works, before his deeds of old; I was appointed from eternity, from the beginning, before the world began.' This hymn clearly asserts that Christ is the fulfilment of all that can be found in these passages about wisdom. What wisdom was, Christ is – and more.

But what is claimed of Christ goes far beyond anything claimed for wisdom. He is much greater than the mere fulfilment of the idea. He exceeds it. Wisdom, we are told, was present at creation, and even a 'master worker at his side', but not the agent and goal of creation in the sense that this hymn attributes those roles to Jesus. 'Wisdom is a personification not a person; a means not an end.'[8]

Perhaps Paul is using some of the ideas which were popular in his time as a means of communicating the truth about Jesus to the Colossians. It would be surprising if he was not. But if he is, it does not mean that that is where he got the idea from, or that he was restricted in what he said about Jesus by them. He exploits them and goes much further than they do in what he declares about Christ.

In fact, it is just as likely, that the background to these claims about Jesus lies not in the Wisdom literature but much earlier in

the Old Testament. The words recall the claims made about Adam
being created in the image of God. So, Paul may well be drawing
a parallel between the first Adam and Christ as the second Adam.
But even here, it has to be said that Christ surpasses the model of
the first Adam in every way.[9]

So, here are claims which outstrip those made of any other
human being, including Adam, or any other concept or idea, such
as that of wisdom. Jesus Christ is unique in his relation to God as
his perfect likeness and honoured Son. He is unique in his ability
to reveal God. He makes the invisible visible, the distant near,
and the unknowable known.

2. Christ and the original creation (verses 16-17)

From describing who Christ is and his role in making God known,
the hymn turns to look at the role of Christ in the creation of the
world. Once more, staggering claims are made for one who not long
before had been a human being and lived among them.

He is its agent (v. 16)

Proverbs makes it clear that wisdom assisted God in creation but
that it was always God who was the Creator. But here the claim
about Christ is greater. *By him all things were created.* The whole
vista of creation is in view. As Paul's eyes sweep the cosmos
there is nothing which is left outside of the creative power of Christ.
The smallest subatomic particle, the DNA helix, the great mountain
ranges of the Himalayas and the largest galaxy of stars came into
existence at his command and through his agency.

It is not the only time this claim is made about Jesus in the
New Testament. It parallels John's claim in the prologue to his
Gospel that 'through him all things were made; without him
nothing was made that has been made.'[10] Commenting on this
verse, Peter Lewis has pointed out the significance of it for our
own times:

> In the past two hundred years Western man, especially, has attempted
> to understand and explain his world in terms of an impersonal physics.

Consequently he has left himself in a cold mechanistic universe in which humanity has no ultimate or objective meaning or purpose. John here gives us the clue we threw away. He tells us the ultimate explanation of creation, the supreme fact of all created reality, is not a formula but a person: 'all things were made through him and without him was not anything made that was made.'[11]

It is at this point that some think, for stylistic reasons, that Paul has added to the original hymn the words *things in heaven and on earth, visible and invisible, whether thrones or powers or rulers or authorities*. No one can be sure. The words are, indeed, so applicable to the situation he is seeking to address at Colosse that it is easy to see why they conclude that he has inserted them just here. The Colossian believers were being encouraged by the advocates of the mix-and-match folk religion around them to attribute power to all sorts of angelic beings, spirit powers, principalities and authorities, in spite of their faith in Jesus Christ. Indeed, they reduced Jesus to the level of these other 'powers'. They said that he was one among them and not one above them. Consequently the Colossian believers were also being encouraged to appease these authorities through all sorts of religious rituals and by keeping all sorts of regulations, as we shall see when we study chapter 2.

In the face of this false teaching Paul wants to encourage them to have faith in Jesus Christ as the one who alone has authority and creative power. Not one of this hierarchy of heavenly powers has any power in comparison with Jesus. He is the one who determines whether things exist or not. So, he is superior to them all. Furthermore, his word is surer than theirs will ever be. So they should look only to him and not be distracted by these mini pretenders. They should listen only to him and be deaf to all other voices.

He is its goal (v. 16)

Bringing creation into existence out of nothing is one thing. But there is more. Creation exists, Paul tells us, not only *by him* but *for him*. He is not only its agent but its goal. The purpose of it is that it might bring him pleasure and do his bidding. He gives it meaning and provides it all with the purpose of its existence. Apart from him it is a meaningless, directionless void.

In recent days it has become common to talk about (and to criticise) the anthropic principle of the universe. Building on the observation that the creation of human life demanded some extraordinarily fine tuning when the 'big bang' occurred and the universe began, some have concluded that human life must be the reason and purpose of the universe's existence. Without such literally split-second timing at the point of origin the necessary conditions would not have been there to create human life. Stephen Hawking, who does not support the principle, expresses it like this. 'This means that the initial state of the universe must have been very carefully chosen indeed if the hot big bang model was correct right back to the beginning of time. It would be very difficult to explain why the universe should have begun in just this way, except as the act of a God who intended to create beings like us.'[12] This view of the purpose of creation is an advance on some of the older evolutionary views which suggested the universe was random and pointless in the extreme. It speaks of a purpose and of design. It recognises the extraordinary significance of human life as the climax of creation and suggests a creator who brought the universe into existence in just the right way to create life. But we must be wary of jumping out of the frying pan into the fire. The danger of this principle is that it makes human beings the centre of the universe and the reason for its existence. The Christian claim is that Jesus Christ is the centre of the universe and the reason for its existence. He is the goal of creation.

He is its sustainer (v. 17)

The third great claim about Christ and the present creation is that he not only brought it into existence and is the reason for its existence, but that he also sustains it. *And in him all things hold together*. Jesus Christ did not create the universe and then leave it to its own devices. He is not like the manufacturer of a washing machine who puts it together and then sells it on but really has no continuing interest in it – especially when it goes wrong. For the most part you don't need the manufacturer of your consumer goods to come and live with you to make them work. They're made to function without continuing dependence on their makers. Not so the cosmos. Its continuing existence, its present vitality and good order depends on Jesus. He remains involved in sustaining the creation. That is probably what Jesus was referring to when he said to the Jews who were criticising him for healing on the sabbath, 'My Father is always at work to this very day, and I, too, am working.'[13] If he were not, the universe would collapse in upon itself or spiral out of control away from itself. He was the Creator and is still creating the planet on which we live and the universe of which we are such a tiny part.

It is due to him that the stars remain in place and do not move about randomly and chaotically, as if the universe was a gigantic bumper-car ride at the cosmic fun-fair. It is due to him that planet earth remains the right distance from its sun, neither burning to a crisp as it strays nearer, nor freezing to a wasteland as it strays further from its source of light and life. It is due to him that the regularities of day and night can be trusted. It is due to him that stability marks the created order and not chaos. It would be a very haphazard, unpredictable, random and unstable place to live apart from him. He is the source of the very air we breathe and the life we have. 'For in him we live and move and have our being.'[14]

And he holds it all together, providing it with cohesion and preventing it from spiralling into disintegration. John Wesley remarked that, 'He is the cement as well as the support of the Universe.' While J. B. Lightfoot remarked that, 'He impresses upon creation that unity and solidarity which makes it a cosmos instead of a chaos.'[15]

The words *hold together* have the overtone of uniting that which is fragmented, and they may well anticipate the reconciling of all things to which Paul is going to come in verse 20. Already, in the way in which Christ providentially governs his universe, we have an early sign of the holding together of all things which will come at the end of time.

Contemporary cosmology has enriched our understanding of

Christ as a continuous Creator even more. 'We now know,' as Richard Bauckham points out, 'that nature itself has a history, very much longer and more dramatic than human history, extending from the "big bang" through the still continuing process of the expanding universe.... Nature is an unfinished process, continually productive of novelty.... God's creative activity must be a continuing activity in the whole process of nature, not only sustaining and renewing what already exists, but continually bringing new things into existence out of old.'[16] If this is so, then the role of Christ in sustaining our universe becomes even greater than Paul could have appreciated when he penned these words to the Colossian Christians.

The absolute superiority of Christ over creation is thus established. He is the reason for its existence in three senses: he brought it into being in the past; he is its purpose and goal; and, he continues to sustain it and give it existence in the present. The creation has no rationale outside of Christ.

It is in the light of verses like this that *An Evangelical Declaration on the Care of Creation* can 'urge individual Christians and churches to be centres of creation's care and renewal, both delighting in creation as God's gift, and enjoying it as God's provision, in ways which sustain and heal the damaged fabric of the creation which God has entrusted to us.'[17] The role of Christ in the original creation means that no Christian should be indifferent or hostile to that creation. We, of all people, should be the first to exercise care of it and to exercise wise (not exploitative) stewardship over it, since we are the ones who have made the earth's Creator the Lord of our lives. We should, then, be in the vanguard of moves which seek to reduce the pollution of the environment, to combat the degradation and deforestation of the land and the rape of the non-renewable resources of the earth. It is a standing rebuke to the church that others, especially those with New Age commitments, appear to have a more positive evaluation of creation than we have and so show a more passionate concern to preserve it. Since 'the earth is the Lord's, and everything in it,'[18] the Lord's people should value it highly.

3. Christ and the new creation (verse 18)

The original creation was soon marred and distorted by sin. Adam
and Eve chose to live independently of their Creator's instructions
so turning life into death, good into evil, and order into chaos.
This did not take God by surprise and so he put into action a plan,
which had been his 'before the creation of the world',[19] to create a
new humanity, called out from wider humanity, where his Lordship
would be a present and actual, not virtual, reality. The early
outworking of the plan can be seen in the call of Abraham and the
election of Israel. But it came to fulfilment in the creation of the
church of which Jesus Christ is the Head.

He is its head

Without giving up any of his role within the wider creation, Christ
brings into being a new creation. Three significant things are said
of this new creation. He is its Head. It is his body. And this body
is the church. The focus is on his headship. Paul had spoken of the
church as a body several times in his writings, most notably in
Romans 12:4-5 and 1 Corinthians 12:12-31. The focal point of
his teaching on those occasions had been on the organic nature of
the church, where each member was significant, and where each
member had a gift to offer to the wider body, and each member
was in a living and coherent relationship with other members of
the church. Michael Griffiths encapsulates the teaching in a
pungent illustration when he writes 'that a body is something quite
different from a pile of minced meat!'[20] But here there is a
development in Paul's thinking. His concern is not so much with
the nature of the body as the place of its head.

They did not view the head, in Paul's day, in quite the same
way in which we do today. Many of the physiological and
reasoning functions of the brain which we attribute to the head
they associated with the heart. But by referring to *the head* two
things would have been in mind. First, the head was the source
and origin of something. We still speak, for example, of the source
of a river as the head of a river. So, Jesus Christ is not only the

source of all creation but the source of the new creation. It is he who gives life to it. That leads naturally to the second aspect of *the head*.

In the Old Testament, the idea of headship involved the concepts of honour, primacy, authority and control. It was akin to being chief, leader or lord. So Christ not only brings the church into being but continues to have the place of supremacy within it and exercises control over it. The point is spot on. The Colossian Christians were being tempted to listen to other voices of authority and think that some aspects of their life and well-being might depend on keeping in favour with other authorities. Paul's none too subtle implication is that since Christ *is the head of the body, the church*, it is him and him alone that they should obey and look to for direction. Their continued existence depended on being in a vital relationship with him. 'As the body of Christ the church is vitalised by his abiding presence and his risen life.'[21]

The amazing thing is that Paul connects this great creative power of Christ with the little bunch of Christians who met in Colosse. They were *the body*, and *the church* of whom he speaks. The word 'church' has come to mean many different things to us – a building, an institution, a local church, a denomination, a universal church, the invisible church and the church triumphant. But its primary meaning in the New Testament was of a local congregation of believers meeting together. Occasionally it has a wider reference to a body which is universal, but when Paul wants to speak of more than one church he usually uses the plural, churches. Some would argue that in Colossians Paul has a concept of a heavenly church since believers are already 'raised with Christ' and seated where he is 'at the right hand of God.'[22] But even if the meaning here is that wide, Paul never loses sight of the earthly expression of the church in the local Christian community. So, however wide the reference might be, Paul is here making the staggering claim that this small, feeble and uncertain group of Christians in Colosse are none other than the creation of the Lord of creation and that they are ruled over by him. It was a breath-taking claim. That these people should be so special, that they should be part of God's rescue plan for creation, that they should be members of the new creation and herald the future of a totally renewed creation was nothing short of astonishing.

The church which looks to Jesus as its head is one he brought into being and is going to be vitalised by his presence, energised by his power, governed by his authority, used as his instrument and jealous of his honour.

He is its beginning

Just as Christ was the initiator of the physical creation, so Paul emphasises that Christ is the initiator of the new creation. It is already implicit in the idea of headship, but now he spells it out explicitly. He is its *beginning*. The word he uses is *arche* which draws attention not only to his priority in time but, again, to his supremacy and honour. Down the road in Ephesus they used the word as a title for their rulers. Here, says Paul, is the reason why Jesus Christ is worthy of the title of *head of the body*.

Without him the church would not have come into existence, the new humanity would not have started. Without him the original creation would continue to struggle against the forces of chaos which seek to destroy it. Without him we should still be awaiting a rescue plan. But through him a decisive change in the fortunes of the world has taken place. A new chapter has opened. Things are not the same as they were. Through him a new start has been made, a new order of creation has been ushered in, a new humanity is in the process of formation and a process has been triggered which will one day climax in the restoration of all things in him. So he is worthy, not only of the title of 'arche' but of the obedience and the adulation which goes with it.

He is its firstborn

Paul has already stated that Jesus Christ is *the firstborn over all creation* (verse 15). Now he asserts that Christ has the same status over the new creation since *he is...the firstborn from among the dead*. Just as he held the place of honour, like the older son in a family, over creation, so it was essential that he should occupy the same place of honour in the new creation. The new humanity is a community of the resurrection. It is the community of those who defeat death, the ultimate force of chaos and destruction in the original creation. As such it was appropriate that Jesus Christ should pioneer the way forward. Unless he has manifestly overcome the forces of death by meeting them head on and defeating them, how would we know that he was the one who was supreme in the universe? However good his teaching or effective his miracles, without the ultimate deed of power in the resurrection, would we not be left with a lingering doubt that death and not Christ had the last word? To establish his supremacy it was necessary that he should die and rise again in triumph over the grave.

As *the firstborn from among the dead*, Christ is the model of the resurrection which all believers will one day experience. But he is more than that. He is also the source of it. As Peter Lewis so rightly says, 'Our resurrections shall issue from the power of his original and definitive resurrection. Our life from the dead will be the outflow of his risen life as the Son of God in power. Our eternal place will be alongside our elder brother who is the author of the life we share.'[23]

Here is a second reason why Christ is *the head of the body, the church*. He is its head by virtue of being *its beginning*, but also by being its prototype for and source of resurrection. Together these claims lead Paul to the conclusion that the purpose of it all was *so that in everything he might have the supremacy*. There is nothing left outside of his control and nothing in which he comes second. Both in the creation of the world and the creation of the new humanity he is, in every possible way, the one who takes precedence over all and is unsurpassed. Preachers have often used the words *so that in everything he might have the supremacy* as an exhortation to Christians to yield their lives completely to Jesus Christ and give him the pre-eminence in everything. But, we need to note that the words are not an exhortation but an explanation; not an imperative but an indicative. By virtue of his role in creation and in recreation Christ has the supremacy already. He is not dependent on us to give it to him. This is first and foremost a statement about what he already is, not a statement about our need to make him something he is not (that is, supreme in our lives). Of course, it is a logical deduction to build the imperative (give him supremacy in our lives) on the indicative (he is supreme over all). But whether we yield him that supremacy or not makes no difference to the fact that the priority over all in the cosmos is already his and his by the right of who he is and what he has done. The Christian, then, is invited to submit to Christ in recognition of the facts rather than as a means to changing the situation.

4. Christ and the ultimate creation (verses 19-20)

The story of the work of Christ does not end with the establishment of a new humanity who are reconciled to God and who will one day enjoy unhindered relations with God in heaven while others suffer eternal torment in hell. That is far too individualistic a picture. Paul never narrows the focus of his vision to concentrate on a few elect people who enjoy the benefits of salvation for their own good irrespective of what happens to the rest of creation. His lens is always a wide angle lens which keeps the whole of creation in view. The new creation of the church is a step in the plan of God towards the renewal of *all things*. It is this third movement of creation to which Paul now comes as he reaches the climax of his hymn concerning Jesus Christ. Just as he was the Creator of the original earth and the Creator of the new humanity so, in due time, he will be the Creator of a new heaven and a new earth. You and I might wish to know the process by which this present creation will be restored and renewed. We might especially wish to know something of the timescale. But Paul's concern, in keeping with the situation he is seeking to correct in Colosse, is different from ours. He wants to remind them why Jesus Christ is qualified to bring about this ultimate form of creation. So, he starts this section by talking of:

The person he is (v. 19)

These verses about Christ conjure up the experience of climbing in a range of mountains. As we reach a peak, thinking it to be the very pinnacle of the range, a new vista opens before us, beckoning us to even higher summits, which had previously lain hidden. Many feel that the crown of the poem has been reached in verse 18, with the words, *so that in everything he might have the supremacy*. But Paul has more to say as he goes on to voice the further claim that God *was pleased to have all his fulness dwell in him*, that is, in Christ. The Colossian false teachers may well have spoken a lot about fulness. To them, the fulness of God was probably found only in the sum total of the powers and authorities, rulers and hierarchies, angels and spirits they feared and sought to appease, not in any one being or even one kind of being. They believed that Jesus was merely one among the motley bunch. To be sure, he'd make his contribution to the fulness of deity, but he did not possess it in himself. In strong disagreement Paul says that God had deliberately chosen to have his divine fulness embodied in Jesus. And this was no mere passing visit. He had moved in permanently. The 'totality of divine essence and power has taken up its residence in Christ. In other words, He is the one mediator between God and the world of mankind, and all the attributes and activities of God – His spirit, word, wisdom and glory – are displayed in Him.'[24] So the Christians need not live in fear of other powers or spirits who were supposed to possess some of the divine essence. Jesus was the sole appointed Mediator. It had been God's pleasure to choose him. And he was well equipped to sort out the antagonism between God and his creation and to bring about a complete reconciliation, since he did not possess a little of the divine power but all of it. Nothing further could be required.

It leads to the conclusion so succinctly expressed by Dermot McDonald:

> Jesus Christ is the ultimate. There is none before him, nought beyond him and nothing without him. Other than Jesus will not do; less than Jesus will not suit; more than Jesus is not possible. More than all in him we find. Everything of God is to be found in him and little of God is to be found apart from him.[25]

The plan he has (v 20)

And what does God want to do through this one who possesses his fulness? *To reconcile to himself all things, whether things on earth or things in heaven.* The panoramic view from this mountain top is magnificent in its extent. His purpose was not to reconcile a few Christians to himself. His purpose was nothing less than the reconciliation of the entire spectrum of creation itself. His goal is the renewal of not only planet earth but the entire cosmos.

The fall affected not only human beings but the whole of creation. The judgment which fell on Adam and Eve did not fall on them alone but on the serpent and the ground. The cursed ground would, henceforth, be the place of painful toil, where thorns and thistles would conspire against humanity and where food would only be produced through 'the sweat of your brow'.[26] John Milton imaginatively described the scene as the sentence was carried out on the earth:

> Some say he bid his angels turn askance
> The poles of Earth twice ten degrees and more
> From the sun's axle; they with labour pushed
> Oblique the centric globe;[27]

From that time, the harmony of the earth has been ruptured, its functioning distorted, its systems disrupted and its relationships split asunder. While the beauty and promise of the earth is apparent everywhere, so too is its fallenness. We see it in the savagery of raw nature as seen in the animal kingdom; the absurdity of floods that destroy whole communities while others burn in forest fires; the extremes of bitter winters which kill, jostling side by side with scorching temperatures which also claim their victims; the bad temperedness of the unannounced earthquake or of the sudden eruption of the volcano; the bizarre sight of some of the world struggling with the problem of obesity while much of it is condemned to famine.

The world is fallen indeed, 'subjected,' as Paul says to the Romans, 'to frustration, not by its own choice, but by the will of the one who subjected it...'. But then he adds, the subjection is 'in hope'. He compares the experience of the earth to that of a pregnant woman. The groaning of the world is like the groaning of labour pains.[28] The frustration and the pain are signs that this is not the final state but that new life is on its way. Now, to the Colossians, he reveals that God's plan is to overcome all its pain through the creative power of Jesus.

When my young son has his friends over to play, his bedroom easily descends into chaos. Tidiness rapidly becomes a thing of the past as cupboards are opened, drawers pulled out, boxes emptied and bed clothes turned into tents. Once his friends have gone, the job of clearing up begins, usually carried out by Mum or Dad. What a wonderful relief it is when the chaos is defeated and everything is put back in its rightful place once again. That's the picture of what Christ will one day do to our universe – put everything back in its rightful place in relation to the Creator.

It is often thought that this verse is commending some form of universalism, that is, a doctrine which states that it doesn't matter whether you believe in Jesus Christ as Saviour or not because everyone will be saved at the end. But it is quite wrong to draw this conclusion from these verses and even more so as the doctrine is flatly contradicted by other parts of Scripture. This verse is not about the salvation of men and women but the renewal and restoration of creation. Furthermore, they do not give us the fine detail as to what it means for *all things* to be reconciled to Christ. There is more than one way to bring about reconciliation. F. F. Bruce points out that 'peace may be freely accepted or it may be compulsorily imposed'.[29] It includes the idea of pacification. The key is that all will be subjugated to Christ and unable, any longer, to resist his will or his power. He will triumph over all that is wrong, and so reconcile things to his Father.

By his reference to *things on earth or things in heaven* Paul undoubtedly has the angels and principalities which seem so threatening to the Colossians in his sights. At the present time they may well be standing out against God but one day they, along with the totality of creation, will be brought into submission to him.

So, Paul sets out a vision of a renewed creation. It is not one, as Richard Bauckham points out, which merely puts things back as they were at the beginning. It is better than that. 'Salvation is both restorative (repairing the damage done by sin) and progressive (moving the work on to its completion).'[30] The new heaven and the new earth will be new in nature and quality and be the very climax of God's purposes and plan for creation. It will be the home where righteousness dwells and where sin will not be able to enter. And where, at long last, men and women will be at home with their Creator.

The peace he achieves (v. 20)

This new creation may legitimately be described as a place of peace, if, by the word peace we mean what the Hebrew word for it, 'shalom,' meant. It will be a place where there is no conflict. But more than that, it will be a place of deep harmony, one where all men and women are in perfect accord with themselves, with nature and with their God. But the way in which this peace is achieved is anything but peaceful. It is brought about by the violent death of the man Jesus Christ on the cross. Peace comes at the cost of blood being shed. Elsewhere in the letter Paul will explain a little more as to how such a death can bring about peace.[31] For the moment he is simply concerned to assert it. It means that creation and redemption are not two separate concerns of God, but one integrated concern. The new creation comes about by the redemption of the cross. Salvation means not just the redemption of individuals but the re-creation of the earth and the restoration of the universe to its proper relation with God. It's a far grander vision than we have often had. The individuals who now submit to the Lordship of Christ have a crucial part to play in the unfolding of this cosmic drama of restoration. Paul tells the Romans that 'the creation waits in eager expectation for the children of God to be revealed.'[32] But they are not the end of God's purpose. His purpose is nothing less than a totally restored creation put back in harmony with him. And it was all to be brought about by the cross. It means that, 'there will be no part of God's renewed universe that will remain unaffected by the cross – nowhere where Calvary is irrelevant!'[33] Eugene Peterson paraphrases it like this: 'All the broken and dislocated pieces of the universe – people and things, animals and atoms – get properly fixed and fit together in vibrant harmonies, all because of his death, his blood that poured down from the cross.'

It was a breath-taking vision that the early Christians had of Jesus of Nazareth. It was a bold claim they made for him. Jesus Christ was the key to resolving the disharmonies of the world and remedying the hostilities of humankind.

- In relation to God he is the image.
- In relation to the original creation he is the agent and goal.
- In relation to the church he is head.
- In relation to the new creation he is reconciler.

Many seek to compare Jesus Christ with other great persons. Just after the revolution I joined a small delegation, of religious leaders, to the President of Romania to talk about religious rights on behalf of the Evangelical Alliance in that country. As we were talking one of our number spoke of Jesus Christ. President Iliescu replied respectfully saying that, of course, we must listen to Jesus as we must listen to many of the great and wise teachers of the world among whom he listed Socrates, Plato, Mohammed and Marx! But Paul has given us enough reasons to see Jesus, quite simply, as the incomparable one. John Stott warns us against any comparisons:

> To relegate Christianity to one chapter in a book of the world's religions is to Christian people intolerable. Jesus Christ to us is not one of many spiritual leaders in the history of the world. He is not one of Hinduism's 330 million gods. He is not only one of the forty prophets recognised in the Qur'an. He is not even, to quote Carnegie Simpson, 'Jesus, the Great', as you might say of Napoleon the Great or Alexander the Great....To us, he is the only. He is simply Jesus. Nothing could be added to that. He is unique.
> He has no peers, no rivals, no successors.[34]

Quite so.

3

The Gospel of Christ
Colossians 1:21-2:5

[21]Once you were alienated from God and were enemies in your minds because of your evil behavior. [22]But now he has reconciled you by Christ's physical body through death to present you holy in his sight, without blemish and free from accusation – [23]if you continue in your faith, established and firm, not moved from the hope held out in the gospel. This is the gospel that you heard and that has been proclaimed to every creature under heaven, and of which I, Paul, have become a servant.

[24]Now I rejoice in what was suffered for you, and I fill up in my flesh what is still lacking in regard to Christ's afflictions, for the sake of his body, which is the church. [25]I have become its servant by the commission God gave me to present to you the word of God in its fullness – [26]the mystery that has been kept hidden for ages and generations, but is now disclosed to the saints. [27]To them God has chosen to make known among the Gentiles the glorious riches of this mystery, which is Christ in you, the hope of glory.

[28]We proclaim him, admonishing and teaching everyone with all wisdom, so that we may present everyone perfect in Christ. [29]To this end I labor, struggling with all his energy, which so powerfully works in me.

[1]I want you to know how much I am struggling for you and for those at Laodicea, and for all who have not met me personally. [2]My purpose is that they may be encouraged in heart and united in love, so that they may have the full riches of complete understanding, in order that they may know the mystery of God, namely, Christ, [3]in whom are hidden all the treasures of wisdom and knowledge. [4]I tell you this so that no one may deceive you by fine-sounding arguments. [5]For though I am absent from you in body, I am present with you in spirit and delight to see how orderly you are and how firm your faith in Christ is.

1. The gospel: experienced by the Colossians (verses 21-23)

What they were (v. 21)
What they are (v. 22)
What they need (v. 23)

2. The gospel: preached by Paul (verses 24-29)

A sufferer for the gospel (vv. 24-25)
A servant of the church (v. 24)
A steward of the mystery (vv. 26-27)
A struggler for the believers (vv. 28-29)

3. The gospel: threatened by troublemakers (verses 1-5)

Paul speaks of his purpose (vv. 1-3)
Paul speaks of his anxieties (v. 4)
Paul speaks of his pleasure (v. 5)

In a way I feel sorry for 70-year-old Ted Jeffries of Porthallow, in Cornwall. He boasts that he owns the most southerly vineyard in Britain and that it bottles a fine table wine. But between 1991 and 1994, due to the weather, there were no grape harvests in Cornwall. Not surprisingly, when an inspector found a bottle of wine bearing the label '1992 Vintage' he became suspicious. How could this be, since there had been no harvest? His investigations revealed that, in order to save his business, what Mr. Jeffries had done was to use a home wine-making kit and brew up some cheap plonk which he then passed off as the real thing. The magistrates fined him £6,000 for his deceit. His defence was interesting. 'No one,' he argued, 'had complained. They were happy with the wine they bought. So, what was the problem?'

Paul had learned of a similar problem at Colosse. Instead of holding true to the genuine and vintage gospel, the Colossian Christians were beginning to enjoy a cheap substitute which was being passed off as the real thing. Unfortunately, like Mr. Jeffries' customers, many of the Colossian believers couldn't tell the difference! In 2:4 Paul mentions 'the deceivers' explicitly for the first time. Later in the chapter he is going to expose their deception. But first he wants to remind the Colossians of the vintage gospel. He jogs their memory of the real so that they can more readily recognise the false.

This very personal section of his letter is all about the vintage gospel: experienced by them (vv. 21-23), proclaimed by Paul (vv. 24-29) and now threatened by others and in need of defence (vv. 1-5).

1. The gospel: experienced by the Colossians (verses 21-23)

It is impossible to separate the person of Christ (who he is) from the work of Christ (what he has done). So, as Paul came to the climax of his wonderful hymn, he focused on what this marvellous Christ was doing in reconciling all things once more to God (v. 20). What was true on a cosmic scale was also true on a personal level. So, Paul applies it to the Colossian believers who, because of their faith in Christ, are already in the process of experiencing reconciliation with God. They have done so as a sort of first instalment of the fuller work to come. Paul takes nothing for granted. As a skilled teacher he goes over the ground carefully, just in case they've previously misunderstood or missed anything.

What they were (v. 21)

He begins by reminding them of their state before they became Christians. They were *alienated from God*. They may have lived in God's world, but they did so as strangers to him and he to them. They enjoyed none of the benefits of friendship, intimacy and ease with God which had been his original purpose for creation. If they knew him at all it was at a distance. As such, the image they had of God would have been distorted or blurred, if not thoroughly faulty. Here, long before Marx thought of alienation, the Christian gospel speaks of it as the key to the ills of the world.

What was the cause of this alienation? Paul's analysis is searching. Doing, thinking and being are all involved. The way they behaved affected the way they thought and the way they thought put them in a position of hostility towards God. They were *enemies in (their) minds because of (their) evil behaviour*. He spells it out more fully to the Romans. In a stunning critique of the lustful, greedy, destructive and immoral culture of his day, Paul puts the blame on the way they thought, or rather didn't think, about God. 'For although they knew God, they neither glorified him as God nor gave thanks to him, but their thinking became futile and their foolish hearts were darkened. Although they claimed to be wise, they became fools.... Therefore God gave them over in the sinful desires of their hearts to sexual impurity for the degrading of their bodies with one another. They exchanged the truth of God for a lie, and worshipped and served created things rather than the Creator – who is for ever praised. Amen.'[1]

In his letter to the Romans Paul seems to make warped thinking the cause and evil behaviour the effect. In Colossians it appears the other way around. No matter. In reality, human beings are integrated beings and it is difficult to separate out one aspect of our nature from another and insist that one aspect is always cause and another always effect. Bad thinking leads to evil behaviour, but equally bad behaviour might lead to futile thinking.

The application to today is almost too obvious to mention. The same marks of alienation from God, futile thinking and evil behaviour, are writ large everywhere you look.

What they are (v. 22)

But there is an answer. God can be known, our thinking can be sorted and our behaviour transformed. The broken relationship with God can be healed. So, Paul speaks first of the fact of our reconciliation. John Stott comments that of all the metaphors of salvation in the New Testament, reconciliation is 'the most popular...because it is the most personal'.[2] How we long for reconciliation in Northern Ireland – a deep coming together and a true overcoming of hostilities that results in genuine friendships. How we long for a genuine reconciliation between black and white in post-apartheid South Africa. How many people long for reconciliation within their own families? Perhaps not all are in the extreme position of Mr. and Mrs. Wearing of Worksop who, some years ago, had to send their son Ernest, who was then twenty, and their daughter Julie, who was nineteen, a solicitor's letter ordering them out of the house, because of the foul language and the abusive and violent behaviour they used against their own parents. The Wearing's solicitor commented that he was involved in six such cases. How many long for reconciliation at work, where broken relationship can make the daily grind a daily nightmare? These are but symptoms of the key broken relationship which needs restoring – that between people and their God. And the good news is that reconciliation in that relationship is possible. Indeed, God longs for it!

Paul makes it clear that we are unable to get out of the predicament ourselves. The initiative lies with God. God is the offended party who, in grace, takes steps to remove the obstacle of sin which his creatures have erected to block him out. *But now he has reconciled you.* Paul's choice of words here is emphatic and decisive. Something definite has changed. Things are no longer what they were. That was then and this is now. The tense of the verb *reconciled* is an aorist tense stressing the completeness of what has taken place. So, Paul speaks first about the fact of reconciliation.

Secondly, Paul speaks of the means of reconciliation. The means by which God brought about this reconciliation was by Christ's physical body through death. It is the sacrifice of his Son which has effected reconciliation. All sorts of analogies come to mind to try to explain why God chose to do it this way. You may know of Don Richardson's story of the Peace Child.[3] The Sawi people of New Guinea belonged to a culture which idealised violence. It was riddled with treachery, headhunting and cannibalism. No village could trust another and 'every demonstration of friendship was suspect'. But there was one way in which hostilities could be overcome, the spiral of violence interrupted and trust established. If one of the warring parties took the initiative and presented a son to their enemies as a gift, that man could be trusted. An exchange of sons would follow and peace would be restored. As the ritual unfolded, alienated villagers would be invited to lay their hands on them as a sign that they were forsaking violence against their enemies.

It is a moving story. But, like most analogies, it fails to do justice to what God did for us in Christ. For the cost of our reconciliation with God was not the giving of a son who remained alive and unharmed, albeit permanently cut off from his own family, as in the case of the Sawi, but the giving of an only Son over to death. The most helpful way to understand what God chose to do here is, in fact, to see it through the lens of the Old Testament, where the death of the sacrificial animal was the means by which atonement was made. Atonement means that divided parties are at one again.[4] Perhaps God could have devised another way for reconciliation to take place. But this is the way he chose. And one can see why. It is a way which takes the enormity of the offence and the seriousness of the disruption of relationship into account and does not make light of them. It is a way which graphically portrays the cost of genuine reconciliation where the offence is not ignored as if unimportant. It is a way in which a substitute can be provided to bear the outworking of alienation which we could not bear ourselves. Reconciliation costs, as ordinary experience testifies. Here, God was prepared to pay the greatest cost of all that we might be friends with him again.

Paul's stress on *Christ's physical body* – literally, body of flesh – here is unusual. Many in the ancient world thought the body unclean and consequently would have doubted that a holy God could have used that which was physical to effect salvation. This idea was to be found in the early church at various stages and it could well be that Paul is stressing the physical death of Christ because a version of this particular teaching was circulating at Colosse. It led some to question the reality of Christ's death. In the face of such tendencies Paul affirms what has been the united position of Christ's followers since the beginning; that he died a real, painful and physical death. He did not escape from the cross at the last moment. His death was not an illusion and his body was not substituted by a spirit, as some teach. And mercifully so, for only a real death could achieve anything other than an illusory salvation.

There are still forms of Christianity around which want to devalue the body and escape from it as quickly as possible to what is thought to be the higher plane of the spirit. I've often heard people praying about leaving the body behind and getting caught up, out of the body, in the spirit in some mystical experience or other – perhaps like that which Paul refers to in 2 Corinthians 12:2-6. But it should be clear by now that Jesus is Lord, not just of the church and the spiritual, but of the creation and the material. It is not a true Christian understanding to denigrate the physical and seek to escape it. It is in our bodies, on this earth, that we are called to live out our Christian lives and serve our incarnate Lord. The physical body of Christ was the vehicle of God's redemption, and necessarily so, because it was through the physical realm that humanity had sinned. And the punishment must fit the crime, so to speak. If we had sinned in all our flesh and bloodness and God had only saved us in the spirit, our salvation would be woefully inadequate.

Having spoken of the fact of our reconciliation, and the means of our reconciliation, Paul mentions, thirdly, the purpose of our reconciliation. It is, *to present you holy in his sight, without blemish and free from accusation.* Although salvation is assured – we are reconciled – it is not yet complete. We are not yet perfect, as must be all too obvious to everyone, including ourselves. In practice we are not yet fully what we will be one day in Christ. There is progress to make. And we dare not remain content with the status quo. We are not reconciled in order that we can go on living as we used to. Our restored relationship with God is no mere legal transaction that leaves us unaltered. Far from it. We are now in a restored relationship with him and that relationship will change us, as all close relationships do. We should want to please him in every way and it will take most of us time to learn how to do that.

The language calls to mind the Jewish sacrificial system once more. The purpose of Christ's death is so that he might *present* his followers *holy in his* (that is, God's) *sight,* just as a priest presented a sacrifice to God. Then, too, just as the sacrificial animal was required to be without blemish,[5] so we are to aspire to be *without blemish and free from accusation.*

Within the space of this one verse Paul has alluded to two sacrifices. There is the sacrifice of Christ, who as our sacrifice of atonement was the perfect sacrifice, without any sin or blemish.[6] But then there is the thought that having been reconciled to God by Christ's sacrifice, every believer is also to become a sacrifice. In view of what Christ has done for us, our calling is now to become living sacrifices[7] and so we must, with the Holy Spirit's assistance, strive towards the goal of being free from blame.

What they need (v. 23)

It is a high standard which has been set before the believers at Colosse, and so before us today. What is the secret? How can we work towards such perfection, even if it is clear that we shall never reach perfection this side of the grave or the second coming of Christ? Is there some secret formula yet to be discovered? Is there some special experience which will help us get there? Is there some new truth, yet to be unlocked, which will aid us? Is there a quick fix we can take?

Paul's answer to all these questions is an emphatic, 'No!' There is only one thing necessary and it is already well known. It's not a secret we're still waiting to be revealed. The one thing is to continue in the faith received; to persevere with the gospel which we have learned. Those troubling the church at Colosse may be offering some new version of the gospel, some short-cut way to perfection, some new and improved version of 'how to be holy in twelve easy steps'. But such offers are attractive delusions. Believers already have in Christ all that is necessary. We have, to use the words of 2:10, *been given fulness in him*. He and his gospel are completely adequate. So we must resist the temptation to look elsewhere and we must keep going back to the gospel, building on it and staking our lives on our relationship with Jesus and him alone.

Almost every week some novelty or other is being taught. Our age is restless and discontented with things learned in the past. We get bored very easily. Our education system trains us to make 'an original contribution' to our discipline, to push the boundaries and work at the frontiers. Unoriginality is the original sin in the academy. The theologian Thomas Oden, who was once a slave to pursuing such novelties, has recently exposed the folly it can lead to. He speaks with bemused glee about dreaming one night of falling over his own tombstone in a New Haven Cemetery. On it he read this epitaph: 'He made no new contribution to theology.' He said he woke up feeling deeply reassured, for he'd been trying to follow the mandate of Irenaeus, one of the ancient fathers of the church, who directed his followers 'not to invent new doctrine'.[8]

Of course, we need constantly to come to a renewed understanding of old doctrine and a renewed application of the old truth to our own day. But that is different from changing the gospel itself and seeking a new gospel. The danger in discovering that which is new (or worse, merely inventing something which is novel) is that we come up with that which is not true. That was the situation in Colosse. So, don't chase novelties, however exciting. *Continue in your faith, established and firm, not moved from the hope held out in the gospel*. The little town of Colosse suffered some devastating earthquakes in AD 60 and 61, and knew what it was to be moved, unexpectedly, dramatically and involuntarily. But when it came to their faith, the believers there were not to live in the earthquake zone. They were to put down roots, establish strong foundations and be earthquake proof.

The gospel which the Colossians originally experienced is the one true gospel which is adequate for all their needs, and ours. It is the gospel of Jesus Christ, and him crucified.

2. The gospel: preached by Paul (verses 24-29)

In the opening section of Colossians, one thing leads to another. Talking of the gospel leads Paul to talk of himself as a servant of the gospel. The gospel they heard in Colosse is the same one which is being preached effectively around the world and of which Paul had become a servant. These next verses reveal Paul's deep understanding of his calling as a missionary pastor. They paint a picture which stands in sharp contrast to the slick tele-evangelists of our day with their smooth presentations, manipulative techniques and successful business empires. The verses can be approached in a number of ways, but I highlight four aspects which would have appeared on Paul's job description, and should appear on that of anyone commissioned to preach the gospel.

A sufferer for the gospel (vv. 24-25)

He begins with rejoicing – *now I rejoice* – although you and I might wonder why. Being addicted to comfort, as most of us are, we are unlikely to find talk of suffering a matter of pleasure. But for Paul, although he was no masochist, suffering for the sake of the gospel was a privilege in which he often rejoiced[9] because it led him to be more closely identified with Jesus.

His words have caused some confusion down the years. What does he mean when he says *I fill up in my flesh what is still lacking in regard to Christ's afflictions?* Surely he is not saying that somehow the work of Christ was deficient, since that would be to run counter to what he had just stated and what he was going on to develop more fully later in chapter 2. Indeed, throughout his writings the sufficiency of the work Christ did on the cross for our redemption is affirmed. So, the meaning of these verses must lie elsewhere.

The Jews,[10] of whom Paul was one, held a view that the Messianic Age, the age in which the world would make a transition from the present evil age to the golden age to come, would be characterised by trouble, just as surely as a woman's experience of labour, as she gives birth to a new life, is characterised by pain. Paul speaks in these terms in Romans 8:18-27. So, he is not surprised that as an agent of this new age, inaugurated by Jesus Christ but not yet fully realised, he should experience suffering. He is, in fact, placing his ministry in the wider scheme of things. He has a role in the whole unfolding drama of the fulfilment of God's plan. But it's a role which inevitably involves suffering.

Then, Paul seems to be playing on words a bit and again assuming a typically Jewish understanding of things. The Jews had an idea concerning a corporate personality, as distinct from our modern idea of individual personality. They did not necessarily make the sharp distinction between the individual and the group which we do. Here, there is a reference to Christ (the individual) which is followed immediately by a reference to his body (the corporate). The personalities are so enmeshed that what is true of him will also be true of them. So, he is likely to be meaning not that Christ's work as a historic individual on earth lacked anything but that Christ's body, the church, had still not exhausted the suffering which was to be their lot.

Paul frequently sees suffering as a mark both of authentic Christian ministry and more widely of authentic Christian experience. Suffering identifies the messenger with the one who is the message; just as Christ suffered, so his disciples might expect to suffer too. As he walked the road to Calvary, so our calling is to walk the same road. It is the only road which leads beyond, to an empty tomb and glorious resurrection. So, there's no point in escaping it. As Luther starkly put it, 'If I want to be a Christian, I must wear the colours of the court...suffering there must be.' The cross is 'the natural pattern of the Christian life'.[11]

A servant of the church (v. 24)

Paul has spoken of being a servant of the gospel. Now he speaks of himself as a servant of the church, for the church is brought into being and sustains its life by the gospel. His suffering is *for the sake of his body, which is the church*. There is, as James Dunn points out,[12] a neat little paradox here. In verse 22 we read of Christ giving his body of flesh. In verse 24 we read of Paul giving his flesh for Christ's body. We have already learned, in verse 18, that Christ is the head of the body. Now in a different way the close union between the exalted Lord and his people who meet in an assembly on earth is spelled out, for the body is none other than Christ's own.

These are great claims to be making about the little group of believers who met in Colosse or, for that matter, about any feeble and fallible group of believers who meet today. They seem, as they always have done, so insignificant from the viewpoint of the world and so easy to criticise. I am writing as the Lambeth Conference of Bishops is convened and the press are full of complaints about the church being out of touch. Sadly many Christians have connived in these assaults. Theologians have delighted in downplaying the significance of the church and emphasising by contrast that God still works outside the church within the world and more broadly within his kingdom whose boundaries are not co-terminus with the church. That is true, but it should not be used to devalue the church. Then, many post-modern Christians struggle with the church as an institution, longing to find meaningful relationships within her but failing to do so. Consequently, they get impatient with the institution and reject it. The church is the butt of so much denigration and criticism.

It is time for the balance to be corrected. 'Christ loved the church and gave himself up for her.'[13] Certainly Paul did not think the church unimportant. His vision of the church is that it is so intimately connected with the Lord himself that he delights in being its servant, even if that means putting up with suffering, inconvenience and discomfort. How different from what we hear so much of today.

A steward of the mystery (vv. 26-27)

Being a servant of the church does not mean Paul is there to do its every beck and call. He takes his orders from a higher source. He has received a *commission* from God himself to *present to (them) the word of God in its fulness*. The message he presents is not one which they determine but one which God has already determined and revealed. His task is to explain it to them more and more fully so that they might grasp it in all its detail. They already know it a little, but not sufficiently, or else they would not be attracted to the false ideas which are beginning to make headway among them. Given that he is going to question some of the things they are coming to believe, it is not surprising that he should emphasise the divine origin of his appointment.

Paul has been chosen to be a steward in the house of God. His task is to manage what has been entrusted to him well. The precious object committed to his care is *the mystery* which has been kept hidden for centuries (*ages and generations*). But now *the mystery* is an open secret and it was his task to make it known.

Mystery religions were popular in the ancient world and there is some suggestion, because of the wording used in 2:18, that the source of some of the trouble in the church came from that quarter. These pagan mystery cults kept secrets they did not want others to know. They initiated people through private ceremonies into a fellowship of hidden rituals and confidential beliefs.

But the mystery Christians follow is not kept hidden from people's view. It has nothing to do with covert ceremonies or secret doctrines. Far from it. Rather, it has to do with the divine purpose which has now been made plain to all. That purpose was, as Ephesians 1 explains more fully, that the Gentiles should be joint heirs with the Jews of his *glorious riches*. For God to dwell among Israel as his chosen people was taken for granted. That God should also choose, as history unfolded itself into the new age of the Spirit, to dwell equally among the Gentiles was strange, indeed, outrageous. What we may now take for granted was revolutionary when first preached. It took some getting used to. Peter had to be convinced by a vision he received on the rooftop of the house of Simon in Joppa.[14] As a good Jew he naturally resisted such an unclean suggestion to start with. Paul, equally, had to have his worldview revolutionised in a dramatic way. For him it happened in Damascus where he first learned from Ananias that he would be the messenger God would use to announce this mystery to the Gentiles.[15] The mystery was that those Gentile Colossians belonged to the same family as those who had the rich Jewish heritage of faith behind them. The church is constantly composed of outsiders who become insiders, because the only qualification for entry is nothing other than faith.

How did they know this to be true? By the risen Jesus who was already living within and among the Gentiles. He lived among them as a pledge of the final glory of God which one day they would fully experience. That is why Paul says, Christ in them was the hope of glory. In Peterson's words, 'The mystery in a nutshell is just this: Christ is in you, therefore you can look forward to sharing in God's glory. It's that simple.'

A struggler for the believers (vv. 28-29)

Here, in a nutshell is Paul's view of ministry. Condensed within these two verses is the message, method, manner, motive and means of Christian ministry. The message is none other than Jesus Christ: *we proclaim him*. The Christian pastor can never dispense with the message of Jesus and the Christian believer can never outgrow the message of Jesus. It is not that we begin with the simple gospel about him at our conversion and then progress to more complicated doctrines and spiritual experiences subsequently. He is not to be discarded as an adult might discard the toys and cuddly teddies of childhood. He and he alone is at the start of our Christian journey and sufficient for our pilgrimage right to the end. Perfection, Paul claims here, is reached when one is presented at the end to the Father. That is the climax of our Christian experience. And Christ is central to the whole process, for this perfection is not perfection as we might aspire to it from a human or worldly perspective but perfection *in Christ*.

As to method the key issue is flexibility. All must be included in our admonition or teaching. None must be neglected. But our method must be matched to the person whose maturity we are seeking to encourage. Like Paul, the early church fathers were acutely conscious of the differences between the people to whom they ministered and sought to find the approach which would produce the desired end. Gregory of Nazianzus, for example, put it graphically:

> Some are led by doctrine, others trained by example, some need the spur, others the curb; some are sluggish and hard to rouse to the good, and must be stirred by being smitten with the word; others are immodestly fervent in spirit, with impulses difficult to restrain like thoroughbred colts, who run wide of the turning post and to improve them the word must have a restraining and checking influence.[16]

Exactly! Paul would agree.[17] Some people need *admonishing*. The word *noutheteo* which he uses here is one he frequently uses[18] and means 'to set the mind in proper order' or, in other words, 'to correct the wayward.' But not all immaturity derives from error. Much derives from ignorance. And such people require *teaching* or instructing rather than *admonishing*. These two approaches do not exhaust Paul's pastoral approach[19] but they are representative of it and particularly relevant here. There can be little doubt that Paul saw the teaching of the faith as the primary means of Christian growth from early days onwards. But his view of teaching would have been wide. It was not limited to using verbal instruction; to using cerebral content in a classroom setting. Much teaching was by example and done on the job. But whatever the form, there would have been an emphasis on the explanation of the faith and the need to communicate its truth effectively and conscientiously. We can sense here that Paul is no mere professional teacher, setting out solely to earn his living from his teaching. He is passionate about what he teaches and wishes to impart it with a conviction that means no one will be able to take it lightly.

The manner in which he imparted his teaching was with *all wisdom*. Undoubtedly wisdom is mentioned because it was part of the background to some of the discussions in Colosse about the faith. The false teaching which was beginning to circulate certainly boasted about high flown ideas which seemed so wise. Colossians 2:18 and 23 says as much. In contrast to these ideas, Paul says true, godly wisdom was to be found in Christ and was within the reach of all people. Cleverness and wisdom should never be confused.

But there may have been a more down-to-earth reason for speaking of wisdom. Given the practical, grounded and ethical nature of much Old Testament wisdom it is legitimate to apply this verse to the way in which ministry is conducted. How many pastors and teachers lack wisdom! Instead of producing maturity some get people all excited about mere speculations and non-essentials. They promise the moon spiritually, although it can never be delivered, and whip up emotions without foundations. Still others lack wisdom in their handling of personal relationships and either misuse their position of trust or abuse their position of power. Too many, sadly, lack basic wisdom in the handling of counselling situations and get too close to members they are seeking to help, especially if they are of the opposite sex, with disastrous consequences. We need to rediscover wisdom in ministry today.

Paul's motive is to produce maturity. Note that he is not selective, as some are, in his pastoral care. Three times in these verses he stresses his ministry is to everyone, not just some. He cares for 'all the flock of God' which the Holy Spirit has entrusted to him.[20]

His goal for them all is that he might present them *perfect in Christ. Teleios*, the Greek word translated 'perfect' means mature, complete. It would have been the word used to describe an apprentice who was thoroughly trained by his teacher. We must not think it means to be sinless, but rather to be wholehearted. It speaks of being wholehearted in one's trust in Christ and not given to being blown off course by strange teaching. It means living the faith in an appropriate moral and ethical way. It means a disposition that strives after holiness.

Contemporary pastoral theologians are greatly influenced by modern psychology. Consequently they sometimes erroneously interpret this perfection in Christ to mean a personal and interpersonal maturity as defined by the present day human and social sciences. So, it comes to mean being at ease with oneself and having an ability to function adequately and with self-sufficiency.[21] But one might be all those things and still adulterous or unbelieving. Spiritual maturity does not necessarily equate to psychological maturity.

Paul's motive is future in its orientation. He looks forward to the day when he will present these people to his God. The thought of the judgment seat is never far from his thinking when it comes to analysing why he ministers in the way he does. His ministry has as much to do with the next world as with this.[22]

Finally, these verses speak of his means. He's serious about this ministry. It's not a holiday cruise or a day out at the theme park. He presses athletic imagery into service to describe the way in which he struggles, toils, sweats and exerts himself for the sake of producing maturity. He puts effort into it. He's a struggler. But, significantly, he qualifies what he says. He does not struggle with the energy which he generates in himself but rather *with all his energy, which so powerfully works in me*. To throw oneself into ministry relying on one's own skills, gifts, plans and ambitions can quickly lead to burnout, as many have found. Only hard work which is guided by the Lord and resourced by the Spirit can produce the sort of stamina needed to achieve the grand objective of *presenting everyone perfect in Christ*.

John Newton, centuries later, expressed the same understanding of and passion for ministry. His words, taken from a meditation written in 1758, make an apt summary of Paul's teaching. Ministerial character requires,

> 'zeal, courage, diligence, faithfulness, tenderness, humility and self-denial', an extensive knowledge of Scripture, a large stock of 'divine experience', and discernment and prudence. To this must be added a thirst for God's glory and the salvation of souls; a ready ability to share what one has personally learned of God; a desire to wrestle in prayer privately, in assemblies and in families; a willingness to converse with hearers upon what has been preached publicly; and a determination to use every opportunity to extend the gospel into adjacent, perhaps even distant places.[23]

Newton's biographer adds, for understandable reasons, 'No wonder then that he not only felt his own insufficiency for the ministry, but realized that anyone wishing to become a minister would have to depend on a divine calling and assistance.'[24]

3. The gospel: threatened by troublemakers (verses 1-5)

Paul continues to write autobiographically, but the focus shifts a little away from himself and latches on to those who are causing trouble in the church at Colosse. Even while he continues to write in the first person, it is the troublemakers that he really has in his sights and who determine his agenda.

Paul speaks of his purpose (vv.1-3)

With the church at Colosse Paul now couples the church at Laodicea which was about ten miles further down the River Lycus. Unlike Colosse, Laodicea was a wealthy place, wealthy enough, for instance, to rebuild itself from its own resources and without outside help after the earthquakes of AD 60, 61. Its wealth, as we know from the letter written by the exalted Lord to the angel of the Laodicean church, recorded for us in Revelation 3:14-22, could have a spiritually debilitating effect. But here, it is not its wealth but the threat of false teaching which is in view.

False teaching takes its toll on spiritual health. We should never view it merely as an offer of an alternative set of opinions to be put alongside those of others, as we are tempted to do in a tolerant and pluralistic age where we can always see two sides of the argument. We should unmask it for what it is – a cancer which destroys a healthy spiritual body. Paul does so here, at least by implication. In setting out his desires for these believers he tells us what the symptoms of false teaching are for which we should look out. It will cause discouragement, since it doesn't provide the nourishment needed for spiritual vitality; division, since it is moving away from the original teaching and introducing the novel and distorted; confusion, since people will no longer be sure of their beliefs; and, insecurity, since their hold on Christ will be weakened. Paul's therapy was to contact them, by letter and through messengers, with the antidote of the true gospel because he longs to see the cancer of false teaching defeated and its symptoms reversed. If the first symptom was discouragement, he wants to see them *encouraged in heart*. If the second symptom was division, he wants to see them *united in love*. If the third was confusion, he wants to see them *have the full riches of complete understanding*. If the final symptom was uncertainty, he wants to see them *know the mystery of God, namely Christ*.

Christ, he reminds them, is like a rich mine which conceals a wealth of precious minerals. They have not yet begun to quarry it, still less exhaust it. So it is foolish for them to turn away from him so soon to other forms of teaching and mount a quest for other forms of religious experience. What they must be encouraged to do is to dig deeper into Christ so that they might discover *all the treasures of wisdom and knowledge* which are hidden in him. They should stay with what they have rather than being seduced by false teaching. They should seek to understand the gospel more. They'd soon find that it answered all their needs.

So, his purpose is that they might have encouragement in their hearts, unity in their fellowship, understanding in their minds and an assurance in their relationship with Christ.

Paul speaks of his anxieties (v. 4)

His fear is that they may be misled *by fine-sounding arguments*. False teaching usually comes dressed in a very attractive fashion. Satan has a whole armoury of weapons at his disposal and most of them are subtle. He knows that a full frontal assault on the faith will often be rejected outright. It's too obvious and can easily be rebutted. We human beings don't believe what is implausible. Augustine was right. 'No one, indeed, believes anything, unless he previously knows it to be believable.'[25] So, the strategy of the enemy is usually to twist, distort and add to the true faith, rather than oppose it totally. This way he can gradually move us so far away from our original moorings that we are cut adrift in a sea of error without noticing it.

That was certainly Satan's strategy in Colosse and Laodicea. The features of the emerging false teaching had some appealing religious elements to it; like, the fact that it gave some practical rules for living, advocated some interesting religious rituals and possessed some recognisably Jewish features. Any of these would have made it attractive. The false teachers were not concerned to undermine the gospel the Colossians had received but simply to supplement it in parts where it seemed weak. Whether their teaching was true or not did not really matter because it certainly *seemed* to be true. And there were plenty of popular speakers around, very skilled in the art of communication, no doubt, who could put these perversions of the truth over in persuasive ways.

The threat at Colosse had not yet reached the level that it had in Galatia. There is not the same sense of urgency in Paul's writing in this letter as he shows in his letter to the Galatians. His concern is nonetheless real. Here he is engaging in more preventative pastoral work. It's like the little acorns which get planted in my garden, courtesy of a nearby oak tree. If I pull them up immediately they're not too bad to deal with. But if I leave them and they get their roots down they're a frightful job to remove. Paul is warning the Colossians: don't let these persuasive false teachers get embedded in the church. Deal with them while you can.

We really should take the threat of false teaching more seriously than we do. Tolerance, pluralism and relativism are the hallmarks of our age and have deeply affected attitudes in the church. Dogmatism, certainty and absolutism are considered the evils of our age. But when it comes to the gospel we cannot compromise and that for two reasons. First, a gospel other than the revealed apostolic gospel taught in Scripture is, in Paul's word to the Galatians, 'really no gospel at all.'[26] Secondly, and just as significant, to compromise the gospel is to compromise the honour and glory of Jesus Christ who alone is pre-eminent. For both reasons we must beware false teaching.

Paul speaks of his pleasure (v. 5)

As a wise pastor, Paul ends this personal section of his letter on a positive note. He doesn't leave them with a negative taste in their mouths or they might not have had much of an appetite for the good diet of teaching which he is shortly going to serve up. He has, he says, a strong sense of being spiritually present with them even though he is physically distant and, indeed, has never met them. There is a oneness in spirit which the Spirit gives which binds believers together regardless of how geographically close they are to one another or how well they know one another. That's why you can travel across the world and visit a fellowship you've never been to before and feel instantly at home.

This close relationship causes Paul to observe two things about them which give him pleasure. *I...delight to see how orderly you are and how firm your faith in Christ is.* Both are military terms. Soldiers who maintained their positions in the rank when marching or fighting an enemy were *orderly*. Those who defended their position without retreating when facing an attack were *firm*. So the church at Colosse, though facing a threat which was potentially dangerous, was, at this stage, basically sound. As a fellowship their relationships were still intact and their faith still in Jesus. If they remained orderly and firm they would be able to resist the enemy. But nothing could be taken for granted and so Paul needed to set out the true gospel in contrast to the false teaching with care, as he now goes on to do.

The thread that binds this largely personal section of the letter together is the thread of the gospel. It is a gospel that:

- can be experienced, as it has been by the Colossians;
- must be preached, as it was by the apostle Paul;
- ought to be defended, as it is in this letter.

It would be a mistake to think of this as merely an interesting note in the history of the early church. These things are not recorded so that we might have an insight as to how they lived and thought but so that they might have contemporary impact. This letter is not an exhibit in a religious museum but a living communication from a gracious God. So, these words are written to impress themselves on us. They might do so in various ways, depending on where we stand.

If God is still a stranger to us, the words invite us to be reconciled to God. They invite us to overcome our distance from him, to trust in what he did for us through the death of Christ and to experience the decisive shift in our relationship with God which the cross has made possible.

If we are believers, then these words set out for us a grand vision and a great requirement. The vision is that we are saved in order that we might become holy. Our salvation is neither for our private indulgence, nor to assure us of a comfortable place in heaven while others will be damned. The purpose of our salvation is to transform us so that we become pure and spotless. The requirement is that we continue in the faith that we have received and refuse all seductive advances to alter, add or renege on the gospel.

If we are preachers, missionaries, pastors or teachers we must examine ourselves to see how our lives match up to Paul's understanding of the task. Do we rejoice in suffering as a sign that we are Christ's authentic messengers? Do we willingly serve the church? Do we take the gospel to the outsiders, who don't seem to fit, for the mystery is that in Christ God has chosen them? Do we have our eyes on the goal of producing maturity in Christ with all the energy he inspires within us?

If we are members of a church, are we on our watch against false teaching and are we defending the gospel? Or, have we become so *laissez-faire* in our spiritual attitudes and indifferent in our doctrinal commitments that anything goes – particularly if it's entertainingly communicated. If so, the time has come to 'urge you to contend for the faith that was once for all entrusted to the saints'.[27]

The gospel is:

- ■   too precious to ignore: believe it;
- ■   too precious to relinquish: be faithful to it;
- ■   too precious to hide: proclaim it;
- ■   and, too precious to betray: defend it.

4

Fulness in Christ
Colossians 2:6-15

[6]So then, just as you received Christ Jesus as Lord, continue to live in him, [7]rooted and built up in him, strengthened in the faith as you were taught, and overflowing with thankfulness.

[8]See to it that no one takes you captive through hollow and deceptive philosophy, which depends on human tradition and the basic principles of this world rather than on Christ.

[9]For in Christ all the fullness of the Deity lives in bodily form, [10]and you have been given fullness in Christ, who is the head over every power and authority. [11]In him you were also circumcised, in the putting off of the sinful nature, not with a circumcision done by the hands of men but with the circumcision done by Christ, [12]having been buried with him in baptism and raised with him through your faith in the power of God, who raised him from the dead.

[13]When you were dead in your sins and in the uncircumcision of your sinful nature, God made you alive with Christ. He forgave us all our sins, [14]having cancelled the written code, with its regulations, that was against us and that stood opposed to us; he took it away, nailing it to the cross. [15]And having disarmed the powers and authorities, he made a public spectacle of them, triumphing over them by the cross.

1. Founded on Christ (verses 6-7)

    The basis they had (v. 6)
    The challenge they faced (vv. 6-7)
    The spirit they needed (v. 7)

2. Freedom through Christ (verse 8)

    From deceptive philosophies
    From human traditions
    From basic principles

3. Fulness in Christ (verses 9-12)

    Who he is (vv. 9-10)
    What it means (v. 10)
    How it works (vv. 11-12)

4. Forgiveness from Christ (verses 13-15)

    He cancels our debt (vv. 13-14)
    He defeats our enemies (v. 15)

Leroy Eimes, the veteran leader of the Navigators, tells a story that we can all identify with. He was visiting Florida on a hot summer's day and was longing for a drink, so he went into a restaurant and asked for an orange juice. Since he was surrounded by oranges in this Orange State it was a simple enough request. 'Sorry,' came the reply, 'we can't give you any – our machine has broken down.' There were millions of oranges all round. Getting the juice out of an orange is relatively easy. But he wasn't able to quench his thirst because 'the machine had broken down'.

Jesus Christ is a rich resource for every believer. The central message of Colossians is found in verses 9 and 10. *For in Christ all the fulness of the Deity lives in bodily form, and you have been given fulness in Christ....* Why is it, then, that so many Christians seem only to get a faint dribble of juice out of their faith? Where do they go wrong? Why has 'the machine broken down'?

From the introduction – a lengthy and meaty introduction to be sure – Paul turns in these verses to the substance of his letter and sets out for them the foundation for Christian experience and a comprehensive guide to Christian living. He starts at the beginning by reminding them that they are founded on Christ. He challenges anything which would take away the freedom they have received through Christ. He gets them to look carefully at the fulness that there is in Christ and reaches a climax as he speaks of the cross and the forgiveness that flows from Christ.

1. Founded on Christ (verses 6-7)

The basis they have (v. 6)

Whatever may be going wrong at Colosse Paul does not doubt that the members of the church are genuine Christians. He makes the point by using the simplest and earliest definition of what it is to be a Christian. They *received Christ Jesus as Lord*. The tense of the verb is significant. It is an aorist tense. It is a past, completed, definite transaction which has taken place, not a tentative or vague exploration. Jesus is their Lord.[1] Most people quite legitimately take time to investigate the Christian faith before committing themselves to it. The journey from the point of being introduced initially to the Christian faith to a point of public commitment, we are told, takes on average four years.[2] But however long it had taken the Colossians to reach this point they had done so. They were no longer hesitant about the question of who Jesus was. He was the Lord and he was their Lord.

To name him Lord was to recognise him as the authority in their lives. It was to have made him 'the boss'. The word was a common one in the ancient world. The Jews in the Greek-speaking synagogues used it as a substitute for Yahweh, the sacred name of God. So when Paul uses it he is claiming that Jesus was God. Others used it to describe a whole range of relationships between a superior and an inferior person, whether it was a master and his slave, a king and his subject, or a god and his worshippers. In Paul's writings it comes to occupy a special place for the Christian. He uses it some 230 times in his letters as a title for Jesus Christ and invests it with an intensified meaning. The Lord whom Christians acknowledge was not one who was relatively superior but one who is absolutely supreme. He is the divine Lord described in 1:15-20, not a Lord that they had dreamed up or invented. His relationship with God, role in creation, position in the church and significance for the future is without comparison. He is peerless. This was a cause of great celebration for the early Christians. No other power they faced, whether the power of oppressive governments, economic forces, natural disasters, demonic beings, or that great enemy death, was supreme. Jesus was. He was Lord over it all.

In view of this, while people might normally owe multiple allegiance to several lords – to a father, a master, a magistrate or a king – simultaneously, this Lord, who is unique and supreme, claims an allegiance over all others. One cannot confess him Lord while also seeking to serve other gods or spiritual masters. As the old saying goes, 'If he is not Lord of all, then he is not Lord at all.' Nor can one say, as one wit is supposed to have prayed, 'Lord I want to serve you, but only in an advisory capacity.' There are plenty who want to do that. But it is to fundamentally misunderstand what it means to say that he is Lord. If he really is

Lord then he is the master and we are his servants who set our lives at his complete disposal. The Colossians had once understood all this, but now they were in danger of compromising on it.

Before we pass on we need to look a little more carefully at the way Paul puts it. He tells them that they *received* Christ Jesus as Lord. Receiving Christ looks a familiar enough idea. We think we understand it. It's what happens when someone responds to the evangelist's invitation. It's what happens when the moment of decision comes at the end of a youth house party. The convert passively accepts Jesus into their lives and receives him as Lord. Well, not quite. The word he uses is interesting. It is the word *paralambano*[3] in the Greek and it relates to the word 'tradition'. Receiving Jesus in this way meant not a passive acquiring of a personal relationship with Jesus but the active entering into a tradition concerning him. The word rules out the idea that anyone can be an isolated believer. We're not in this alone but we join countless thousands of others who belong to the same tradition. We're part of the church, like it or not. Furthermore, it rules out any idea that being a Christian is a matter of opinion, or that we have the ability to pick and choose what suits us about the Christian faith. The Christian is one who has entered into a tradition where the body of belief is already formed and now is being handed on to us. The tradition needs to form us, rather than us the tradition.

The challenge they face (vv. 6-7)

Since they have a solid foundation, the challenge they faced was to build on it. Some were saying that the foundation they laid in Christ was all right but the house they needed to build on top was to be constructed of different materials. The message of the gospel was OK for beginners, as an elementary starting point. But now they needed to refine it by supplementing it with other religious ideas and practices. To stick with the message of the gospel as if it was the sole and total answer was, so they said, a bit naive.

'On the contrary,' says Paul. 'All you need you will find in him, so *continue to live in him*. Nothing else is necessary. You need to make progress but it is progress within the relationship you already have with Jesus the Lord, not progress away from him to something else.' Paul amplifies his point by using three metaphors. First, there is an agricultural one, *rooted*; second, an architectural one, *built up*; and, third, a commercial one, *strengthened*.

The agricultural metaphor is the transition metaphor which moves them away in their thinking from where they are to where they should be going. Their roots are already established. Again, he acknowledges what has already happened. They have roots, they don't need to be digging over the ground to prepare to plant something new. The roots may need to go deeper so that their faith will be able to withstand all the storms of heresy, persecution, temptation or discouragement which might blow on them, but the roots are there. So, on the one hand, the message is, don't uproot and plant yourself in a different part of the spiritual garden. That will only lead to death. On the other hand, the message is, let your roots go deeper into the soil of the gospel. Don't be content with the somewhat shallow footing which you have as yet.

Paul is a great one for mixing his metaphors, so he easily switches from thinking about roots and trees to foundations and buildings. The architectural metaphor looks forward. The foundations are secure, so there is every reason to build confidently on them. A strong building can be erected by their keeping close to Jesus and by their growing in the knowledge of their faith.

Then he switches to a commercial metaphor, somewhat hidden under the English translation of *strengthened*. It's actually a word from the marketplace. He's talking about the receipt; the confirmation that goods have been bought or that property has been sold. 'Now,' he says, 'the transaction has taken place. You have given yourself to Jesus who has bought you with a price. Now confirm the transaction by affirming your faith in him. Confirm it, by having a firmer, not lesser grasp on him. Don't try to fill your minds with other ideas or think you'll find greater satisfaction through other rituals. There's nothing wrong with him or *the faith as you were taught* it. The gospel of Jesus will satisfy your deepest longing and defeat your greatest enemy. What's wrong is your hold on him. So, strengthen your grip.'

The spirit they needed (v. 7)

I don't know if they were a particularly grumpy lot in Colosse, but Paul certainly keeps stressing the need for them to be thankful. Six times[4] in this short letter he tells them they must be thankful. Here they are encouraged not simply to be thankful but to be *overflowing with thankfulness*. Perhaps they suffered from the negative mindset at which, it seems to me, the British excel. If we ever do win a test match, triumph in international football or defeat our opponents at rugby, our newspapers can always explain the victory away or give bigger headlines to another sport where we lost! We're never happier than when we can rubbish a team, ridicule a manager and wallow in defeat.

It all reminds me of a neighbour I once had. Harry was as dour as they come. Shortly after we moved in next door to him we had a terrific amount of rubbish to dispose of, so we put it out in black sacks for the dustmen to collect. 'Oh,' he said to me as I went off to work, 'they'll never take that lot you know.' 'Well,' I replied, 'if they don't they don't, but it's worth a try.' When I came home from work Harry was still leaning over his garden gate. The rubbish was gone. And he greeted me with the words, 'They took it, then. But they'd have never taken it if you'd lived in Watford' (which we didn't). Such is the power of negative thinking.

To be a thankful person can make you profoundly counter-cultural, at least in British society. What a powerful Christian witness it can be. But given how much we are shaped by our surrounding culture, as the Colossians were shaped by theirs, maybe it is a spiritual discipline we have to learn. The old hymn may seem quaint now, but when it taught us to 'Count your blessings, name them one by one; count your blessings, see what God has done! Count your blessings, name them one by one; and it will surprise you what the Lord hath done,' it certainly had a point. Cultivate thankfulness.

I suspect that Paul's real reason for encouraging them to *thankfulness* lies elsewhere. The exhortation to be *built up* and *strengthened* in their faith could be read the wrong way. They could have become terribly introspective and self-critical when they read those words. 'Paul's putting all the blame on us,' they might have said. 'We're not good enough or strong enough.' It's certainly the effect many zealous, well-meaning evangelical preachers have. They leave their congregations deflated with the feeling that they don't believe enough, pray enough, give enough, witness enough, do enough, attend enough and it's all their fault. But that's not Paul's intention. So, he balances his exhortation to grow with a hint that whatever is currently deficient in their spiritual growth as yet, still they have so much for which to be thankful. It encourages them to look away from themselves to all that they have already experienced of the grace of God. It encourages them not to strive with grim determination for progress, but to develop with a free and joyful attitude. It encourages them away from the negative mind-set of spiritual postmortems to the positive mind-set which appreciates amazing grace.

2. Freedom through Christ (verse 8)

What might stop the Colossians from continuing in their faith and building healthily on the foundation they have in Christ? Verse 8 tells us explicitly for the first time (although it was hinted at in verse 4) what the problem is. People are trying to take them *captive through hollow and deceptive philosophy, which depends on human traditions and the basic principles of this world rather than on Christ.* Just as old lags suffer from gate fever – the fear of freedom – when they have been institutionalised for so long, so Christians, having been set free in Christ, sometimes yearn to return to the captivity of other religious answers. It's exactly what the children of Israel did after they were set free from Egypt.[5] They soon forgot how dreadful their lives in Egypt were and foolishly cried out to return to captivity. So it sometimes is with Christians.

Deceptive philosophies

Paul doesn't name the gaolers outright here, but he does describe the prison bars that would restrain them. There seems to be three: *hollow and deceptive philosophy*; *human tradition*; and *the basic principles of this world*. Whether he is referring to three different things is questionable. One seems to grow out of another. They overlap.

Hollow and deceptive philosophy is the overall problem. Not all philosophy is hollow and deceptive, but there is plenty that is. The ancient world was full of popular philosophers who would go and stand on a street corner or hire a hall and peddle their beliefs. Much like the media commentators of our day or the TV chat show hosts they were considered entertaining and educative at the same time. You get a glimpse of it in the New Testament when Paul visits Mars Hill in Athens and speaks to the meeting of the Areopagus. Luke comments that, 'the Athenians and the foreigners who lived there spent their time doing nothing but talking about and listening to the latest ideas.'[6] Colosse would have had its fair share of such philosophers. They would have made persuasive speakers, but Paul dismisses them as *hollow and empty*. He doesn't write this out of prejudice, nor is he dismissing them too glibly. As one trained in the best of Jewish (a former student of the respected Gamaliel) and Greek culture, who had grown up in Tarsus which was well-known as a cultured university city, he had investigated these philosophies and knew what he was dismissing. It was just that here was not the place to unmask them in depth or he'd lose sight of his objective, which was to keep his eye on Christ.

Our own culture is based on a number of philosophies which we should also question as Christians and unmask as in opposition to Christ. There is the philosophy of individualism, so brilliantly exposed by the chief Rabbi Jonathan Sacks in his book *The Politics of Hope*. He shows how no society can survive on an individualism which has gone to seed, as it has done among us today. We have lost the true understanding of personal identity as set forth in Genesis 2 because we have lost any understanding of covenant and relationship. 'We have our being in relationship with others and we breathe a common air. There can be no articulate "I" without a coherent "we".'[7] We have replaced a covenant belonging to one another with a contractual using of one another. And from this rampant individualism all manner of evils follow. Individuals are isolated and lonely. The family no longer serves as 'the crucible of character'. Children roam in a moral wilderness seeking revenge on an older generation who seem to have neglected them. We have become a 'rights' society where everyone makes demands but few are willing to give. Choice has become addictive. A true morality has given way to moralising. 'We suffer from the privatisation of morality and the nationalization of responsibility.'[8] How can we care for people in the community when there is no community? And so the disturbing analysis of a society based on the philosophy of individualism gone mad goes on. Yet we remain hooked on this deceptive philosophy.

It is not the only empty and illusory philosophy around. There is the philosophy of relativism, of pluralism (in the sense that pluralism is a virtue to be pursued rather than as an observable fact), of scientism (as opposed to science itself). Or, take the victim culture of which we're a part, which seems to believe that people are trapped by their past and unable to do anything about it. All of these philosophies are popular and seem to hold much promise for the emancipation of humankind. But all they really do is imprison people in a cage of their own making.

Human traditions

Paul says that the deceptive philosophies of his day were dependent on *human tradition and the basic principles of this world*. These human traditions might well refer to what was coming out of the Jewish synagogue as much as what came from elsewhere. The reason for saying this is twofold. The Greek word he uses for *captive* is *sylagogeo*. Though it means 'to be taken off as a prize of war', it sounds suspiciously like the word 'synagogue'. Was he hinting that what he was about to say had reference to the synagogue? Then, when he comes to spell out the features of the false teaching, in verse 16 onwards, he clearly refers to practices which sound very Jewish in character. So, part of what he had in mind by these *human traditions* would have been some of the rules and regulations which came from a very worthy source and which had centuries of tradition behind them, and consequently they would readily commend themselves as a way of knowing

God. But regardless of the pedigree, the teaching was still erroneous because it was *human* in origin rather than stemming from divine revelation. Spiritual truth is not always to be found in the hallowed halls of venerable religious tradition.

These *human traditions* probably also included traditions that came from the mystery cults and beliefs about magical rites and superstitious practices which were thought to be necessary to appease the powerful and hostile supernatural forces of the world. Many of these had found their way into the Jewish synagogue by Paul's time. They were not confined to the pagan religious practices of the Gentiles. So it was probably through the synagogue that they too might well have influenced the church and created the problem. Whether from a Jewish stable, or from an obviously pagan one, human traditions may have seemed to make sense, but they were a very faulty foundation on which to build in comparison with the divine revelation which had come to them in Christ.

How much we're still saddled with the influence of human traditions both within and outside the church! Inside, it's fish on Fridays, or AV only, or teetotalism, or dressing in a certain way, or observing special days. Outside, superstition still stalks boldly across the land as people try to appease fate by avoiding their unlucky number, not walking under ladders, throwing salt over their shoulders or touching wood. Sociologists tell us that common religion outside the church is largely characterised by superstition.[9] Human traditions may range from the major to the trivial. They're still common and they're still significant, because they continue to draw people away from Christ.

Basic principles

The third element in the construction of the prison is that of *the basic principles of this world*. 'Basic principles', which translates the Greek word *stoicheia*, has given rise to a host of interpretations. It essentially means 'to set out in rows' or 'to mark off a boundary'. But the word came to be used in a variety of ways. It came to refer to the basics of the 'A, B, C'. It referred to the rudimentary principles of a trade or discipline. Or, it referred to the four basic elements of the world: earth, water, fire and air. Then, some used it to refer to the spirits who ruled the sun, moon and stars.

Given both the general thrust of the letter, and the details of the false teaching he is opposing, Paul is almost certainly using it of personal spiritual beings, like astral deities, angels or spirits who were thought to exercise control in the universe and over individual lives.[10] These supernatural beings were supposed to bring about sickness, misfortune, war and conflict or prosperity and good luck. No wonder people wanted to treat them with respect. But the respect too easily became a cringing fear or a kowtowing to their existence. They tied people up rather than setting people free. Only Christ, who had triumphed over them, as Paul asserts in verse 15, was able to grant such freedom.

It ought to be said that many scholars today have ridiculed the idea of supernatural beings and interpret these *basic principles* not as spirits or supernatural beings from another world but as the elementary structures of this world; by which they mean the structures of government, of economics, of military power, of nationalism, or of big business. They take this line largely on the basis that belief in supernatural beings doesn't fit easily into a world like ours which has been shaped so much by scientific rationalism. But they also base it on the understanding that there have been demonic and destructive forces, like war or the holocaust, which have fatefully shaped our modern world so much and that these forces are, at least arguably, more in evidence today than personal evil intelligences. They argue that whatever former ages believed about the existence of mythological creatures, the best, and most realistic way, of interpreting the word *stoicheia* today is to understand it as the non-personal structures of our world.

Several things might be said in response to this. First, there can be little doubt that whatever we might believe today about the existence of supernatural spirits, the word in its original context was used to refer to supernatural beings by those who did believe in their existence. In our interpreting of this word, or any other part of Scripture, we should never read back our own position into it without first seeking to understand what it originally meant.

Second, the dismissal of a belief in the existence of supernatural beings may have been popular among western intellectuals for whom it is an unsophisticated idea, but thousands of ordinary men and women believe in such powers and influences, as is evidenced by the popularity of horoscopes, mediums and the superstitious practices which still abound in an attempt to ward off evil influences. Many feel their lives are controlled by real, personal powers outside of themselves. Even among western intellectuals today, the cold rationality that once dismissed the dimension of the supernatural is crumbling, since it seems an inadequate way of understanding the world, at least if used to the exclusion of all other schemes of interpretation.

Third, there is no reason to think, even if the word *stoicheia* was in its original context primarily a reference to supernatural beings, that it might not also include a reference to the institutions and structures of oppression that equally today keep people in fear. What is not legitimate is to replace the one idea with the other and dismiss the idea of the existence of evil powers as a result. Nigel Wright's inclusive view of the word is probably a wise guide. He writes that the word 'refers consistently to genuine power realities which are heavenly and earthly, divine and human, spiritual and political, visible and invisible, good and evil'.[11]

These philosophies, traditions and principles were, in reality, great confidence tricksters. The bars were an illusion and the prison gate was not locked. They kept people under restraint when they really had neither the right nor the power to do so. Believers had been released from their clutches by Christ, who had exposed their deception and disarmed them from whatever power they might have been able to muster. It would have been folly, indeed, for believers to voluntarily put themselves back behind bars when there was no slither of a reason for doing so. The believer who is correctly founded on Christ can genuinely experience freedom through him.

3. Fulness in Christ (verses 9-12)

I understand that Rolls Royce will never disclose the bhp of their cars. There is an old preacher's story, which obviously contains a grain of truth, that a man bought a Rolls Royce and took it overseas where he ran into a spot of bother with it. He took it to a local garage for repair and they, dazzled by its technological brilliance, began to ask all sorts of questions about it. Eventually they asked what its bhp was. No matter what information they looked up they couldn't find the answer. So they sent a telegram to Rolls Royce in England to ask for this additional piece of technical data. When the reply came it consisted of a single word, 'Adequate'.

That's Paul's message about Jesus. No matter what powers are ranged against you, what authorities seek to imprison you, what philosophies seek to trick you or what traditions want to enslave you, Jesus Christ is an adequate deliverer and sufficient Saviour. He is so because of:

Who he is (v. 9)

He is the one in whom *all the fulness of the Deity lives in bodily form*. Others may have insights into God, or a touch of God about them. But he is God himself. In the incarnate Christ, God has made, as Handley Moule put it, 'a settled and congenial home.'[12] Jesus Christ is not less than God, but fully and uniquely God come in human form. What more could you want? Any other route to God is bound to be inferior and less complete than the way through Jesus. For, 'everything of God gets expressed in him, so you can see and hear him clearly. You don't need a telescope, a microscope, or a horoscope to realise the fulness of Christ, and the emptiness of the universe without him.'[13]

Dermot MacDonald expresses this in a mind-expanding, worship-inducing way: 'In him all fulness dwells. He is the fulness of wisdom and knowledge. He is the fulness of space, for in him and through him and unto him are all things. He is the fulness of time, for he fills eternity.... There is nothing before, nothing after, nothing more, He has no "before" or "after". Jesus Christ is the Ultimate.'[14]

Once again, as in 1:22, the stress is on God coming *in bodily form*. Obviously they were worried about that and thought it somehow impossible or unworthy that God should have assumed a physical body. They assumed that to do so would have reduced God or made him unclean. But, as we have seen, it was essential that he should have done so 'for,' as Gregory of Nazianzus pointed out centuries ago, 'that which he has not assumed he has not healed.'[15]

What it means (v. 10)

Paul presses home the implication of Christ's coming in this way for the believer. If there is fulness of deity to be found in Christ then we can find fulness of salvation in him. For we *have been given fulness in Christ*. So, how erroneous it is to think that Christ can only meet some of our needs or that to find protection from some authorities or to gain deliverance from some powers we need to turn elsewhere, as the Colossians were doing. There is nothing missing that we should need; nothing short that we should have to supply from elsewhere; nothing inadequate that we must supplement from another source. We need only to look to him, and him alone.

How it works (vv. 11-12)

Here then is great medicine. But how is the medicine to be taken so that it might do its work and effect the cure? Here is valuable treasure. But how is the treasure to be cashed in so it has some current value for us? The medicine is to be applied by *faith*. The goods are to be exchanged by *faith*. Faith is to trust yourself completely into the hands of the powerful God who raised Jesus from the dead, just as you might trust yourself wholly to a surgeon if you are sick, or trust yourself wholly to the pole if you are a pole-vaulter charging down the track towards the bar. It means to put your whole weight on to Christ and to lean on him.

This kind of faith leads to some inner changes which Paul illustrates in reference to the ceremony of circumcision and the ceremony of baptism. The false teachers were more than likely advocating that Gentile Christians should submit to circumcision. But Paul explains that in Christ a new meaning has been given to circumcision and the outward rite no longer has the force which once it did. It was the inner transformation which really mattered.

There are two ways to take his reference to circumcision. Circumcision, it should be said, was the initiation rite which provided a Jewish boy with an identity in his family and race and made him a member of the covenant people of God with all the privileges and obligations that entailed. It was only an outward ceremony, although the Jews taught that it should be matched inwardly by a circumcision of the heart.

So, one way to take verse 11, which is the way the NIV translates it, is to say that we do not have to undergo physical circumcision – *circumcision done by human hands* – for Jesus has circumcised us metaphorically and spiritually and caused us to put off our *sinful nature*. By his physical death he has dealt with our sensual natures (the cause of so much trouble and home of so much temptation), broken their power over us, stripped them of their authority in our lives, and initiated us into a new way of living in union with him. It's not the undergoing of any religious ritual which has achieved this transformation in us, but the reality of what Christ has done for us that makes it possible.

But, to be precise, Paul does not write here of our *sinful nature* but of the *body of flesh*. He uses a phrase he has already used in 1:22 where it clearly referred to the death of Christ. So, this might be, in fact, as many have suggested, a reference to Christ stripping off his body of flesh on the cross. The circumcision may be his, not ours. If so, circumcision, in this case, is not the removal of a tiny piece of flesh but a symbol for a violent and gruesome stripping away of his whole body in crucifixion.

Neither interpretation is without problems. But whichever interpretation you choose, the next step in Paul's argument is clear. In verse 12, we see that Christ's death, burial and resurrection are intimately interwoven with our own. He died, his death was sealed by his burial and followed by his resurrection. What happened to him happens, spiritually, to us. As believers we participate in his death by dying to self and to the world and its systems;[16] we confirm that by burying our old way of living and rising to a new way of living with him. We don't die like him but with him; we're not buried like him but with him; we have been raised not like him but with him. This sharing in the death, burial and resurrection of Christ, all of which, note, are spoken of in the past tense as having already happened, is what incorporates the believer into Christ and releases the fulness of his life in theirs. All of this was graphically symbolised by the act of baptism when a convert was buried in water and rose, washed, as it were, from it. Hence his reference to this taking place in *baptism*. It is not that baptism brings this about, but that it portrays a spiritual reality which has already taken place *through faith*.

So, the exercise of *faith in the power of God* renders the outward ceremonies of circumcision redundant, while making the benefits of Christ's work available to the believer and admitting the believer into the closest of relationships with Christ the Lord, who 'died for our sins according the Scriptures... was buried... (and) was raised on the third day according to the Scriptures.'[17]

4. Forgiveness from Christ (verses 13-15)

In moving his argument along, Paul now uses the idea of circumcision which he has just introduced to remind the Gentiles what a dreadful state they were in until Christ came to the rescue.

We need to keep in mind how deep the division between Jew and Gentile was in the ancient world, much deeper than any division we know between black and white or Catholic and Protestant. Quite simply, the Jews were kosher and the Gentiles were not. The Gentiles were uncircumcised and unclean. The absence of physical circumcision was really only a physical symbol of where they stood spiritually. They were left to wallow in their sins, were morally cut off from God and spiritually dead. They were powerless to help themselves, for there was no way they could bring themselves back to life. Only by God stepping in *when (they) were dead in (their) sins* and providing them with resurrection life could they come to life again. This he did through

Christ, who provided the key to unlock their, and our, predicament when *he forgave us all our sins*.

Again Paul summons up two images to help us understand the wonder of Christ forgiving us our sins, which he did through his work on the cross. First, he uses the picture of debts being cancelled. Then, he uses the picture of enemies being defeated.

He cancelled our debts (v. 14)

Sin is pictured in some way as a debt we owe. The bill, which records the amount, as it were, takes the form of a *written code* and until it is paid off it stands over against us and condemns us. The *written code* Paul has in mind could be the code of the law. That would seem to make sense in view of the next phrase where he describes it *as the written code with its regulations*. Ephesians 2:15 seems to back that up, as do the allusions in Romans and Galatians to the role of the law in our lives.[18] There would be plenty in the law which would highlight our offences and our debts to God. In any spiritual court they could surely 'throw the book at us'.

But some have suggested that Paul is talking about a document which it was thought was kept in heaven where names and deeds were recorded. Moses, for example, mentions it when he prays to God following the incident with the Golden Calf. 'Please,' he pleads with God, 'forgive their sin – but if not, then blot me out of the book you have written.'[19] It was a common enough idea. In later Old Testament history the idea had been developed somewhat and it was claimed that the angels kept the book as a place in which people's good and evil deeds were being recorded with an eye to the final judgment.

It is possible that Paul would not have wanted his readers to accept all the details associated with the picture. Whatever the details, it is apparent that sin costs and a price has to be paid for it. That sin costs is often all too apparent. The drunken driver who kills another road user has cost his victim their life, cost himself a gaol sentence and cost others great heartache. Stealing costs the one whose goods are taken as well as costing the reputation and worth of the one who steals. Our greedy lifestyles cost in terms of the depletion of the earth's non-renewable resources and is usually at the expense of the world's poor. The price tag of sin is all too often obvious. But even where it isn't, it is no less real. It always costs, not just us, our fellow human beings and our earth, but supremely God, whose honour is shamed, whose creation is ruined and whose holiness is grieved by our sin.

The wonderful news is that the IOU of sin has been *cancelled*. The document recording our debts has been taken away and ripped up by Jesus Christ. It would be wonderful indeed for most of us if the building society took our mortgage agreement and cancelled it because all that we owe had been paid by someone else. It is still more wonderful that the debt we owe for sin has been paid by God himself in Christ. It is even more marvellous to see how he did so: *he took it away, nailing it to the cross*.

Paul's mind's eye goes back to the scene at Calvary. There, above the cross of Jesus, Pilate had nailed a notice setting out the crime for which he was being executed. This 'titulus', as it was called, was the normal way in which a criminal's indictment would be announced. Pilate, you remember, had written, 'This is Jesus, the King of the Jews.'[20] No doubt it was calculated to anger the Jews. They certainly asked him to reword it so the claim was less direct. But Paul says that on that nail above the head of Jesus as he hangs on the cross he sees a different indictment. It reads, 'This is Jesus who dies to pay the price for the sins of the people.' Just as in the ancient world an IOU, once paid, would have been stuck on a nail as a sign of it being cancelled, so Christ stuck our sins on the nail of his cross and declared them cancelled.

Here, in Luther's words, is a 'fortunate exchange'. 'What is ours becomes his, and what is his becomes ours.'[21] He assumes our debt and we receive the riches of his grace. He assumes our sin and we receive his righteousness.

At last we see how the prophetic insight into the character of God came to fulfilment. Isaiah declared, 'I, even I, am he who blots out your transgressions, for my own sake, and remembers your sins no more.'[22] The debt of sin had been swept away 'like a cloud' and 'like a morning mist'.[23] And the sins are remembered no more.[24]

He defeats our enemies (v. 15)

The second picture of our salvation is that of a victorious Roman general who returns home and celebrates his victory by marching into Rome in triumphal procession to the cheers of the adoring crowds. Behind him displayed, for all to see, are the spoils of war, including the defeated soldiers and their generals. They are stripped of their dignity, rendered powerless, publicly humiliated and held up to contempt.

The Colossians were worried that there were all sorts of *powers and authorities* in their world who had the ability to control them and direct their lives for good or ill. Paul tells them that this is nonsense. It might be so if God, who is the subject of this verse, had not done something to deal with them through Christ on the cross,[25] but he has. They have been rendered powerless (*disarmed*) and he has *made a public spectacle of them*.

What God did on the cross was a delicious irony. As Tom Wright points out:

> The 'rulers' and 'authorities' of Rome and of Israel – ...the best government and the highest religion the world of that time had ever known – conspired to place Jesus on the cross. These powers, angry at his challenge to their sovereignty stripped *him* naked, held *him* up to public contempt, and celebrated a triumph over *him*.[26]

We might add that it was not only the powers of Greece and Rome that conspired to put him there, but all the malevolent powers of the cosmos who took part in that evil alliance. But they did not know what they were doing. Rather than trapping him and doing away with him, they were themselves being caught and defeated. For, as Wright continues, the paradox to be seen in the cross is that in reality 'God was stripping them naked, was holding them up to public contempt, and leading them in his own triumphal procession – in Christ, the crucified Messiah.'[27] Having done their worst, they overreached themselves. Having played their trump card, they were trumped. In the cross the enemy is outwitted and vanquished.

Here is a bold claim. It is a huge reversal of the usual way of seeing the world. We normally think that power is needed to defeat an enemy, but God uses weakness. We generally think that dignity is associated with majesty, but God glories in the shame of Calvary. We are accustomed to think that success must be safeguarded, but in Christ God embraces defeat. We mostly believe that pain is to be eschewed, but in the cross God willingly accepts it. But in the weakness, shame, pain and apparent defeat of the cross there is real victory. His strategy is so much the opposite of ours. Yet his strategy is the one which succeeds.

The point of it all, as James Dunn writes, is that, 'The unseen powers and invisible forces that dominated and determined so much of life need no longer be feared. A greater power and force was at work, which could rule and determine their lives more effectively – in a word "Christ". Triumph indeed!'[28]

For many centuries this perspective on the cross of Christ did not receive a high profile. Other interpretations of the atonement, like that of penal substitution, were more dominant. But here is a true understanding of the cross, that on it Christ is Christ the victor, who defeats and disarms our enemies in battle. Gustav Aulen, who, in his book *Christus Victor* did much to draw attention to this interpretation of the cross once more, calls it the classic theory of the atonement. One thing he stresses remains important. He wrote:

> It is important, above all, at this point to see clearly that the work of salvation and deliverance is at the same time a work of atonement, of reconciliation between God and the world. It is altogether misleading to say that the triumph of Christ over the powers of evil, whereby He delivers man, is a work of salvation but not of atonement; for the two ideas cannot possibly be thus separated.[29]

Aulen is right. The work of deliverance and the work of atonement is all of a piece. In winning the battle against our enemies he also reconciled us to God. In delivering us and giving us freedom he also set us free from the power of sin and its penalty.

On 18th December 1865, the 13th Amendment to the Constitution of the United States was passed, declaring that from that time on, 'neither slavery nor involuntary servitude shall exist.'

The abolition of slavery had been secured at the cost of the sacrifice of thousands of lives in a bloody Civil War which had left the nation in tatters. It had also cost the life of the President, Abraham Lincoln, who was assassinated. But freedom had been won. How tragic then that, as Shelby Foote records in his history of the Civil War, when an Alabaman Negro was asked what he thought of the Great Emancipator, Abraham Lincoln, he replied, 'I don't know nothing 'bout Abraham Lincoln. And I don't know nothing 'bout emancipation either.'

The Christians in Colosse were in danger of forgetting the freedom which was theirs in Christ and of voluntarily slipping back into slavery by submitting to religious rituals and unnecessary rules and regulations. How tragic. As Paul urged the Galatians, 'It is for freedom that Christ has set us free. Stand firm, then, and do not let yourselves be burdened again by a yoke of slavery.'[30]

Here, then, are the basic elements of the Christian faith.

■   We need to be founded on Christ and on him alone.

■   We must receive freedom from Christ for it is available from him alone.

■   We can receive fulness in Christ, for the fulness of God dwells in him. So, our Christian experience may be abundant, not meagre.

■   And it all flows from the cross where forgiveness from Christ is to be found.

5

Falling from Christ
Colossians 2:16-23

[16] Therefore do not let anyone judge you by what you eat or drink, or with regard to a religious festival, a New Moon celebration or a Sabbath day. [17] These are a shadow of the things that were to come; the reality, however, is found in Christ. [18] Do not let anyone who delights in false humility and the worship of angels disqualify you for the prize. Such people go into great detail about what they have seen, and their unspiritual minds puff them up with idle notions. [19] They have lost connection with the Head, from whom the whole body, supported and held together by its ligaments and sinews, grows as God causes it to grow.

[20] Since you died with Christ to the basic principles of this world, why, as though you still belonged to it, do you submit to its rules: [21] 'Do not handle! Do not taste! Do not touch!'? [22] These are all destined to perish with use, because they are based on human commands and teachings. [23] Such regulations indeed have an appearance of wisdom, with their self-imposed worship, their false humility and their harsh treatment of the body, but they lack any value in restraining sensual indulgence.

1. The character of false religion (verses 16-23)

> Special diets (v. 16)
> Rigid calendars (v. 16)
> Ritual humiliations (vv. 17, 23)
> Worshipping angels (v. 18)
> Imposing rules (v. 21)

2. The critique of false religion (verses 17-23)

> Its form: shadow not substance (v. 17)
> Its character: sensual not spiritual (v. 18)
> Its power: severed not connected (v. 19)
> Its future: transient not permanent (v. 22)
> Its origin: human not divine (v. 22)
> Its value: futile not effective (v. 23)

3. The counter to false religion (verse 20)

> Death with Christ

Clever people can sometimes get things very wrong. At the time when sociologists were conducting the funeral rites of religion and declaring their belief in the theory of secularisation, that the world had finished with religion for good, new religious movements were coming to birth as never before. It seems that people are deeply and enduringly religious, whatever enlightenment-trained sociologists might think. People have an innate capacity to reach out after 'god', and if the old 'gods' fail, then they'll invent new ones. It is a day of multiple-choice religion. The shelves of the religious supermarket have never been so well stocked or offered such variety. And if off-the-shelf religions don't satisfy, then there is plenty of material at hand to construct your own designer God.

The same inclination towards religion was evident in the ancient world, as was the same tendency to pluralism, even if not quite to the degree we suffer from at the moment. The pluralism of our day has led Peter Berger to conclude that modern men and women are homeless in their minds.[1] Far from having settled beliefs, the offer of so much choice, so many alternative viewpoints, makes us displaced persons. Like refugees of the mind we travel from one place to another and we don't belong anywhere. We have no settled spiritual convictions or firm interpretations of life. We're attracted by whatever comes along next and always ready to explore another option. What we fail to realise is that being displaced in this way is a very uncomfortable form of existence. Humanitarian organisations spend millions trying to combat the plight of the refugee precisely because it is an evil and should never be the norm. Home is where we belong, where we're intended to live. To be homeless is to be condemned to living in exile in a barren wilderness. What's true literally is also true spiritually.

The Colossian Christians were being tempted to wander. They had recently found a home in Jesus, but now they were being invited to move to another religious address. What made it more tragic was not just the discomfort of being on the move again, but that the alternatives on offer were neither true nor proficient. They were based on a lie. The truth was to be found in Jesus alone. And they were quite unable to deliver people from the fears and powers which enslaved them. They were quite ineffective. Jesus alone could set people free. Yet, elements of this false religion seemed so attractive, as they still do. So Paul sets about unmasking them. In this section of his letter he describes their character – a character we shall find uncannily contemporary. But he doesn't do so in a neutral way. Throughout his description he weaves in a critique of this alternative religion. He shows us why anything other than Christ is not a harmless, interesting substitute but a fatal error. In the middle of it, he gives them the one vital clue as to how they can counter the snare which the slick salesmen are laying for them.

1. The character of false religion (verses 16-23)

Scholars have spent much time trying to identify the precise source of the false teaching. Did it come from the Jewish synagogue? Did it emanate from the mystery cults? Did it derive from pagan practices? Did it arise from Gnostic teaching? Much the most convincing explanation has been given recently by Clinton Arnold in his book, *The Colossian Syncretism*.[2] He shows that much of it would have come from local folk religion, channelled through the Jewish synagogue, with which the early Christians would have had close connections. Elements of paganism, of the mystery cults and of Judaism can all be seen in what Paul describes. And there is no need to say it has to be either this source or that which lies behind the teaching. In the realm of folk religion all sorts of things get mixed up and are to be found together, no matter how inconsistent or incoherent. Only the theological purist will feel the need to choose between contradictory viewpoints, not the ordinary people. The evidence is that even those aspects of the false teaching which don't immediately appear to fit with the Jewish faith, like the worship of angels, did have a home in the local synagogue. So the false teaching came essentially from a Jewish source. The one explanation for which there is less evidence than once thought is that of Gnosticism, a philosophy which was not in fact developed until a later date. So what were the elements which characterised this alternative religion and what relevance, if any, do they have to today? Paul lists five features of the false teaching.

Special diet (v. 16)

His critique begins with *do not let anyone judge you by what you eat or drink*. Throughout their history the Jews had maintained their separateness from others by observing distinctive eating patterns. The Jewish law, recorded in Leviticus 11:1-23, gave a detailed list of animals considered clean and so able to be eaten and those which were unclean and so forbidden as food. It's well known that pork was on the forbidden list, but so too was the camel, coney and rabbit, as well as some fish and birds. Moreover, some came to believe that demons could gain access to a person's life through eating certain foods. Hence the desire to be careful about what they ate.

In the New Testament era, the issue was still a live one and caused tremendous friction in the early church. Many thought that to be a Christian it was vital that the Jewish food laws should continue to be observed. In spite of the Council of Jerusalem resolving the issue[3] and declaring that salvation was through the grace of the Lord Jesus alone, and not by adopting the covenant customs of the Jews, some still persisted in seeking to foist these food laws on Gentile converts. As late as Paul's first letter to Timothy,[4] at the end of the New Testament period, he was still arguing against those who ordered believers 'to abstain from certain foods'.

Some still draw a close connection between spirituality and eating. I'm not thinking here of the command not to overeat. It's clear that gluttony and greed were and are sins.[5] But that's different from what's being suggested both to the Colossians and to many today. Many Jews, of course, still hold to the importance of only eating kosher food. But the contemporary forms of 'the forbidden list' are much wider than this. People have tried to make out that eating all sorts of food and drinking all sorts of drink is spiritually detrimental. Of course, everyone has a different list. I've heard the eating of meat, the consuming of any alcohol, the drinking of coffee, the devouring of McDonalds and even the enjoyment of peanut butter condemned as something no Christian should do. Some wonder how you can possibly be an authentic Christian without sticking exclusively to vegetarianism, to wholefoods, health foods, or non-organic foods. Such foods may possibly be connected to physical health, but they have no spiritual value. Those who advocate their spiritual worth should be reminded of Paul's words to Timothy that God created food to be 'received with thanksgiving by those who believe and who know the truth. For everything God created is good, and nothing is to be rejected if it is received with thanksgiving...'[6] They, perhaps, also need to be gently reminded that such scruples are a luxury in a world where one third go to sleep hungry every night and thousands die every day of starvation.

In the light of God's liberating truth, why is it that people are so keen to enslave themselves with dietary regulations that are quite superfluous to their spiritual lives? Why do they think that observing such restrictions should any longer benefit them spiritually, when the whole thrust of the gospel is that they don't. For, in Christ, God has declared all food to be clean.[7]

Rigid calendar (v. 16)

The Jews also maintained their distance from other nations by observing a special religious calendar. Paul's particular wording here about *a religious festival, a New Moon celebration or a Sabbath day* are the very terms which occur a number of times in the Old Testament.[8] So we know this aspect of the teaching had a Jewish origin. But that doesn't mean to say that those against whom Paul is writing observed these festivals for the purpose for which they were originally designed. They were designed as celebrations of God's activity in history and as reminders of his sovereignty and salvation. But by the time we read of the Colossians observing them, we know that they were doing so as a means of warding off the evil influences which might come from the stars or from angelic beings. Their observance of the festivals had become magical and superstitious. A couple of popular moon gods were worshipped in Colosse. 'Selene' and 'Men' were thought to be able to offer people protection from evil powers if their special days were carefully observed. Further, we know that many of the initiation ceremonies of the mystery religions were held at the time of the new moon.

So, Paul's warning against being held accountable for whether these days were observed or not is more significant than it seems. While some still argue within our churches about the proper way to observe the Christian calendar, similar perhaps to the argument which Paul addresses in Romans 14:5-6 where he regards different evaluations of different days to be legitimate, the issue here is somewhat deeper. It's not a matter of what calendar you observe, if any, but why you observe it. To use it to celebrate the mighty acts of God and the wonderful things he has done in Christ is one thing. To use it superstitiously as a means of manipulating spirits and securing protection and good fortune is something altogether different.

Ritual humiliations (vv. 18, 23)

Paul's next reference is to people *who delight in false humility*. It is an issue he returns to in verse 23, where he talks about the false teaching as having *an appearance of wisdom, with their self-imposed worship, their false humility and their harsh treatment of the body*. At its simplest level, humility is likely to refer to the practice of fasting. Fasting is obviously a practice which was commended both by the example and teaching of Jesus as having some spiritual value – and it was practised beneficially in the early church.[9] But it can be taken to excess and be used not as a free offering of oneself to God but as a way of trying to manipulate him to our own ends. In the world of Colosse it was associated with initiation into a mystery cult, which might be an issue in Paul's thinking here. There are some grounds for believing that his use of the phrase *disqualify you for the prize* is a phrase associated with being accepted or rejected for membership of a mystery cult. The arguments for this are not altogether convincing, so it may be a more general reference that Paul is making here.

Fasting was widely commended as a means of ensuring you received a dream, of securing success in the use of magical rites and of driving away demons.

Given Paul's second mention of *false humility* which he links with the *harsh treatment of the body*, it may be that he has something more than fasting in mind. Various forms of mortification, ranging widely from sleep deprivation, sleeping on beds of nails, wearing hair shirts, taking cold showers, flagellation, chanting and so on, have been advocated over the centuries as a means of becoming more spiritual. But this is not the way in which God has chosen to effect our inner transformation or to make himself known to us.

It is strange, as the great preacher Alexander MacLaren pointed out, that people should think they make themselves more acceptable to God by making themselves uncomfortable.[10] But this curious belief has exercised a strong hold on people down the centuries. Fasting, isolation, and celibacy have all been considered widely as means by which the body could be controlled so that the soul could flourish. One thinks of Simeon the Stylite who sat for thirty-six years up a stone column, living a life of great austerity. The height of the pole was gradually increased until it reached sixty feet! Thousands came to see him and hear him preach. Then, there are some of the extreme positions adopted by some of the Irish Celtic monks of sleeping standing up or praying when standing in ice-cold water neck deep. Somehow or another this was all supposed to subdue the flesh and let the soul dominate. These may be extreme examples, but harsh and humiliating practices of one kind or another always seem to hold a strange attraction.

Coming up to date, one recalls many stories like that of Erica Heftmann who joined the Moonies and described a number of humiliating rituals she endured. One day when on a fund-raising run which was not going well, and for which one member of the team called Pete got the blame, their team leader, Todd, slammed on the brakes of the minibus and got them all to jump out. It was 3 o'clock in the morning. Even so, they were made to climb over a barbed wire fence, stand in a circle in a vacant and frozen field and, with clenched fists and bent bodies chant, A-bo-ji Mansei. Up and down they went as if they were marines until Peter, at least, collapsed shivering and sobbing to the ground.[11] Plenty of other bizarre and humiliating rituals could be described. They're not uncommon among new religious movements. But why should people be deceived by them when the way to God is a whole lot more gracious and a whole lot simpler?

Worshipping angels (v. 18)

The Jews believed that angels played a key role in the struggle against Satan, as Daniel 10:13 suggests. But later Judaism built a major superstructure on this which was perhaps not merited. Angels increasingly became the focus of attention. They were credited with having control over the physical elements of the world. They were looked to for help, particularly in the fight against evil spirits, and to protect graves, avert disasters and provide direction. Whilst initially it was thought that God dispatched them to offer help, the position soon changed and people began to pray to the angels themselves for help. They were sought in ecstatic visions; magic rites and mystical experiences going together. If they didn't actually worship them, and they probably did, they came pretty close to it.[12] At least the Jews and the Christians didn't develop an organised cult of angel worship, as others did.

The chief problem with this worship was that as the reputation of angels grew the reputation of Jesus sank. People were happy to have him as one mediatorial figure between themselves and God, so long as he was not seen as superior or exclusive in any way. So Jesus was devalued to being roughly on the same level as the angels. Clinton Arnold mentions a pagan prayer which has been excavated in the area which reads, 'Hor, Hor, Phor, Eloei, Adonai, Iao, Sabaoth, Michael, Jesus Christ. Help us and this household. Amen.'[13] Jesus, apparently, is no more special than a number of pagan gods or angelic beings.

So, the worst aspect of this false teaching was that it diminished Jesus in the eyes of his followers, rendering him impotent and denying his sole mediatorial role between people and God.[14]

Angels clearly have a place in biblical teaching and cynicism as to their existence is not warranted. But the place they were occupying at Colosse was not consistent with the restrained teaching of the Scriptures about them, and one wonders whether it is in the place being granted to them today by some. Angelology is currently a growth industry. One wonders how long before some enterprising university offers the first B.A., that is Bachelor of Angelology, in the subject. A glance at a recent *Books in Print* yielded the titles of eighteen newly published books on angels. They included *Angel a week*; *Angel Almanac*; *Angel and the Ants: Bringing heaven closer to your daily life*; *Angel at my shoulder*; *Angel decoder*; *Angel in my house*; *Angel in my locker*; *Angel therapy*; *Ask your angels* and so on. The internet even provides an angel tracking service so that you can keep abreast of their movements.

In so far as this is a healthy reaction to the cold rationalism which has ruled out the possibility of the existence of a spirit world, and in so far as it seeks to resurrect a neglected biblical theme, it is to be welcomed. But the infatuation some display with the subject and the extra-biblical claims which many books make for the role of angels, suggests we should be extremely cautious less we too fall into the same mistake as the Colossians were making. Anything which detracts from the pre-eminence of Jesus should be called into question.

Imposing rules (v. 21)

The last characteristic which Paul mentions is that of the rules: *Do not handle! Do not taste! Do not touch!* Religions are very good at creating taboos, and at teaching 'thou shalt not...'. It's always done for the best of motives. It's designed to prevent someone from being defiled as well as to present them pure and holy. But it doesn't work. It produces a very unattractive kind of holiness which majors on the negative. It leads to a measuring line approach to holiness. How close do I have to get before I'm considered to have broken the rule? How much of it do I have to touch before I have infringed the regulation? It's like the supermarket sign I've seen which obviously wished to advertise its submission to the English Sunday Trading laws. So, it declared the store would be open on Saturdays from 7.00 am to 11.59 pm.

Jesus ruthlessly exposed the folly of this approach to spirituality. When he was challenged by the Pharisees about his disciples eating their food with hands which were ceremonially unclean, he pointed out that it's not what is on the outside but what is on the inside that matters. 'Nothing outside you can make you "unclean" by going into you. Rather, it is what comes out of you that makes you "unclean".'[15] That's why the solution to our uncleanness is never to avoid external defilement as an end in itself, but rather to seek inner cleansing and transformation.

Paul not only agrees with Jesus, as verse 23 makes clear, but has other reasons for attacking these legalistic preachers. There are many areas in the Christian's life which are matters of freedom. It is, therefore, quite wrong for people to make them a matter of law. The questions of keeping special days, observing special diets, touching and tasting certain things, fall within this area of freedom. True, as he is careful to mention when he discusses the issue in some depth in Romans 14, we should always act with an eye on the effect our actions will have on our fellow believers, we must always act within the limits of our faith and we must always act as those who are accountable to the Lord. But, within those constraints it is quite wrong for anyone to crystallise even sound advice and wise pastoral guidance into hardened law. Christian experience should be one of freedom, not one of captivity to a new set of rules and regulations. If it is not, then we have failed to appreciate the work of Christ. And that is Paul's most serious objection to the rule-makers. He came to defeat our captors and liberate us from the law.[16] So why are we voluntarily going back into slavery? Again, therefore, as with the worship of angels and the other aspects of this false teaching, the basic problem was that the rule book approach to holiness denigrated Christ.

Manifestations of this legalistic approach are still legion. Sadly, they're not all outside the evangelical church. It's not only modern cults that encourage the strict observance of rules and the sharp separation of converts from their unconverted family and friends.

Many a zealous church has done the same. Pharisaism is the besetting sin of keen churches who are eager to produce ardent Christians. And it's all too open to abuse. Authoritarianism, heavy shepherding, rigid attitudes, the demand for unquestioning obedience soon takes over. Ronald Enroth is one of those who has drawn attention to the potential for churches to abuse. He describes the experience of Tom and Pam Murray, among others, who joined a church and initially welcomed the clear sense of direction and guidance they received from its leadership. It sought to live by 'first-century-church standards' and to elude 'the stain of the world'. Then the leader began to claim he had received revelations and to exercise control over a broad spectrum of people's lives including dress, diet, work habits, entertainment and employment, as well as over some of the more obviously spiritual areas of discipline. Any dissent earned discipline, some of which was extremely humiliating and intimidating. Eventually, as so often, it 'all blew up in our faces' and the Murrays left the church and struggled with God for some time before regaining their balance and rediscovering their freedom in Christ.[17]

In days when people are reacting against the vacuum which the moral and spiritual revolutions of the Sixties have created, they are searching for strong direction, clear moral frameworks and authoritative answers. But that makes many people particularly vulnerable. They are prey to any strong-minded charlatan who seems to have a way forward to offer. Hence, they are liable to abuse. We need to take care.

Even if the preaching of do's and don'ts as a way of knowing God doesn't amount to abuse, it still stands in contrast to the gospel. Therefore it must be resisted and where it is found we must unmask it as erroneous teaching.

It will be evident by now that each of the issues Paul raises needs to be handled with care. Some of the things he talks about seem to relate to healthy spiritual disciplines. Since God created us as united, embodied beings, it's good to eat healthily, avoid food and drink that is damaging, and exercise to keep our bodies fit. Many find the discipline of retreats and keeping some days special so that they can be set aside for prolonged prayer extremely valuable. The acceptance of some discipline may lead to maturity. An awareness of the role of angels may give us a fuller picture of the providence of God in our lives. But the moment we trust any of these things as the means of our salvation, and the moment they usurp the place of Christ as our sole and supreme Saviour, they become a snare and not an asset. They had done so in Colosse. Far from being useful spiritual disciplines they had been distorted beyond recognition and, betraying as they did some very warped views that lay underneath them, they had become a spiritual liability.

2. The critique of false religion (verses 17-23)

As Paul describes the false teaching in some detail, he interlaces his description with criticism. His analysis of it shows us why he evaluates it so negatively and why we must be as careful to avoid it as an alcoholic should be careful to avoid a pub. Six criticisms are mounted.

Its form: shadow not substance (v. 17)

The first criticism on the list is that *these are a shadow of the things that were to come; the reality, however, is found in Christ*. A shadow projects a shaded image of a body when the body gets in the way of the sun. It relates to the body but it has no existence of its own. It is not the body itself. Shadows are fickle and transient. They have no substance or permanence about them. The idea of the shadow is used on a number of occasions to explain how the laws and rituals of the Old Testament relate to the Christian. The idea, for example, occurs a couple of times in the letter to the Hebrews, both in connection with the sanctuary and the law.[18] They are like signposts which point forward to your destination. No one imagines that as you're driving down the M5 in search of Exeter that the first time you see its name on the signpost you've arrived. You haven't. But you know you're in the right direction. The reality is something else.

So it is with the religious laws and customs of the Old

Testament. They are helpful as a way of pointing forward to the real thing which is to come. They are extremely rough sketches of what's to come. They have value but they're not meant to be binding now. They were never meant to be the last word, any more than the signpost should be mistaken for the destination.

By contrast, the substance (literally, the body) is the real thing which we are to expect, and that is Christ. He fulfils all the expectations of the Old Testament. It was all a pointer to him. As J. B. Phillips paraphrased it, 'All these things have at most only a symbolic value: the solid fact is Christ.'

We would consider anyone strange who could easily enjoy the benefits of a modern, full-colour digital TV with Nicam surround-sound but chose to stay with their little black and white set, complete with liquid magnifier, which they bought in the 1950s. Anyone who chose to write his Ph.D. thesis using a manual typewriter instead of enjoying the benefits of a recently upgraded word-processor would be odd indeed. But, in effect, by adopting the approach of these false teachers, that's exactly what the Colossians did, or anyone else who goes down the same road does. Why lurk in the shadows when the real thing is available?

Its character: sensual not spiritual (v. 18)

His next criticism is that though they send out signals of being very spiritual, the truth is that they are anything but. It all sounds so impressive. They *go into great details about what they have seen*. They have plenty of testimonies to give about ecstatic worship in which they have participated and mystical visions they have seen, so you think they must be streets ahead of you spiritually. You feel small in comparison with them and long to be able to reach the religious heights they've reached. It's all very discouraging. Why can't you have the same experiences? Why hasn't the supernatural world impressed itself upon you as it has on them? Why hasn't God shown himself to you in the same way? You begin to think there must be something wrong with you.

But Paul says the Colossians should not be intimidated by such people. What's called for is some hard critical reasoning about the character of their claims. Interestingly, when Erica Heftmann, to whom we referred earlier, left the Moonies, the thing she said that she could not believe was just how much she'd left her mind at the door when she joined them and had been prepared to be brushed off without answers. She wrote, 'My cult experience, as an extreme expression of an entire social trend, focused for me all-pervasive symptoms of a chronic social ailment – lack of critical thinking.'[19]

Paul tells the Colossians that if they think about what these teachers claim, two things will quickly become obvious to them: their minds are arrogant and their ideas are empty. How can they be spiritual if this is so? By any standard they do not measure up. The criteria the New Testament sets out for assessing spirituality are never about how much one has had experience of visions or mystical encounters. When Paul writes about his own experience in this area he writes with great reserve and reticence.[20] The test is normally a test of character. It is of how much the 'love, joy, peace, patience, kindness, goodness, faithfulness, gentleness and self-control'[21] are evident. In contrast to these qualities, the false teachers are known for their arrogance. *Their unspiritual minds puff them up*. They believe themselves to be so knowledgeable that it makes them proud. Unless they exhibit a genuine humility people should question just how spiritual they are. A second test, which they fail just as hopelessly, is the test of truth. Jesus Christ was 'full of grace and truth'.[22] They have neither. Instead of grace they demonstrate arrogance. Instead of truth they are full of *idle notions*. They enjoy speculative discussions and doubtless claim to have everything sorted out. They know the exact formation of the hierarchies of powers and authorities in heaven and have worked out exactly how to appease the star cycle and manipulate the planets to the best effect, or so they think. But Paul dismisses it as futile nonsense. Their views have no foundation either in revelation or in reason. What is more, their views do not live up to their promise. They are powerless to deliver people from fear or to change people so that they can defeat sin in their lives. A close inspection renders the verdict of 'poppycock', a safe one to be handed down on their views. And that's just what Paul does.

Its power source: severed not connected (v. 19)

As I was shaving the other morning, I strayed too far from the power point and my electric razor became disconnected from its cord. Instantly, it ceased to work. It became lifeless. That's how Paul evaluates the false teaching. Using a pre-electric, biological image, he says the false teachers have *lost connection with the Head*. The head is what gives life and direction to the body and once it is severed from the body, as Sir Thomas More or Mary, Queen of Scots, had good cause to know, the body cannot continue to live. It dies. So, their ideas are lifeless. They have no power supply or energy source which can keep them alive.

The climax of his indictment against the false teachers is that they are no longer in touch with Christ, let alone holding fast to him. They were more connected to other people and institutions than to Christ in whom reality is to be found. They were more in touch with popular opinion, with what was being said in the synagogue and with the prevailing views of folk religion than with Christ. But the body of Christ cannot even survive, let alone grow, unless it is joined to him. The Head is the one *from whom the whole body, supported and held together by its ligaments and sinews, grows as God causes it to grow*. If it is united to him, his divine life will energise it and be the source of its strengthening, co-ordination and development. The proof that the false teachers had severed their connection with Christ was that under their leadership the body was being weakened, not strengthened; it was experiencing disintegration, not co-ordination and it was atrophying, not developing.

So, Paul's advice is, keep plugged into Christ. Don't wander from the power supply. There's no life apart from him.

Its future: transient not permanent (v. 22)

The teachings Paul is opposing appear very powerful because they are very popular. So they must be right! They wouldn't meet such a ready response unless they were true. Or would they? The test of truth is never to be judged by the criterion of fashion. Fashions come, and fashions go. You only have to look back at photographs of what you were wearing twenty years ago to realise how transient fashions are. You considered then that what you were wearing was the last word. Now you find it all acutely embarrassing. You wouldn't be seen dead in those outfits today.

The false teaching is just like that. *These are all destined to perish with use.* They may be circulating wildly at the moment, but they won't endure. The garment will wear out; the fashion will change. Or, to change the metaphor, the fireworks will soon be spent, having exhausted themselves.

History is littered with illustrations of Paul's claim. Back in the 1960s it was very fashionable in theological circles to claim that God was dead. His death was considered a cause to celebrate, since it liberated people from traditional views of a God who was 'out there' and introduced people to the 'god' who was the ground of their own being. It liberated people from religion and announced the arrival of religionless Christianity. It released people from dependent servitude as it proclaimed that man had 'come of age'. Now, although the effects of some of that teaching are still with us, no serious theologian still writes or thinks in these terms. The flaws in the fashionable argument were soon discovered, not least, as I heard Professor H. E. W. Turner say in a sermon at the time, that, 'those who are so prolifically writing about the death of God are also inevitably writing the obituary of man.' The death of God theology today is no more than an interesting exhibit in the museum of theological fashion. It perished with use.

The apostolic gospel, by contrast, endures. Down through the centuries and throughout every continent and culture the truth of Jesus Christ continues, as it will go on doing. In fact, its permanence will outlast the present structures of the world. The letter to the Hebrews makes the point like this: ' "Once more I will shake not only the earth but also the heavens." The words "once more" indicate the removing of what can be shaken – that is, created things – so that what cannot be shaken may remain.'[23] What cannot be shaken, what will remain, in the terms used in Hebrews, is the kingdom of Jesus Christ, the mediator of the new covenant. The gospel of Jesus Christ is the one permanent truth which will last to eternity.

So, why be foolish and go for a passing fashion which, by its very nature, is going to fail you in the future?

Its origin: human not divine (v. 22)
The reason why these false teachings are bound to fail, Paul explains, is *because they are based on human commands and teachings*. Their origin is human as distinct from the origin of the gospel, which is divine. Human beings have tremendous capacities of reason and discovery, as the scientific and technological advance of recent times bears ample witness. But their ability to reason is not perfect and their capacity for discovery is not unlimited. The human mind is affected by the fall. Although there should be enough evidence to introduce people to God, they choose not to make use of the opportunity. Paul explains it like this to the Romans. 'What may be known of God is plain to them (to human beings), because God has made it plain to them, For since the creation of the world God's invisible qualities – his eternal power and divine nature – have been clearly seen, being understood from what has been made, so that they are without excuse.'[24] But instead of building on this knowledge so that they might know God, for moral and spiritual reasons people chose to 'suppress the truth'. They preferred to live in wickedness in independence from God. 'They exchanged the truth of God for a lie.'[25] So their minds became corrupted, their thinking futile, their understanding darkened and they became ignorant of God.[26]

No doubt, most modern people will find such an anatomy of their capacity to reason about spiritual issues grossly offensive. We think we're better than that. It seems severe. Surely it is not all that dark. Is there not truth about God to be found here and there? Perhaps. But here is the bottom line. Whatever partial truth we may be able to attain to about God on our own, it will only ever be partial, and is likely to be distorted, and therefore dangerously incomplete. Given the effects of the fall on the way we think about God, there can never be any security in relying on religious beliefs that have their origins purely in a human source.

If we can't argue ourselves to him, then, what we need is for God to make himself known to us; for him to take the initiative and reveal himself. And that is what he has done in sending us Jesus. He has made himself known in a number of ways down the centuries: through creation, through the experiences of Israel, through the giving of the law and through prophetic voices. But Jesus is the final, the complete, the ultimate, the sufficient disclosure of who God is. When Philip, towards the end of Jesus' life asked him, 'Lord, show us the Father and that will be enough for us', Jesus' reply was significant. 'Don't you know me, Philip, even after I have been among you such a long time? Anyone who has seen me has seen the Father. How can you say, "Show us the Father"? Don't you believe that I am in the Father, and that the Father is in me?'[27]

The Christian gospel does not arise from a human source but a divine revelation. It does not arise from men and women seeking to climb up to God on the ladder of their capacity to reason about him. Their immoral lives have corrupted their ability to do that. It's not reliable. The Christian gospel arises from God descending the ladder to earth in the form of Jesus Christ, and making himself known to us. So, why rely on the broken reed of human reasoning when the secure staff of divine disclosure is available?

Its value: futile not effective (v. 23)

Paul's rigorous critique of false teaching comes to an end with one more accusation. If the other punches had not landed up to now, as surely they have, then this must be the knockout blow. The false teachings which the Colossians are beginning to find attractive are simply ineffective. *They lack any value in restraining sensual indulgence*. Paul challenges them, in effect, to go and join up with the false teachers. Will all their practices, their rituals and their disciplines achieve anything? By fasting, enduring ritual humiliations, physical privations, having mystical experiences, sticking rigidly to their diet sheet or their calendar, will they be changed? Will it make any difference to the person they are? The answer is inevitably no.

The reason why they inevitably *lack any value in restraining sensual indulgence* is because the problem of sensual indulgence can't be answered in this way. It's as if they have asked a historical question and got a mathematical reply. The two don't tie up. It reminds me of 'Mr. Clever'.[28] Mr. Clever lived in a very clever house in Cleverland and as long as he stayed there he was fine. But one day he went for a walk and strayed from Cleverland. He proudly introduced himself to a number of people he met in the outside world and they, naturally, thought he would easily be able to answer all their questions. Mr. Happy wanted to know a really good joke. Mr. Greedy wanted to know the most delicious dish. Mr. Forgetful wanted to know his name. But Mr. Clever couldn't answer any of their questions. These weren't the questions they considered in Cleverland. He wasn't equipped to handle them. It was outside of his frame of reference. You can appear very clever, but be quite unable to answer the real questions of life. So it was with the rules and regulations of the false teachers at Colosse.

Paul's point is that the problem of sensuality lies within us. It's not an external problem which can be fixed by external measures; it's an inward problem which can only be fixed by internal measures. Beat the body as much as you like, deprive yourself as much as you wish, but it won't make a difference on the inside. Jerome found that to be true. Like many others in his time who desired to be saints, he took himself off to the desert to live in seclusion. But in a frank confession he admits:

O how often I imagined that I was in the midst of the pleasure of Rome when I was stationed in the desert, in that solitary wasteland which is so burned up by the heat of the sun that it provides a dreadful habitation for monks.

I who because of the fear of hell had condemned myself to such a hell and who had nothing but scorpions and wild animals for company, often thought I was dancing in a chorus with girls. My face was pale with fasting, but my mind burned with passionate desires within my freezing body; and the furies of sex seethes, even though the flesh had already died in me as a man.[29]

Paul's point could not be made more graphically. External disciplines cannot bring about inward change. Only an inward change brought about through the deep cleansing which Christ offers and the inner transformation which is brought about by dying and rising with him can have the desired effect.

So why submit to teaching and practices that are doomed to fail?

In concluding his evaluation of the false teachings, Paul admits that they have *an appearance of wisdom*. But the wisdom is purely cosmetic. Any wisdom you might detect is only skin deep – painted on the surface. It's not for real. What is for real is that it leads to *self-imposed worship*. The NIV translation of the word *ethelothreskia* is perhaps a bit narrow. Paul is really saying that this worship is a self-made, self-induced, self-willed worship. As such, its claims are bogus and its offer phony. Erica Heftmann's verdict on the Moonies fits the false teaching in Colosse like a glove. It is a 'heavenly deception'.[30] Paul has given one reason after another to expose the teaching as counterfeit. The cumulative evidence against it is devastating.

3. The counter to false religion (verse 20)

But it's one thing to demolish, another to build. If the way of the false teachers is not the way to know God and experience change within oneself, what is? The answer is introduced here, in verse 20, almost in passing, only to be developed more fully later, as the basis for an appeal he makes to them. *Since you died with Christ to the basic principles of this world, why, as though you still belonged to it, do you submit to its rules?*

The first step on the path to experiencing God is to die to the basic principles of this world. On this occasion Paul lets us know what he means by *the basic principles of this world* because he goes on to explain that they don't need any longer to submit *to its rules*. So the term is used as a general reference to the false teaching and particularly to the rules and regulations aspect of it which people voluntarily accept as an obligation.

We've seen how he has already introduced the imagery of death, burial and resurrection. Now he uses it again. When people die, they are no longer able to respond to the obligations and commands which were once appropriate for them when they were alive. So, when I die, the tax inspector won't be able to get at me personally, even though, given the state of computer technology, she might well try to do so. She can't chase me beyond the grave because she has no jurisdiction there. She can write to me all she likes, threatening the most dire of consequences if I don't respond. But she still won't get an answer and her threats won't mean a thing. In the same way, when people put their faith in Jesus Christ they die to things which previously exercised a hold over their lives. Literally, they 'come out from under' the authority of the powers and influences which belonged to their former situation. Their status has changed and with it they are deaf to old voices and attuned from then on to new ones.

'Remember that,' Paul tells the Colossians, 'and you're on the road to freedom. Be deaf to the voices of pseudo religion that would claim your allegiance. Don't respond to them. You've no need to do so since they have no claim over you.'

Later he is going to expound both what it means to die with Christ and to live with him. Death will be followed by resurrection and resurrection by setting our hearts and minds *where Christ is seated at the right hand of God*. But death to the voices of this world is the necessary first step to freedom.

Once again, Paul is telling them of something which has happened in their lives. They have died with Christ. It is a past event, a completed action, a definite experience which has occurred. *Leadership* journal once carried a superb cartoon of a home Bible study group sitting around discussing this or a similar verse. The woman speaking commented, 'Well, I haven't actually died to sin, but I did feel kind of faint once.' But there can be no freedom without this first step. Dying is essential if the hold of tyrannical voices is to be broken and the freedom of Christ is to be experienced. Vaguely drifting in and out of consciousness, sometimes following the voice of Christ and sometimes following the voice of other teachings will not do. Nothing short of death is required.

And having died, we need to remember that we have done so and act according to our new status. Like the children playing cowboys and Indians who shoot one another and shout, 'You're dead, so lie down', we need to do exactly that. Lie down and not stand up in answer to any other voice than Christ's.

6

Focused on Christ
Colossians 3:1-11

¹Since, then, you have been raised with Christ, set your hearts on things above, where Christ is seated at the right hand of God. ²Set your minds on things above, not on earthly things. ³For you died, and your life is now hidden with Christ in God. ⁴When Christ, who is your life, appears, then you also will appear with him in glory.

⁵Put to death, therefore, whatever belongs to your earthly nature: sexual immorality, impurity, lust, evil desires and greed, which is idolatry. ⁶Because of these, the wrath of God is coming. ⁷You used to walk in these ways, in the life you once lived. ⁸But now you must rid yourselves of all such things as these: anger, rage, malice, slander, and filthy language from your lips. ⁹Do not lie to each other, since you have taken off your old self with its practices ¹⁰and have put on the new self, which is being renewed in knowledge in the image of its Creator. ¹¹Here there is no Greek or Jew, circumcised or uncircumcised, barbarian, Scythian, slave or free, but Christ is all, and is in all.

1. Living with Christ (verses 1-4)

Our position (v. 1)
Our priorities (vv. 1-2)
Our predicament (v. 3)
Our prospect (v. 4)

2. Living in Christ (verses 5-11)

Vices to be renounced (vv. 5, 8-9)
Truths to be remembered (vv. 6-7)
An image to be renewed (v. 10)
A community to be remodelled (v. 11)

Little things can sometimes have a great impact. I was once driving my car down a hill in Wales when it shuddered to a halt and refused to start again. Everything in the car was fine, except one little nut which had worked itself loose in the engine and caused a cable to disconnect. The whole car refused to go because of that tiny nut. Little words can sometimes carry great significance. A 'theology of prepositions'[1] doesn't sound very interesting. But those little place words, like, 'in', 'with', 'through', 'under' and 'for' unlock a wealth of meaning about our Christian experience. They help to focus on the different places in which a believer stands in relation to Christ. Hence, they become 'signposts to profound theological truths'. And, as John Stott has rightly pointed out, by examining them 'our relationship with Christ is thus displayed as a multi-faceted diamond of great beauty'.[2]

Colossians 3 begins to unpack for us the practical nature of Christian experience. Christ is at the very centre of it all. All our experience of Christian living must be drawn from his risen life, lived under his liberating authority and lead to his greater glory. This is not to displace the Holy Spirit's role in the experience of the believer, which is, indeed, great. If he is not mentioned much in the letter to the Colossians it is not because he is unimportant, but because teaching about the Holy Spirit is not the problem in Colosse and so not the issue which Paul is addressing in this letter. The work of the Holy Spirit is alluded to directly or by implication in the letter on more than one occasion,[3] but he is not the one in dispute and so is not central. The Spirit is the one who makes the divine connection, who empowers the Christian, who makes the truths of Christ live. But the spotlight here, as it ever should do, falls on Jesus Christ. Christians must never seek to drive a wedge between Jesus and the Holy Spirit. Their relationship is inseparable. The Holy Spirit is always the Spirit of Jesus whose task, as Jesus himself said, was 'to bring glory to me by taking from what is mine and make it known to you'.[4] So, with John Stott, we may affirm 'that Jesus Christ is the centre of Christianity, and therefore both the Christian faith and the Christian life, if they are to be authentic, must be focused on Christ'.[5]

Throughout chapter 3 Paul expounds the meaning of authentic

Christian experience and authentic Christian living. The rich truth he sets out can be understood by using various prepositions. It involves: living *with* Christ (vv. 1-4); living *in* Christ (vv. 5-11); living *like* Christ (vv. 12-14); living *under* Christ (vv. 15-16) and living *for* Christ (v. 17). In this chapter we shall look at the first two of these.

1. Living with Christ (verses 1-4)

The first aspect of authentic Christian experience which is mentioned here, is that we live *with* Christ. Living with someone may sound like a very casual relationship – you just share a house together as two independent people and carry on doing your own thing. But, even in the most casual of arrangements, living with someone has an effect on those involved. More often than not it has a profound effect. We had someone living with us for a time who was struggling with a crippling depression. It was not long before we felt guilty when we laughed and the grim mood took its toll on us. We began to get depressed! To use a more positive example, every parent knows, like us, the impact of bringing a few pounds of flesh home from the hospital and beginning to live with a baby in the house. Things are never the same again! A room is decorated in a style you'd never dare use for anyone but a baby. Independence becomes severely curtailed. Sleepless nights become routine. Nice clean clothes and handsome furniture become the places where baby kindly deposits sick. Tidy rooms become hazardous obstacle courses as lethal toys are left lying around. And then there is the joy, the sheer unadulterated pleasure, that this bundle of life brings which nothing else can surpass. Life and lifestyle gets totally transformed by living with a baby. So it is with the Christian and Christ. To live with him is to invite a transformation of life and lifestyle – only, in this case, the transformation is wholly positive.

Our position (v. 1)

Chapter 2 ended on a down note. It was a necessary and sharp reminder that authentic Christian living begins only when a person has died *with Christ*[6] and no longer responds to the other voices which clamour for attention and allegiance. To be dead to all those pestering voices of the false teachers must have been a blessed relief to the Colossians. They no longer had to worry about, still less obey, their petty and ineffective regulations. To be dead and buried, however, may be a relief, but it's not a life. And Christianity is about life, a life which comes about through death and resurrection. So, having spoken about death this chapter moves on and begins with the words, *Since, then, you have been raised with Christ...* . After Good Friday came Easter Sunday. The one without the other is an inadequate gospel. They belong together. And both are part of the believer's experience. Christ came not to rob us of life but to give us a new, and better, life.

Paul set the issue out more fully in his letter to the Romans when explaining the meaning of baptism:

> We were therefore buried with him through baptism into death in order that, just as Christ was raised from the dead through the glory of the Father, we too may live a new life. If we have been united with him like this in his death, we will certainly also be united with him in his resurrection.... Now if we died with Christ, we believe that we will also live with him.... In the same way, count yourselves dead to sin but alive to God in Christ Jesus.[7]

It is important to note that Paul states this as a fact of Christian experience, not as a condition of it. This is the very basic truth about what it is to be a Christian. It is the case that a Christian shares in the death and equally the resurrection of Jesus Christ. It is not something one has to work up, psych oneself up for, or graduate to after a certain degree of holiness has been achieved. This newness of life in Christ is ours through his resurrection and by the fact that we have joined ourselves with him.

The resurrection is not the end of the story, for after Christ's resurrection came his ascension and exaltation to the right hand of God the Father. So, now he sits in the throne room of heaven, at the control centre of the universe. His throne is the nearest to the Father's throne. No one comes between him and his Father. There are no other mediators or intervening hierarchies to which believers either can or should resort. Jesus is *seated at the right hand of God.*

The pictorial language reminds us that he has conquered his enemies and now reigns with liberating power over all. So, no lesser power, of whatever sort, has any right to intimidate the Christian believer, especially not the sort of make-believe authorities to be found in the folk religion of Colosse which feigned power over the believers there.

But the truth Paul is setting out is even more amazing than that. The position that Christ occupies in heaven is one which believers share with him. Ephesians 2:6 expresses in a succinct way the truth that Paul is explaining here. It says, 'And God raised us up with Christ and seated us with him in the heavenly realms in Christ Jesus.' The seat of victory in heaven is not only his but ours as well.

If we are to tackle any of our enemies, real or otherwise, or face any threats, actual or imaginary, we need to know where we stand. And where we stand is with Christ in heaven, who has defeated all our enemies – those of death and judgment, sin and Satan, demons and oppressors – through his resurrection. Since we now share the risen life of the exalted one we need not be disturbed by them. One of the reasons why believers are living such defeated lives is that they do not have the confidence which comes from knowing what their true position is in Christ.

Our priorities (vv. 1-2)

Our position should determine our priorities. If persons accept positions in a company they then shape their lives accordingly. They spend time going to work for that company and not for someone else. They work to its agenda, show loyalty to it and defend its interests. It is exactly the same with being a Christian.

Since we now live with this risen and exalted Christ we should *set (our) hearts on things above* and similarly *set (our) minds on things above, not on earthly things.* The heart includes both our will and our emotions. The mind refers to our intellect. We are willing, feeling and thinking creatures and each dimension of our being is to be concentrated on Christ. Paul's invitation is all-embracing. The intentional, emotional and intellectual aspects of our lives are all to be brought into line and submitted to Christ. To be all heart but mindless does not bring honour to Christ. Nor, equally, do we honour Christ by being all intellect while refusing to bring our wills and emotions to his transforming throne.

Paul's language indicates that it may not be easy for us to do this. Using not one but two different Greek words – *zeteo* and *phroneo* – he urges us to aim at, keep seeking, be intent on, fix our thoughts on and give our minds to things above. The fact that *we have been raised with Christ* does not mean that we have become instantly perfect. We have not become dehumanised, lost our ability to think, take decisions and make choices. This means that temptation still tempts us, lesser motives still attract us and things which can be seen in the material world, as opposed to things which are in the unseen world, can still seem more real. Consequently, we need to demonstrate real determination if we are to overcome sin and establish a new set of priorities which relate to eternal and heavenly things. Without effort on our part the things of this world will eventually smother our life in Christ.

If this is so, what is the point of our saying *we have been raised with Christ*? What is it worth if effort is still required on our part? The value is just this: that if God had not granted us new life in Christ our effort would have been futile. We would not have been able to achieve any worthwhile transformation in our characters, and it would not do us any eternal good even if we had. But the life of Christ in us gives us the power we need and guarantees that it is ultimately worthwhile. God may not make it too easy for us, but he does make it possible.

The priorities we need to establish are those which relate to *things above*, which simply means spiritual things. In encouraging us to have a spiritual agenda for our lives, Paul does not wish us to become 'so heavenly minded that we are of no earthly use'. I have known Christians who are so sold out for Christ that they spend their time gazing into the sky in the belief that he will come again at any moment. As a result they have no time to work to earn a living. To support themselves in the meantime they sponge off long-suffering Christians. Quite apart from the fact that such a lifestyle is in flat contradiction to Paul's instructions in 1 Thessalonians 4:11 and 2 Thessalonians 3:10, as well as to the spirit of Ephesians 4:28, it demonstrates a misunderstanding of who Christ is. If we learned anything from that hymn about Christ, in 1:15-20, we surely learned that he is the Creator of this world and has a passionate commitment to it. The spiritual agenda which Paul is speaking about here, then, must work itself out in the arena of creation and not remove us from the sphere of the ordinary, material, economic, social and political aspects of life. It should simply make us handle them differently, as the rest of the chapter will show.

Our predicament (v. 3)

Paul continues to be realistic in talking about our Christian experience and so explains a predicament we face. If living with Christ is such a good thing, why are believers in such a minority? Why aren't Christians understood and recognised in a positive light? Why don't people flock to become disciples? Why doesn't everyone agree with the gospel? The reason is that for the moment our lives are *now hidden with Christ in God*. The divine mystery, which has been disclosed to believers, has not been revealed to everyone and the truth lies concealed to many. If the truth of God's plan is hidden to them, then it follows that the true identity of the people at the centre of God's plan will also remain hidden to them.

   Some say that this phrase is essentially saying that the believer is secure in Christ, beyond the reach of harm. Bishop Handley Moule spoke of being hidden *with Christ in God* as a life which was safe-guarded by 'a double rampart, all divine'.[8] There may well be shades of this security here. But that is not really Paul's primary meaning. He is really voicing the perplexity we all feel at being caught between times. The kingdom of God has already been established but it is not yet consummated. Salvation is already a present reality but it has not yet been completed. So, on the one hand, we can speak with great confidence about being saved, having died and having risen with Christ. On the other hand, we know that we have not yet arrived and there is much of salvation we have yet to experience and much of the risen life of Christ which we have not begun to tap.

In one sense there is often a difference between facts and experience. For example, in October 1991, Germany was united again into one nation. The Berlin Wall had come down, the laws had been passed, proclamations had been issued, governments had been joined and unification was a fact. But reality took some time to catch up with fact. If you had stayed shortly afterwards, as I did, in old East Berlin and wished to make a phone call to West Berlin you would still have found it necessary to make an 'international' call. The phone system still functioned as if Germany were two nations. Unification was inaugurated and sure, but its implications had not yet been fully worked through. So it is with our salvation. The facts need not be doubted but the experience seems, sometimes, to deny them. The puzzles, perplexities and dilemmas of living as a Christian in this world, and our continuing struggle with sin and Satan will remain until Christ returns and the kingdom of God and his salvation are consummated. Then, we will no longer live in the tension of the 'already' but the 'not yet'. Then, all will be fully ours. In the meantime, much will remain *hidden*.

Our prospect (v. 4)

It is with that future vision that Paul brings this part of his argument to a climax. If at the moment our lives are *hidden with Christ in God*, one day it is all set to change. *When Christ, who is your life, appears, then you also will appear with him in glory*. The truth will no longer be concealed. Believers will no longer be unrecognised and Christ will no longer be unacknowledged. His second 'glorious appearance'[9] will be in magnificent splendour. Then, the glory of his person and his majesty will be seen by all and 'at the name of Jesus every knee should bow, in heaven and on earth and under the earth, and every tongue confess that Jesus Christ is Lord, to the glory of God the Father'.[10] The curtain of heaven will be drawn back and all will see the truth about Jesus.

And with his coming, the false teachers in Colosse will also see the true identity of the little group of seemingly insignificant Christians whom they were seeking to win back to the local folk religion. Their hidden period will be at an end, just as squirrels come to an end of hibernation after winter, and they will appear for all to see. In that day they will share the glory of Jesus, just as they have shared the life of Jesus up to then. That glorious day will mark not only their personal vindication but the end of the struggle of creation itself and the ushering in of the restored and renewed creation.[11]

In a passing phrase, Paul describes Christ to the Colossians as the one *who is your life*. That sums it up. Apart from Christ they do not have life, just existence. To them and us, Christ is the centre, the source, the dynamic, the focus, the meaning, the glory and the goal of the Christian life. He is the all-sufficient one.

These are great truths which should be the very foundation of our Christian experience. Sadly, too often, they appear to have been forgotten. The way we frequently live our Christian lives reminds me of a press cutting I read, years ago, on a wintry summer's day on a Scottish island. I was on holiday and had taken refuge from the rain in an old crofter's cottage, turned museum. Electricity had only come to the island, from memory, in the 1960s and shortly afterwards a journalist had asked one of the crofters what difference the electricity had made. 'Och,' came the reply, 'it's marvellous. Every night when it gets dark I can turn on the electric light. It's so much easier to light my oil lamp that way. Then, when the lamp is lit I can turn it off again!'

We should be those living in the blazing light of these great facts of the faith. We *have been raised with Christ*. He is *seated at the right hand of God*. Our lives are *now hidden with Christ in God*. And, *when Christ appears...then (we) also will appear with him in glory*. We are united with him in his death, resurrection and exaltation, and will one day be united with him in his glorification. That is a powerful battery of spiritual facts to support the one appeal which Paul makes. Since (not, if) this is so, we ought to keep our eyes fixed on heavenly things. Just as a compass seeks out true north and constantly returns to it, so the believer should seek his or her true north in the exalted Christ.

He may have waxed a little lyrical about it, but perhaps Bishop Handley Moule had a point when he wrote:

> Here is St. Paul's programme, his prescription, for the blessed life, the transfigured life, at Colosse. Live in heaven, that you may really live on earth. Live in heaven, not in the sense of the poet but in that of the believer. Live in recollecting and conscious union with him who is there, but who is at the same time in you, your life. Live in the continual confession to your own souls that you died in his death, and live his life, and are with him – by the law of union – on his throne; and then bring *this* to bear upon the temptation of your path. *Use* these things. Take them as facts into life, exactly as life is for you today. You shall find that in them, that is to say, in him, you can be holy. You can walk in perfect liberty, and you can walk (with the same steps) in perpetual and delightful service.[12]

That's what it means to live with Christ who is seated at the right hand of God.

2. Living in Christ (verses 5-11)

Our identity shapes our behaviour. Hide it as you may, the Englishman abroad is soon given away, the Scotsman soon stands out in London, and the American can rarely disguise his origins. Who we are shapes us. It governs our accent, subtly determines our dress, moulds our table manners, and fashions us in all sorts of indefinable ways. The Christian's identity in Christ must, no less, shape the way the Christian lives. Our being and our doing are all of a piece. Or, to put it another way, our theology and our ethics cannot be separated. So, it is not really a change of agenda when Paul turns from the elevated thoughts of heaven to talking about the need for the Christian to shun lust, idolatry and lies and to be renewed in the image of the Creator. Here he 'fleshes out' what it will mean in practice to set our hearts and minds on the things which are above. It takes us, as we shall see, to the realm of some very down to earth speaking on Paul's part. Living *with* Christ will lead us to live *in* Christ. Here Paul tells us something of what it means to live in Christ.

He begins with the negative. There are:

Vices to be renounced (vv. 5, 8-9)

For a couple of reasons our initial response to the way Paul begins this section of his letter is probably one of curiosity. First, he has just been teaching the Colossians that they *died with Christ*. Now he tells them to *put to death* certain things in their lives. How can both be right? Secondly, he has just asserted that *Christ is our life* and the whole direction of the chapter seemed to be going in an upbeat, life-enhancing direction. But now he seems to be back-tracking and talking about death again. How can a celebration of life start with the words of a death sentence?

There is no conflict between his saying that a believer is someone, on the one hand, who has died with Christ and that a believer must, on the other hand, *put to death...whatever belongs to (his or her) earthly nature*. His use of the word *therefore* in the middle of the command gives us the clue as to how to understand it. It is because the believer has died and is risen with Christ that he or she is in a position to put to death these ugly characteristics of ungodly behaviour which he is about to name. Without having been united with Christ's death and resurrection Christians would be powerless to do so. They would be fighting a losing battle. But from the position they already occupy with Christ they can face and defeat these vices with confidence. It is, as mentioned before, a bit like the children's game where they cry, 'You're dead, so lie down.' Because the believer is dead, these evils can be repudiated and made to lie down.

As to the second puzzle, again the answer is not difficult. Death is often a gateway to life. A patient who is terminally ill with cancer needs the cancer cells to be put to death if he or she is to live. Bacteria often need to be destroyed in order that life may flourish. So it is in the spiritual realm. The new life which is ours in Christ can only be experienced to the full if the vices which are incompatible with it are destroyed.

Paul leaves Christians in no doubt about the necessity of getting rid of these things from their lives. He uses several strong images to make the point. In verse 5 he uses the image of execution. We are to put them to death, to kill them. In verse 8 he uses the image of refuse. We are to rid ourselves of them as we might throw out the rubbish. In verse 9 he turns to the image of the wardrobe. We are to take off the old self, as we might discard a worn, dirty and crumpled suit of clothes. Each picture witnesses to a definite and thorough act of renunciation on our part. We are not to toy with them, but to destroy them. We are not to half-kill them, only then to resuscitate them. We are not to put them out for the refuse collector, only subsequently to bring them in again. We are not to partially undress, but to strip them from us thoroughly. The Christian who seeks to compromise here will never be able to enjoy all the riches of Christ which should be their right. They will live in the half-light of the old oil lamp mentioned above, rather than rejoicing in the full light of resurrection morning.

Paul details the characteristics which need to be renounced in two lists, each of which contains five evils. The pattern and content of the lists have suggested to some that he has only taken up and used lists of vices (and later of virtues) which were in common circulation among the philosophers of his day, especially among the Stoics. But, even if that were so, it completely ignores the fact that Paul grounds his appeal in the union which the believer experiences with the death and resurrection of Christ. His appeal has a completely different basis to it than any found elsewhere. Moreover, most contemporary ethical appeals were addressed to individuals, whereas Paul's concern, as will become evident, is life in the new community.[13]

The first list, in verse 5, consists of *sexual immorality, impurity, lust, evil desires and greed which*, he explains, *is idolatry*. The second list, in verse 8, consists of *anger, rage, malice, slander and filthy language*. To this list he then adds, in verse 9, a prohibition against lying. Dermot McDonald has made the interesting observation that, 'the second list goes in the opposite direction to the first. That began with actions and went upstream to desire: this one begins with emotions and comes down to actions.'[14] It is a catalogue of self-indulgent but ultimately self-destroying and certainly socially destructive behaviour.

The individual characteristics are worth some comment. We often pass over them quickly, perhaps out of fear of embarrassment or out of a sometimes mistaken assumption that 'we know all that'. But taking these lists for granted can lead to a casual attitude towards them and to our being less than serious about our abhorrence of them. *Sexual immorality* originally referred to relations with a prostitute but later came to include any genital sexual activity outside of marriage, which means both adultery and fornication. *Impurity* again refers to sexual sin and relates to indecency,[15] of thought as well as of act. *Lust* speaks of passion, sensual craving and of desire which is not under control. The term *evil desires* is broad in scope, but the adjective reminds us that not all desire is evil. Desire, in itself, may be a good thing. It depends whether what we desire is something which is wholesome and legitimate. Desire turns sour and becomes evil either when what we want is unworthy (like pornography which degrades a woman) or when what we want should be beyond our reach (like another person's marriage partner, or a partner of the same sex.) The final characteristic here is *greed*. This word is the widest one in the list and reminds us that desire may be evil when it fixates not just on unworthy or illegitimate sexual objects, but when it latches onto anything, not just sexual objects, which is either unworthy or illegitimate. It relates to coveting anything which does not rightly belong to us. Paul immediately goes on to identify greed with *idolatry*. Its connection may escape us, but it would not have surprised those who were used to thinking along Jewish lines. What greed does is to make the acquiring of things and the gaining of satisfaction into gods which have to be served. Hence, it becomes idolatrous.[16]

All evil behaviour destroys community. The first list of vices, no less than the second, has social implications, but the second list is more obviously social in its orientation. Christians who pride themselves on their sexual purity, which may in practice have

more to do with their inhibited upbringing than their growth in
genuine holiness, and who would never fall foul of the first list,
except perhaps when it came to greedy materialism, may well
find themselves distinctly more uncomfortable with this second
list. *Anger* means a quick and uncontrolled temper. James mentions
it as a trait which 'does not bring about the righteous life that God
desires'. He tells us that its antidote is to be 'quick to listen, slow
to speak'.[17] *Rage* denotes not a chronic state of anger but 'a passionate outburst of anger'.[18] Christians who appear saints at church
have been known to throw crockery and furniture around at home.
If Paul were writing today he might well be alluding to some of
the physical and sexual abuse which takes place even, sadly, in
Christian homes. *Malice* is spiteful behaviour which arises from a
lack of forgiveness and a desire to hurt. *Slander* means to speak
maliciously of someone and to destroy someone with scurrilous
words. It literally means blasphemy. Why, then, is it translated in
a way which suggests it is speech directed only at fellow human
beings rather than at God? Tom Wright explains the connection
helpfully like this: it is 'speech which dishonours God himself –
in this instance, by reviling a human being made in his image.'[19]
Filthy language is any foul language including smutty talk, sexual
innuendo, swearing or any other form of unwholesome vocabulary.

Having completed his list of five vices, Paul links it to the next
part of his discussion by speaking of another form of bad speech.
Lying is equally a sin. Contemporary society may well say it's all
right providing one isn't caught out. Contemporary governments,
with their craving for 'security', may well prefer softer terms for
it, like being 'economical with the truth' or 'disinformation'. But
the blunt command of Scripture is *do not lie to one another*. Where
any of these forms of emotion or speech are found it is impossible
to enjoy good relationships with one another. They inevitably
destroy fellowship.

These vices, then, must be repudiated by Christians. What is
the best way to do that? Margaret Thatcher once spoke of starving
terrorists of the 'oxygen of publicity'. We need to starve these
vices of the oxygen that gives them life. This should be our starting
point. The flesh will be quick to exploit any opportunity we give

it to indulge in these vices. And they soon become habit-forming. So let's not give them the opportunity. Let's not read the magazines, watch the videos, go to the places where the sexual vices, spoken of in verse 5, can find a foothold in our lives. Let's not put ourselves in situations where, if this is our particular weakness, we have the opportunity for sexual activity outside of marriage. Let's avoid the streets, the homes, the times alone with those with whom we are tempted to go too far. Let's live wisely. It is the lack of wisdom, so well set out in the book of Proverbs, which leads many into trouble. Too often we make the excuse that we can't help ourselves when, quite frankly, we can, especially with the Lord's help.

We may not always have the opportunity to avoid the situations which provoke us to anger and rage. But we must never think of these as unfortunate qualities about which we can do nothing. If we're serious about renouncing them, perhaps we can get a friend to help us and point out to us situations where we reacted sinfully or spoke out of turn. A close friend, to whom we hold ourselves accountable, can help us pray through situations and review them so that, again with the strength of the risen and exalted Christ, we might respond to them differently in the future. The primary problem for most Christians in forsaking vice and developing virtue is not our inability to change but our unwillingness to change. It is our lack of conviction about the need for change in our lives. If only we were more convinced that sin was sin, and more passionate about being like Christ, greater changes of character would occur. We need to renounce these sins.

Paul then turns to:

Truths to be remembered (vv. 6-7)

God is a gracious God who, although he does not need to explain himself to us, frequently backs up his commands by giving us his reasons. Paul does that here. Both these lists of wrongs are followed by him giving arguments as to why we should renounce them. Verses 6 and 7 mention two grounds for doing away with the vices of verse 5. The first reason is that they invite the wrath of

God on our lives. *The wrath of God*, he writes, *is coming*. It is not that God suffers from the anger or rage which Paul is to condemn in believers just a few verses later. God's wrath is not like ours so often is. It is not an uncontrolled personal pique that delights in getting its own back. Nor is God vindictive because it makes him feel better. His wrath is the just and measured reaction of a righteous and holy God against all that is unworthy, all that mars and destroys his good creation, and all that runs contrary to his good will and design. It is an aspect of his love for mankind. Because he loves us he opposes that which would ruin us.

The interesting thing is that Paul writes of this *wrath* in the present tense. It is not something which is way off in the distant future but something which, if not actually present now, is imminent. Romans 1:18-32 serves as a commentary on this verse. It explains that the judgment of God, though still to be faced finally in the future, is already at work in the world. Twice in that passage the awful sentence is announced: 'God gave them over.' The judgment of God against sin starts with God saying to people, 'If that is the way you want to live, independent of me, worshipping the created thing rather than the Creator, indulging in all kinds of immorality, so be it. Painfully, I will step aside and let you do it. But see where it leads you.' The process of judgment climaxes at the throne of God when, after death, all people will face their Maker.[20] So, to indulge in these vices is both to experience now, and in the hereafter, the anger of God. Surely, we want to avoid that at all costs.

The second reason Paul gives for Christians repudiating such sins is that they belong to the past way of life. *You used to walk in these ways, in the life you once lived*. But now things are different. You've moved on. You don't live at that address any longer, so why keep pretending you do?

It's an interesting debate as to how much of what we are is due to nature and how much is due to nurture. Whatever side you take in that debate you must allow some place for the importance of nurture. However much life might be determined by our genes, nurture plays a part. The family and social setting into which we are born, the friends we have, the company we keep all shapes us, at least to some extent, and many would believe to a considerable extent. Every parent who has ever sought to buy their child a pair of trainers or a present for Christmas knows the power of peer pressure. Any shoe will not do, especially if it is cheap. The only shoe which will do is the one with the right designer label on it. Paul is acknowledging that much of our behaviour is influenced by our social environment. The values of the company you used to keep, he says, were the values of the sewer. But you're not in those circles any longer. So don't still practise their customs either. You have entered a new culture. Live according to the virtues and practices of your new culture. Allow yourself to be influenced more by the new social environment in which you now live, by the new company you now keep, than by those of the past.

Two things, then, are to be remembered as we face the strong pull of slipping back into a pre-Christian way of life: the awesome wrath of God and our definitive change of life. They should be powerful incentives which encourage us to disown the ugly catalogue of vices he condemns.

An image to be renewed (v. 10)

The story so far may seem awfully negative. Unapologetically, Paul has been telling us that there are things Christians must give up. 'Don't' is writ large in these verses. And rightly so. If our Christian lives are to have any integrity, then there is no place for the wrong-doings, the wrong reactions and the wrong feelings which he mentions. But the story has not ended yet. There is something gloriously positive to come. Much harm has been done to the Christian faith by people putting a full stop where there isn't one and by ending the story too prematurely. Christianity has often come over as judgmental moralism which tells everyone off for doing wrong but doesn't tell them anything about how they might do right. In verse 10 Paul begins to unpack the positive. He's going to spell it out much more from verse 12 onwards, but he makes a start here.

Jump leads need to be connected both to the negative and the positive terminals of a car battery if a dead car is to spring into life. In like manner Christians need to be connected both to the negative *and* the positive if they are to experience life in Christ. The negative on its own is empty and depressing moralism. Taking up Paul's metaphor of taking off the old clothes, Michael Griffiths once commented in his usually graphic way, 'There is a kind of Christian negative holiness which rejoices in discarding various forms of worldliness, but which leaves the individual stark naked. True Christian holiness demands also the putting on of positive virtues like a suit of beautiful new clothes.'[21]

In New Testament Christianity the negative is always balanced by the positive. Verses 9 and 10 state it clearly. ...*You have taken off your old self with its practices and have put on the new self.* Paul is reminding them of what happened when they were baptised. They stripped off to be baptised and dressed in a new set once they had been baptised. There was a deep symbolism in that. That's exactly what they had done with their lives. They had deliberately laid down one way of living (without Christ) and taken up another (with Christ as Lord). They had had, to use Jesus' words, to lose their lives in order to save them.[22]

The point of discarding the old wardrobe is so that you can wear a new one. The point of putting certain practices to death is so that you can let other practices live. The point of getting rid of some forms of behaviour is so that you make room for new forms of behaviour. The tired old leaves fall from the trees in the autumn in order that new fresh leaves may come in the spring.

So, what is the *new self* which the Christian has *put on*? It is one which *is being renewed in knowledge in the image of its Creator*. What a wealth of meaning that phrase contains for the believer.

It tells us that the change which is taking place is a process. The believer *is being renewed* – present continuous tense. The process has begun but has not yet been completed. The transformation doesn't take place overnight. Christians are neither suddenly transported into the presence of God, with whom one day they will dwell permanently, nor into a state of perfection, which one day they will attain irrevocably. The process will only be complete on the day of Christ. But we can have the assurance now that the process is real and that we will make progress until it is complete. We need not doubt the transforming power of the new life within, however slow the progress may sometimes appear to us. It is a change, sometimes almost imperceptible, that moves us 'from one degree of glory to another'.[23] Like Magnus Magnusson, the famous Mastermind Quiz Master, God says to us, 'I've started, so I'll finish.' You can be confident that 'he who began a good work in you will carry it on to completion until the day of Christ Jesus'.[24] So do not be impatient, either with yourself or with your fellow believers.

This verse tells us that the renewal of life is God's doing. The verb is passive. We are not renewing ourselves but *being renewed*. It is something which is being done to us. We must be careful how we handle this. It does not provide us with an excuse for spiritual indolence or moral lethargy. We are not inert substances in whom God works a change whether we want it or not, co-operate or not. It must be clear by now that Paul's robust commands to *put off* some forms of behaviour and *put on* others means that there is something for us to do. We need to be active Christians and not those who laze around in some spiritual deck chair waiting for God to revolutionise us before we get up and do anything for him. That's not the way it works.

Nonetheless, the truth we must affirm is that whatever part we play, it is God who renews us. We cannot do it on our own, nor even do we take the major role. Paul puts it neatly to the Philippians, 'continue to work out your salvation with fear and trembling, for it is God who works in you to will and to act according to his good pleasure.'[25] He alone can do it because he is the Creator and the origin of all life. Just as he sustains and renews the physical creation, day by day, just as he gives us physical life and renews it every day, so he is the originator of the new life believers have in Christ, and he sustains and renews them daily too.

This verse tells us next that the *new self* is being renewed in *knowledge in the image of its Creator*. That's an interesting phrase. To remake us in the image of the Creator is God's fabulous purpose in salvation. His goal is to renew in us what we lost through Adam and Eve in the Garden of Eden. We are damaged masterpieces and he, the great artist of the universe, longs to restore us. We are sick creatures and he, the great physician of the soul, longs to heal us and remove the blemishes caused by sin and Satan so that they are no longer evident in our lives.

But why does Paul include the word *knowledge* in this sentence? Would it not have been simpler for him to say that we are 'being renewed in the image of the Creator' and leave out the word *knowledge*? The most likely reason he mentions it is that knowledge played a key role in the original fall. It was when Adam and Eve ate the forbidden fruit of 'the tree of the knowledge of good and evil'[26] that they triggered the consequences of their disobedience and set death in train. If forbidden knowledge was instrumental in their fall, true knowledge must be instrumental in our restoration. Renewal, says Tom Wright, 'is to result in the true knowledge of God,'[27] and that knowledge of God will lead to us living true Christian lives.

A community to be remodelled (v. 11)

One of the immediate effects of the fall, according to Genesis 3:7, was that the pure, innocent and open relationship which Adam had enjoyed with Eve was ruptured. They recognised their nakedness and 'sewed fig leaves together and made coverings for themselves'. It was a graphic portrayal of the masks and disguises people would adopt from then on to hide themselves from one another. Human beings, who were made for community, would now have their relationships cursed by disputes, envy, fear, hatred, power struggles and hierarchies. The repercussions of sin were to be felt not just in men and women as individuals but by men and women as social beings, who were designed for relationships.

Given this, it is not surprising that Paul immediately applies the renewing of God's image in us to the area of our social relationships. God does not renew his image in us so that we might be personally pure and privately pious while permitting our social relationships to carry on unaffected. He renews us so that we might demonstrate to the world what his image looks like both in a new person and in a new community. His design is a community design as much as a personal one. The twin agenda dare not be prised apart.

One of the primary marks of the new community, where the old socially destructive patterns of immorality and vengeance have been put to death and where the knowledge and image of God has been renewed, will be that the common but tragic divisions of the world will be transcended. *Here there is no Greek or Jew, circumcised or uncircumcised, barbarian, Scythian, slave or free, but Christ is all, and is in all.* Although he makes the same point elsewhere,[28] his choice of vocabulary here is unusual. His words highlight that the divisions he has in mind are particularly to do with the ethnic and cultural divisions of the world. Greeks divided the ancient world into the civilised, that is themselves, versus the rest, all of whom were scornfully dismissed as barbarians. Jews divided the world into the circumcised and the uncircumcised, the clean and the unclean. The Scythians were a strange people from northern Asia who became a byword for those who were uncivilised and coarse. Slavery and freedom was another of the great status divisions of the ancient world. Slaves might be very cultured and quite influential, but if they were slaves a stigma was attached to them which they could not shake off. But in Christ, all these yawning chasms have been bridged. They no longer have any significance. Being reconciled through Christ is the overwhelmingly significant thing that every person in the new community shares, whatever their background. Christians are so focused on him, for *he is all and is in all*, that these distinctions which once mattered so much, as they still do to those outside of Christ, are quite eclipsed.

These verses will always be both a frightful embarrassment and a standing rebuke to any church which models itself on racial, ethnic or social lines. A white church, or a black church; a Serbian church, or a Bosnian church; a graduate church, or a church for the educationally challenged is a nonsense. Any church which seeks to perpetuate the divisions of the world only serves to demonstrate that its members have not understood the gospel which, at its heart, as Paul has already explained, is about reconciliation. How can such churches demonstrate that they are the renewed community while perpetuating the divisions of an unreconciled world? Furthermore, such a church displays that its members are not sufficiently focused on Jesus. If they were they would not be seeing each other through the spectacles of the world and ranking each other according to ethnic or social status. They would be so caught up with the wonder of their new life in Christ that they would consider the colour of a sister's skin, the nationality on a brother's passport or the signs of a fellow member's status quite irrelevant.

To live, then, in Christ means that there are vices to be renounced, truths to be remembered, an image to be renewed and a community to be remodelled.

These verses, which introduce what it means practically for Christ to be our life, remind me of those visual illusions. You know the ones? You're confronted by a picture which you can see either as two faces peering at one another or as one candle stick in the middle. One is foreground and the other is background. You can't capture them both at once. Or, there is the other picture that you can see two ways in which you can see either a beautiful swan or an old hag. You can't see them both at once. One will always be in the forefront of your vision and the other in the background. Many look at these verses and make the negative commands the foreground. They see it as a chapter all about 'don'ts'. But I believe they need to reverse the image. The foreground should not, as it were, be the old hag but the beautiful swan. This is a chapter all about life. Verse 4 sets the tone. Christ, we are told, is our life. The rest is about living the new life we have in him and the restoration of life as God originally intended it should be. It is a life which, to be sure, has no room for behaviour which abuses others, destroys community or demeans self. So there are things to be 'put off'. But, it is equally about what we are to 'put on' – the new life of Christ, which is a gift from God that enables us to live in harmony with him, at peace with ourselves and in unity with others. It is a life where Christ is the centre of our focus. It is one where he eclipses all that is unworthy. It is a life where we live with him and in him. Who wouldn't want a life like that?

7

Living for Christ

Colossians 3:12-17

[12] Therefore, as God's chosen people, holy and dearly loved, clothe yourselves with compassion, kindness, humility, gentleness and patience. [13]Bear with each other and forgive whatever grievances you may have against one another. Forgive as the Lord forgave you. [14]And over all these virtues put on love, which binds them all together in perfect unity.

[15]Let the peace of Christ rule in your hearts, since as members of one body you were called to peace. And be thankful. [16]Let the word of Christ dwell in you richly as you teach and admonish one another with all wisdom, and as you sing psalms, hymns and spiritual songs with gratitude in your hearts to God. [17]And whatever you do, whether in word or deed, do it all in the name of the Lord Jesus, giving thanks to God the Father through him.

---

1. Living like Christ (verses 12-15)

> Imitating his character (v. 12)
> Continuing his forgiveness (v. 13)
> Wearing his love (v. 14)
> Realising his peace (v. 15)

2. Living under Christ (verse 16)

> Through the word
> In our worship

3. Living for Christ (verse 17)

> Totally for him
> Worthily of him
> Gratefully to him

There are some Christians who remind me of stainless steel. They are clean but cold, and not very appealing. They do little wrong. They are very good at avoiding the vices condemned in the first part of Colossians 3, as well as a good many others not mentioned there. But they are not very warm or winsome. Their holiness is a sort of holiness by numbers. They've learned the rules and are painting their lives within the lines. But they're not very personable or attractive. Religion seems to have made them anxious, inhibited and hard. They are the sort of people Mark Twain talked about as 'good in the worst sense of the word.'[1]

How different is genuine Christianity. To be a Christian is to have Christ within and surely, in spite of the real moral strength which was evident within him, he was one of the most attractive, warm and winsome of individuals who has ever existed. To be a Christian is to imitate him.

Three further aspects of our relationship with Christ are unfolded in this chapter. Christians are to live like him, the subject of verses 12-15. But that is only possible if they also live under him, that is, under his rule and authority (verses 15-16). And the point of it all is so that they might live for him (verse 17).

1. Living like Christ (verses 12-15)

The Christian life is one of imitation of Christ. Rather than simply leaving us with the general principle, Paul helps us understand what it is to imitate Christ by setting the matter out in some detail. It will mean we seek to become like him in character, we will relate to others as he did, with both forgiveness and love, and we will let his peace rule in our lives.

Imitating his character (v. 12)

To appreciate Paul's teaching about being like Christ we need to grasp something about the differences between Paul's society and ours. There has been a shift in our culture in two important, and connected, respects. First, there has been the shift from a concern about character to a preoccupation with personality. Secondly, there has been a shift from a concern about virtues to a preoccupation with values. The significant issues for Paul are to do with character and virtue. Modern people are caught up with questions of personality and values. The difference is profound.

Character has to do with the moral worth of the person and the enduring qualities of virtue which belong to them. Personality has to do with style and image. No one has spelled out the shift better than David Wells in his book *Losing our Virtue*. Quoting Warren Susman, he writes:

> The adjectives most commonly used to describe personality became 'fascinating, stunning, attractive, magnetic, glowing, masterful, creative, dominant, forceful.' None of these words could easily be used to describe someone's character. Character is not stunning, fascinating, or creative. Character is good or bad, while personality is attractive, forceful or magnetic. Attention therefore was shifting from the moral virtues, which need to be cultivated, to the image, which needs to be fashioned. It was a shift away from the invisible moral intentions toward the attempt to make ourselves appealing to others, away from what we actually are and toward refining our performance before a public that mostly judges the exterior.[2]

A little later he illustrates the shift from character to personality further:

> Nowhere is this disengagement between personality and character more plain than in the way that celebrities have replaced heroes in our culture, and in the way that villains have disappeared. A hero was someone who embodied what people prized but did so in such a way that others wanted to emulate him or her. A celebrity may also want to be emulated, but the grounds of the emulation have now changed. A celebrity usually embodies nothing and is typically known only for being known. Fame, in our world of images and manipulation, can be manufactured with little or no accomplishment behind it. In Daniel Boorstin's rather caustic comparison: 'The hero was distinguished by his achievement; the celebrity by his image or trademark. The hero created himself; the celebrity is created by the media. The hero was a big man; the celebrity is a big name.'[3]

We're all desperately afraid that our friends may regard us as a dull or inadequate personality. That's why we are concerned so much about our image. But New Testament Christianity was much more concerned about character and, above all, a character which is pleasing to God.

Behind this shift from character to personality lies the shift from virtue to values. Without this latter shift the former would not have been possible. The word 'values' is surprisingly modern. Until this century people spoke of virtues, not values. Virtues had the ring of qualities which were agreed to be morally right. They were concerned with moral excellence and goodness. They had a 'firm, resolute character'[4] to them and carried an authority and gravity which is altogether lacking in the word 'values'. As Gertrude Himmelfarb, a recognised historian in this area, points out, values, 'can be beliefs, opinions, attitudes, feelings, habits, preferences, prejudices, even idiosyncrasies – whatever any individual, group, or society happens to value, at any time, for any reason.'[5] We can all clarify our values, but we can never judge between one set of values and another. Values are whatever people choose.

The change in vocabulary, then, is not a neutral updating of language but a deep modification of our understanding of what matters to people. And all sorts of implications flow from it for our spiritual and moral lives. So, it is important to understand that what Paul is writing about to the Colossians is the subject of virtues, which lead to the formation of Christian character, not values which lead to the creation of personalities. The former, not the latter, is the currency in which eternity deals. Christians can leave unbelievers to trade in the currency of values and personalities which may one day prove as worthless as the Russian rouble in the summer of 1998.

Paul's previous lists of vices each contained five components. Now, he balances them with one list of positive virtues which is also made up of five components, the structure being according to the custom of his day. But there is nothing customary about the way he writes about them. His plea is not addressed to society in general but to those who are *God's chosen people, holy and dearly loved.* Unless the wearers are chosen, set apart and deeply loved by God, this uniform will be an uncomfortable fit. It will be obvious that the suit was made for someone else. But if people fit this description then this uniform is for them: they are required to wear it and will gladly do so.

The virtues are those of *compassion, kindness, humility, gentleness and patience.* The meaning of the words is simple enough. It is the practice which is difficult. *Compassion* means to feel with a heart of pity. It is the opposite of being hard-hearted, of living according to the law of 'ungrace' and the language of rights and of just desserts. The Gospels record Jesus as being moved with compassion for the crowds and for individuals. It led him to miraculously feed thousands who were hungry; to heal blind men, to cure a man with leprosy and to raise a widow's dead son.[6] Compassion was what the Samaritan felt for the victim of violence on the road from Jerusalem to Jericho.[7] Compassion was what the waiting father felt for his wayward son when he returned home.[8] Compassion means to be moved in the emotions – to feel pity. But, interestingly, in all these examples from the Gospels, compassion led Jesus and all who felt it to action. Feelings were not divorced from doing something to change the situation of those for whom pity was felt.

Perhaps the most remarkable woman in our day to demonstrate the meaning of compassion was Mother Teresa of Calcutta. She was once taking part in a talk show in Canada with a brilliant Nobel prize-winning biologist. He was speculating on what future breakthroughs there might be in DNA research which might lead to everlasting physical life. The host turned to Mother Teresa for a comment. She simply remarked, 'I believe in love and compassion.' The biologist couldn't understand the relevance of the remark. But those on the streets of Calcutta could. She has demonstrated over and over again the impact which compassion can have in our world. What a difference it can make, as great as any that can be made by a renowned research scientist.[9]

Compassion is followed by *kindness.* The word for 'kindness' comes from the same Greek root as the word 'Christ'. But the word 'kindness' is used by New Testament writers to describe

God the Father as well as Jesus Christ the Son.[10] Kindness is
goodness of a practical kind, a goodness that issues in generous
behaviour. It is a sweetness of character which means one's natural
reaction to people is to give to them and to bless them. The great
Augustine was won to Christ by the preaching of Ambrose but,
like so many others down the course of history, it was not the
preaching that first attracted his attention but the kindness of the
preacher. Kindness remains not only a reflection of the character
of God and of his Son Christ Jesus in our lives, but also a
persuasive communicator of the gospel.

Next on the list comes *humility*. To be lowly in your thinking
about yourself was no more welcome in the ancient world than it
is in our own. As a virtue it is profoundly counter-cultural. It is
the antithesis of pride, which lies at the root of so much sin and
opposition to God, as it refuses to submit to him and his law. It is
the willingness not to 'think of yourself more highly than you
ought, but rather (to) think of yourself with sober judgment.'[11] It
is, as James Houston points out, no more than 'moral realism'. It
faces us up to the reality of human sinfulness and failings as we
stand before a righteous and holy God.[12] It will mean a willingness
to associate with people most would not consider their equals,[13]
for it teaches us, as Dostoevsky is reported to have said, not to lie
down but to stand up in someone else's shoes.

In our image-addicted world hubris reigns. We boast about
our achievements and our children, our purchases and our
possessions. Have you noticed that no one is ever average or
ordinary? The way our language has become inflated betrays us.
We no longer have our rubbish removed by dustbin men but by
Refuse Disposal Officers. No one ever seems to be a worker;
everyone seems to be a director. No student is ever pedestrian,
they are only ever brilliant. The modern world breeds pride and
has a corrosive effect on humility. But humility is the trademark
of those who are *God's chosen people, holy and dearly loved*.

The fourth virtue is that of *gentleness*. Like *humility, gentleness* does not fare well in the present climate. The image of 'gentle
Jesus meek and mild' went out of the window of most churches
long ago and with it, rightly, the slightly effeminate picture of

Jesus it epitomised. That picture of Jesus has been replaced with a more robust and masculine image of him which is more in tune with the age. But like it or not, gentleness is included in this list of qualities which the Christian is to cultivate. It is mentioned too in the list of the fruit of the Spirit and elsewhere as a mark of Christ's work within us.[14] So, we cannot escape it. It seems to be important. What does it mean?

In Classical Greek the word was applied to animals, as well as humans. It was used, for example, of horses which had been tamed and could be bridled. They were hardly weaklings! They retained tremendous power. But once 'broken in', the power which had been undisciplined and destructive became disciplined and was channelled so that it was useful. The horse which had been broken in could pull carts or carry riders when the unbroken horse would be quite unable to do so. That, I find, is a very helpful picture of what the biblical word 'meek' or 'gentle' means. It doesn't require me to give up my convictions, deny my strength or be denuded of power. It does require me to control them and channel them, with the help of the Holy Spirit, so that my strong feelings are expressed in helpful and constructive ways. Moses was no effeminate weakling. Anyone who led the rabble of Israel out of Egypt and through the wilderness for forty years must have been a person of real strength and determination. Yet the Bible describes him as a very meek man.[15] For the most part his tremendous strength was well controlled and the people benefited from his leadership. That's the sort of gentleness to imitate.

The final virtue is that of *patience*. To be patient is to be long-suffering with people and forbearing in adverse circumstances. Many of us are far more patient with ourselves than we are with others. We need to learn to redirect our willingness to put up with ourselves towards other people. The virtue of patience is a natural outcome of the four qualities which have already been mentioned. *Compassion, kindness, humility and gentleness* will lead to it. It is also an indispensable quality if the instructions to forgive in the following verse, verse 13, are to be obeyed. *Patience*, then, plays a crucial role in the development of a Christlike character.

Continuing his forgiveness (v. 13)

We shall soon be disappointed if we join the church and expect to find it perfect. We need to remember (but alas we often forget) that the church is only made up of people who are just like us. We know our own failings and the continuing struggle we have with sin, so why should we expect others to be free from them? The church may be composed of people who are already saints from God's vantage point, but to us they are still very much saints under construction. The remodelling has by no means finished. Since this is so, it is likely that we shall soon be offended for one reason or another. We'll hear gossip that hurts. We'll be disappointed by the lack of spiritual zeal. We'll feel let down when we're not loved and understood enough. We'll be shocked at the sexual immorality we discover. We'll get frustrated at the unChristlike behaviour we observe. Before long the grievances will mount and, if we do not deal with them in a proper fashion, they will soon lead to disillusionment with the church.

We need to be sure that we have realistic, and biblical, expectations of the church, which is only ever composed of saints still very much under construction. That may help to defeat cynicism and dissatisfaction. But the upsets will still be there and there is only one way for Christians to handle them – and that is by forgiving them, by letting them go, in the name of Christ.

It seems so elementary but it is amazing how necessary such simple instructions are, now as then. I know of Christians who felt themselves snubbed by fellow church members and have sat at the other side of the church stewing in resentment for years afterwards. The 'offenders' were probably not even aware that they had caused offence! How is it that such basic Christian teaching is so flagrantly ignored in so many churches? Paul tells us we are to *forgive whatever grievances you may have. Whatever* is a pretty comprehensive word. Every grievance is included. None, no matter how petty or how great, how recent or how old, how understandable or how inexcusable, is to be omitted from the spiritual discipline of forgiveness.

The reason why we must forgive is obvious, when we stop to

think about it. We are to *forgive as the Lord forgave you*. We are only continuing the forgiveness of Jesus. As it has flowed into our lives from the cross of Calvary so it must flow through us into the lives of others. We must let go of the wrongs people do to us, because Christ has already paid the price for their sins as well as ours. It should be obvious that we should treat others as God has treated us. Every time we pray the Lord's prayer we recognise the link between the two: 'Forgive us our trespasses as we forgive those who trespass against us.' Philip Yancey quotes Charles Williams as saying, 'No word in English carries a greater possibility of terror than the little word "as" in that clause.' It is terrifying because Christ 'plainly links our forgiveness by the Father with our forgiving-ness of fellow human beings.'[16] Jesus clearly said that if we do not forgive, we will not be forgiven. The church must be the place where forgiveness freely flows back and forth between its members.

Wearing his love (v. 14)

Love is the crowning virtue. If all the other virtues reflect the character of God, or Christ, love does so even more. 'God is love.'[17] We are, then, to wear love above any of the other characteristics which have been mentioned. If we do, they will soon follow in train. Love is the most comprehensive virtue of all. It demands a self-giving which goes beyond anything which has been called for up to now. For, according to the Bible, the Christian under-standing of love is defined by the cross of Christ. John says, 'This is how we know what love is: Jesus Christ laid down his life for us.'[18]

Eugene Peterson picks up the thrust of Paul's exhortation well when he translates verse 14 like this: 'And regardless of what else you put on, wear love. It's your basic all-purpose garment. Never be without it.' Love completes the wardrobe which God has chosen for us. Here is the set of designer clothes we are to wear. And love is its designer label.

Love, Paul says, is important because *it binds them together in perfect unity*. That has given rise to the picture of love as a belt which holds everything else in place. It may be that he means that love gives the other qualities a coherence which they would otherwise lack and brings them into an organic unity. But the original words don't quite say that and even if they did it would be difficult to really see what Paul is driving at. Paul doesn't speak of love like that anywhere else. So might he be saying something different?

Almost every word in the phrase is problematic. Who is the 'them'? The original words speak of love as 'a bond of perfection' but in what sense is the word 'of' being used, and what does 'perfection' mean? Having looked at the arguments,[19] I think the 'them' probably refers to the Christian community, which has just been spoken of in the previous verse. So, it means that love is what binds the believers together and produces perfection or completeness in them. Without love they will be not only half-dressed, but half-finished.

Realising his peace (v. 15)

Jesus Christ was characterised not only by love, but by peace, and we are to make his peace real among us. People have often been misled by the phrase 'in your hearts' in this verse. So we need to look at its teaching carefully. The mention of the heart has led many to believe that Paul is saying that Christian individuals should always feel an unruffled sense of calm and that they should not let anything disturb their sense of tranquillity. Whatever is going on around them they should maintain their composure and exude serenity. They should be able to rest in God and let him work it all out. But that idea is more akin to Stoicism or Confucianism than to Christianity. Jesus Christ, the perfect man, was stirred in spirit at the graveside of Lazarus, moved to anger when he cleansed the temple, got infuriated with religious bigots, and expressed agony in Gethsemane as he faced the cross. He was a full-blooded, passionate man. To adapt Philip Yancey's words, his personality did not match that of the 'Star Trek Vulcan' as he strode spaceship earth remaining calm, cool and collected no matter what he faced.[20] It's not that sort of peace which Paul is talking about.

Our trouble is that as modern Westerners we tend to read everything through the spectacles of individualism. This verse is not about what we feel in our individual psychologies but how we live in our social relationships. Consistent with all that he has been saying in this section of his letter, he envisages situations in the church where conflicts and arguments will arise. His point is that other clubs and societies, political groups especially, can afford disputes and divisions without any lack of integrity, but we can't *since as members of one body, we were called to peace*. Our foundation charter calls us to reconciliation, to peace and to be a united people. Such conflicts, then, would undermine our whole reason for existence, our primary calling and our basic constitution. So, in the church they cannot be permitted; they must be dealt with.

It is there that the *peace of Christ* comes in. His peace is to rule or to be the umpire when such disputes arise. We are to settle them on the basis of what will maintain peace within the fellowship, as he settled disputes by taking the place of weakness, by suffering injustice and by giving himself over to be abused. It's so foreign to our way of thinking that we always need to remind ourselves that this is God's way, not of sweeping issues under the carpet, but of resolving issues. By this means, rather than by the normal route humans choose of upping the conflict, the cross resolved God's dispute with sin and Satan. It did not leave it to fester.

But doesn't that mean that the church will be populated by people like Neville Chamberlain who signed a peace treaty with Hitler in 1938 at Munich, believing Hitler to be open to the persuasion of 'sweet reasonableness', when he should have been preparing for war? No, it most emphatically does not. The fellow church member with whom we are in dispute is not our enemy, but our brother or sister in Christ. The weapons of our spiritual warfare and the strategy of our spiritual war, as we have said, are altogether different from the weapons and strategies of the world. Christ is the head of the church[21] and is active within it through his Holy Spirit. He is capable of sorting out issues which we are likely only to mess up further. And, he has given the gift of leaders to his church whose responsibility it is, if they are properly called and gifted, to lead a church forward toward perfection and not simply to maintain a happy ship which is going nowhere. It is their responsibility to give the church direction and to rule it with integrity and justice. So, have no fear. Let the peace of Christ be the umpire in your relationships and your disputes.

If this verse is all about peace between members rather than peace within a member, what do the words *in your heart* mean? Quite simply, they mean, let the peace of Christ rule deep down in your life. Let it rule not as a matter of outward show but as a matter of inner integrity. Let it rule, not because you must but because the character of Christ is forming in you and his reaction is what genuinely flows out from you when you find yourself in conflict with another church member.

Standing back from the individual items which make up the Christian's wardrobe, we can see that Paul is calling us to live *like* Christ. The call is not to adopt his personality. We may be naturally more or less introverted, more or less humorous, more or less colourful, than he. The call is to put on his character, not his personality. To do so we must not merely identify with his values, for if we do we might soon find ourselves voting for someone else's values. We must commit ourselves to his virtues, to those marks of character which we see in Jesus. Character can express itself through a multitude of personalities, just as God, the Creator of a richly diverse and multi-varied world, intended.

The imagery of clothing is a brilliant analogy but, like all analogies, it is not perfect. We put on and take off clothing daily. Some do it many times a day. These virtues are not to be something we wear externally at our convenience, only to be discarded and replaced when we want to wear something else. We are not to change them with the fashion. They are to become integral to our very beings. They are to be us. Only so can we be *like* Christ.

2. Living under Christ (verse 16)

To live *like* Christ it will be necessary for us to live *under* Christ, that is, under his authority as Lord of our lives. To experience peace in our fellowship we all need to be living under the rule of Christ. Apart from that, any 'peace' we think we're experiencing will be a mere illusion. In order to help us live under Christ's authority God has made two means available to us. The first is the word and the second is our worship.

Through the word

As a Christian you are to *let the word of Christ dwell in you richly*. That is not a piece of pleasant advice to be followed if you opt to do so, but a clear command to be obeyed. *The word of Christ* refers to the teaching of Christ which we have recorded for us in the Gospels. But a full understanding of the teaching of Christ can only be obtained by reading the Gospels in the context of the Old Testament, which leads up to them, and the rest of the New Testament, which leads away from them. In other words, here is a shorthand way of saying that we are to let the whole of the Bible, with a special emphasis on the words of Jesus, live in us.

Paul's language seems somewhat exaggerated. Two strong words are brought into play. *The word of Christ* is to *dwell* in us *richly*. We shall get nowhere with it if it is an occasional visitor with whom we flirt once in a while. If it is to be the means by which we let Christ rule in our lives, we have to treat his word much more seriously than that. The intensity of his language about Christ's words alerts us to both a matter of principle and a matter of practice.

The matter of principle is this. Are we serious enough about the words of Christ to submit to them? Will we listen to them, believe them and then do them? Or will we weigh them against the words of others, filter them to make them more palatable and only obey them when they suit us? The Bible commentator, Matthew Henry, who lived in a previous century, put it like this:

The gospel is the word of Christ, which has come to us; but that is not enough, it must dwell in us, or keep house, not as a servant in a family, who is under another's control, but as a master, who has a right to prescribe and direct all under his roof. We must take our directions and instructions from it, and our portion of meat and strength, of grace and comfort, in due season, as from the *master of the household*. It must dwell in us; that is, be always ready and at hand to us in everything, and have its due influence and use.[22]

To what extent do we let the word of Christ dwell in us richly? Or, as a matter of fact, do we let the words of others influence our lives more? Do we give a more secure place in the home of our minds to them than we do the words of Christ? It's easy enough to test, isn't it? Take almost any topic – our attitude to divorce, our response to our enemies, our feelings about those who offend us, our stance on sexual purity within marriage, our understanding of who our neighbour is, our reaction to the marginalised and the poor, and so on – then ask, how does our position really compare with that of Christ's? It faces us up to the simple yet disturbing question, 'Is he really Lord?'

Another way of testing whether the word of Christ really dwells in us richly is to ask how much time we spend reading and studying it. Here is the second implication of the verse which relates to the matter of practice. As Leroy Eims once remarked, 'We must get into the Word and the Word must get into us. We get into the Word by hearing it preached, reading it, studying it and memorising it. We get the Word into us through meditation.'[23] It won't get into us unless we begin by making it a habit to study it. Surveys of Bible-reading habits among Christians have shown an alarming drop in the practice of daily reading in recent years. This may account for the equally alarming rise in biblical illiteracy which is evident in many of our churches and the low level of spirituality and Christian living which is all too obvious. Reading a portion of the Bible every day, perhaps with the help of some notes which guide us, may not be the only way to get into the word. Nevertheless, there is a biblical precedent for doing so in the Berean church who were described as 'noble' because they did so.[24] Sociological changes to work and family life may make this less practical. Although, one suspects, that it is really the omnipresence of the TV which has eroded Bible-reading habits among Christians rather than the pressures of work and family. But even if the changes in lifestyle make it impossible for us to read the Bible every day, it is incumbent on us to find other ways of ensuring we are fed and taught by the Bible which are just as adequate as the old customs were. The sporadic exposure to it at a conference, the occasional feast at a holiday week, the weekly titbit in a short sermon, is really not an adequate replacement for the more traditional habits, and the church is suffering as a result. So, if in principle you wish to let the words of Christ be the master in your life, how in practice do you set about making sure they are? What pattern have you adopted which ensures that you are regularly informed by the teaching of Scripture and continuously nourished by its truths?

In our worship

Worship is no more an optional extra for the Christian than reading the word is. It is another of the means which God has graciously given us so that we might live under the authority of Christ. Paul teaches us several important things about worship in this verse which gives us a rare insight into how the early Christians went about it. He speaks of its mutual participants, its essential ethos, its varied ingredients and its central focus.

The idea that worship is led by one man from the front while the congregation sit as passive spectators is foreign to the New Testament idea of worship as described both here and in 1 Corinthians 14, which is the other major passage that describes the early church practice. The emphasis in both passages is on participation. *You teach and admonish one another*. There is no hierarchy which dominates and not even a mention of leaders, even if they were there and did exercise some direction. Many in the fellowship were gifted as encouragers, exhorters, pastors, teachers, prophets, and they all had something to contribute. Worship was, and should still be, a mutual exercise where we gain from and learn from one another.

The size of the New Testament churches, which were based in houses and unlikely to have had more than fifty members, obviously helped in forming face to face relations and in the participation factor. But the fact that some of our churches are much larger should not exempt us from seeking ways by which all might engage in meaningful participation. The reason for participation is not sociological (because of group size) but spiritual (because we are all now gifted by the Spirit and members of the body).

The essential ethos of worship is to be one of *wisdom*. The fact that worship is open for many to share may be liable to abuse. It could lead to anarchy if people became so keen on participating that they were not willing to wait for one another. That was the situation in Corinth, where Paul has to encourage them to re-establish some order in their worship times.[25] His concern here is likely to be different. The fact that worship was open might mean that several would take part who were really neither gifted nor qualified to do so. The teaching could easily degenerate into false teaching, as the Colossians knew well. They had been taught all sorts of things about worship which were just not so. Teachers ought to know what they were talking about, but they did not always do so. The church collectively needed wisdom, the wisdom of the Spirit, to lead them into truth.

Admonition might equally be well off-key. Sometimes it is discordant in its manner. Open worship gives the opportunity for people to use the situation to further their own political ambitions in the church, to put others down, to display their own sanctity, or to develop a false authoritarianism. Sometimes, even if the point is right, the spirit with which it is expressed is sour and contrary to all the Christ-like virtues we have studied. It may provide opportunity, too, for some to ride their hobby horses; to rebuke their fellow believers for things which they feel strongly about but which do not clearly arise from the Scripture where God makes known his will.

So, open worship provides an opportunity for folly to reign. That's why those who engage in it must ensure that folly is dethroned and wisdom always given its rightful place.

The next thing to which Paul draws attention is the varied ingredients which compose worship. He refers to singing *psalms, hymns and spiritual songs*. Although we cannot be sure exactly what he would have meant by those different forms, his meaning is probably not too different from what we mean by them. *Psalms* refers to the hymns of Israel and would have drawn on the rich wealth of the book of Psalms, as well as to other poetic worship material which is found in the Old Testament. *Hymns* might refer to more recently composed material of a didactic or credal kind which was addressed to God. By contrast, *spiritual songs* are most likely to refer to the more spontaneous singing which might arise from the direct inspiration of the Holy Spirit. The word *spiritual* usually refers to the Holy Spirit and there is no reason to think that it doesn't do so here. This 'charismatic hymnody'[26] is mentioned in 1 Corinthians 14:15-16 and, again, in Ephesians 5:18-19. Today, all three forms of spiritual singing continue with the addition, too, of another form of spiritual song. Modern spiritual songs are usually shortish compositions which do not develop a theme didactically, as the hymn does, but express praise, gratitude, aspiration or make an affirmation briefly and often repetitively. There is nothing to say that forms of Christian music must be limited to the three forms Paul mentions. His point is rather that there is a diversity in Christian worship and several styles are being used to build up the fellowship.

Christian worship does not need to be musically monochrome. How sad, then, that so many battles in churches have been fought in recent days over precisely this issue. Some denominations curiously think it is anathema to sing anything at all. What they do with this and similar verses I do not know! Others defend the Psalms as the only legitimate expression of Christian music. But this verse is clear in saying that Christian worship is much more varied than that. Still others are going to the stake to claim an exclusive place for the hymn. It is indeed a rich form of Christian music and one which we lose at our peril, but it has no monopoly. Spiritual songs seem to have a particular appeal in contemporary culture and are to be welcomed. The cultural snobbery shown towards them in some circles lacks all the virtues which Paul commended to the Colossians. But to worship using only spiritual songs is to be as deficient in our worship as a diet without any iron in it. Alone they are not adequate. They will lead to a generation of anaemic Christians.

The key point is that we do not have to choose between these three styles of song. When Paul wrote to the Corinthians, who were splitting into factions over who was the best leader in the New Testament church, he told them they were being stupid, because it wasn't a beauty contest where one had to win at the expense of another. '... No more boasting about human leaders,' he wrote. 'All things are yours, whether Paul or Apollos or Cephas...'[27] The choice was simply unnecessary. And so it is with forms of worship and styles of music. We can, and should, benefit from them all. If we don't, it is not because they are wrong but because we are wrong, as we shall see shortly.

Paul's final phrase about worship reminds us of the central focus of worship. It is about expressing *gratitude in* (our) *hearts to God*. He is the centre of it. It is in his direction we should be looking, and we should be doing so with thankfulness and grace. How foreign much recent worship would seem to him. Its focus has often been on one another. Are 'they' lifting their hands, or are 'they' sitting on them? Are 'they' joining in the singing, or sitting in silent protest? Have 'they' got their eyes open when they say the blessing, or not? Are 'they' using the organ or the drums? Is it the green hymn book or the yellow song book 'they're' using today? The effect of it all has been to draw our eyes away from the Lord and to get us to focus on secondary, even unworthy, issues.

Our attitude has certainly not always been one of *gratitude*. The word *gratitude* comes from the word *grace* and it may mean either that we are to worship with thankfulness or in a gracious spirit. Recent worship, all too often, has been characterised by an absence of both of these. The attitude has frequently been that of grumbling and of a hardness of spirit. As David Coffey warned his congregation in an open letter about worship:[28]

- I can bend the knees without bowing to his laws.

- I can raise the hands to the sky without elevating the mind to heaven.

- I can demand silence in worship on Sundays and lead a noisy life during the week.

- I can be on my feet for Jesus at a celebration and fail to stand for him at school.

- I can sing 'Come down, O love divine' and refuse to answer when he knocks.

May God forgive us that our attitudes have been so wrong. Worship, together with the word, was given us by God as a means by which we should bring our lives under submission to the rule of Christ. Our abuse of it has often demonstrated that we have no such intention. Rather than submitting we wish to remain supreme in our own lives.

3. Living for Christ (verse 17)

This whole section concerning the believer's experience of Christ comes to an end as Paul tells us that its purpose is that we might live *for* him. We live *with* him, *in* him, *like* him and *under* him in order that we might live *for* him. He has ranged widely over issues of Christian character and Christian relationships; over practices of spiritual discipline and spiritual worship; over questions of facing temptations and handling conflicts; over matters of the earthly life and the heavenly realm. Now he sums it all up by saying, *and whatever you do, whether in word or deed, do it all in the name of the Lord Jesus, giving thanks to God the Father through him.*

Living for Christ means that we must live totally for him, worthily of him and gratefully to him.

Totally for him

Nothing is omitted. His claim has to have a comprehensive grip on our lives. We cannot compartmentalise our living so that we live for him in church but live for others in our family, for self in our work, for ambition in our study, for self-interest in our politics and for pleasure in our recreation. There needs to be an integrity about believers. And Jesus is to be the integrating factor. He needs to be Lord of whatever we do and say. There are no 'no go' areas for him. It all has to be for him.

When a teenage boy falls in love, strange things begin to happen. Hair which has not been combed for years discovers why combs exist. The bathroom suddenly becomes unavailable to other members of the family as the value of showering oneself with water, soap and deodorants is discovered. The phone bill goes up while the petrol in the car goes down. Things change, all for the new (and probably temporary) love of his life. He'll do anything to please her! In a more mature way, but with no less enthusiasm and joy, we should delight in doing anything to please Jesus.

In the verses that follow (3:18-4:1) Paul spells out some of what that will mean in relation to our family life and employment situation. Comprehensive though the principle is, covering both our actions and our speaking, he brings it down to earth and gives us some practical illustrations so we can understand it. But for the moment his concern is to establish the principle that we are to live for Christ with integrity in the totality of our lives.

Worthily of him

When I was a teenager I was out one day with a friend, who had recently passed his driving test, in his father's car. We'd gone a little further than intended and realised we were about to run out of petrol. Being impecunious school boys, neither of us had any money with us, at least, not enough to buy petrol. What were we to do? My friend suddenly remembered that his dad, who was a well known local businessman, owned an account, and probably some shares too, in a nearby garage. We went in and my friend wound down the window and simply said to the petrol pump attendant (you can tell how long ago this was!), 'Fill her up, please. Swithenbank's the name.' That did the trick. The name caused the attendant to spring into action, the petrol was forthcoming and dad (I hope) paid the bill. We'd have been less happy if we'd had an accident because we had been fooling around and had to confess to the police, 'Swithenbank's the name.' It would have brought shame on the family name.

As Christians we are to do whatever we do and say whatever we say *all in the name of the Lord Jesus*. If bearing his name means we enjoy many privileges, it also imposes on us many responsibilities. We dare not bring disgrace to his name. We must always act in such a way that when people ask us whose we are and whom we represent we can mention the name of Jesus without embarrassment. We must not humiliate our Lord by what we do. Rather we must bring honour to him. Is he pleased to have us associated with his name?

Gratefully to him

Paul comes back once more to the need for thankfulness. It is the third time it has been mentioned in three verses. Verse 15 says that in relating to others we are to be thankful. Verse 16 says that in worshipping the Lord we are to be thankful. Verse 17 says in living the life we are to be thankful. Why is Paul so obsessed with thankfulness?

It is not that Paul wishes to generate a 'feel-good' factor in Colosse. Nor even is it, I think, simply that gratitude to God has such a purifying effect on our lives, even though it does, for as Herbert Carson rightly says:

> Thanksgiving towards God will beget humility, for it develops the awareness that every gift is from him, and so it deals a blow at the self-opinionated attitude which breeds scorn of others. Similarly, by turning the thoughts away towards God, it kills self-pity which is the parent of resentment and bitterness.[29]

But the reason for Paul's stress on thanksgiving is more fundamental than that. Paul emphasises it because, as John Barclay points out, thanksgiving 'describe(s) a community bound together and bound to God in what might be considered the highest human activity, the peak human potential,' namely, that of worship.[30] That's it. To be thankful is to put God in his rightful place and to worship.

These verses have travelled a vast territory. But they boil down to some very simple, but crucial, principles. As Christians we are to:

- Live like Christ in character
- Live under Christ in submission
- Live for Christ in integrity

8

In the Family
Colossians 3:18-21

[18]Wives, submit to your husbands, as is fitting in the Lord.

[19]Husbands, love your wives and do not be harsh with them.

[20]Children, obey your parents in everything, for this pleases the Lord.

[21]Fathers, do not embitter your children, or they will become discouraged.

---

1. Paul's perspective

2. Paul's distinctives

    The principle of Christ's Lordship
    The principle of mutual relationship

3. Paul's directives (verses 18-21)

    Wives: submission (v. 18)
    Husbands: love (v. 19)
    Children: obedience (v. 20)
    Parents: encouragement (v. 21)

A recent British Government discussion document, aimed at looking at how we can strengthen family life, began with these words:

> Families are at the heart of our society. Most of us live in families and we value them because they provide love, support, and care. They educate us, and they teach us right from wrong. Our future depends on their success in bringing up children. That is why we are committed to strengthening family life.[1]

Christians would readily agree about the importance of the family. The Bible made it clear long ago that families are a very special part of God's design for creation and it devotes quite a bit of space to teaching us about family matters. In this next section of Colossians we have a key passage about living in the family and the difference Christ makes to it.

Before plunging into the teaching of this section, however, we need to get our bearings. Whilst it is foolish to try to carve up Paul's letter too neatly – one part flows into another – it's reasonable to say that Colossians falls into three sections. The first section deals with the nature of the Christian gospel (1:1-2:5), the second with the nature of Christian experience (2:6-3:17), while the focus of the last section (3:18-4:18) is that of Christian relationships. This last section begins with some practical guidelines for living in a Christian household (3:18-4:1), goes on to talk of the relationship Christians have with the wider community (4:2-6), and finishes with some personal notes that give us an insight into relationships in the church (4:7-18).

Up to this point Colossians has been saturated with teaching about Jesus Christ. Now Paul offers some more practical advice and jots down some personal notes, yet still his comments are full of Jesus. Christ isn't left behind in the doctrinal sections of the letter; he infuses everything Paul has to say in the more practical and personal section of the letter too. This Christ is not only reality himself, but is concerned with the reality of daily living.

1. Paul's perspective

The questions Paul turns to now are these: How does the fulness of the life of Christ work itself out in the life of a Christian? What evidence can we expect to find which demonstrates that Christ is our life? How will Christ show himself in the way we live?

Time and again the New Testament tells us that the answer to these and similar questions will be two-fold. On the one hand, Christ will show himself in our character. On the other hand, he will show himself in our relationships. If Jesus is Lord, he will impact both who we are and how we relate. In 3:5-17, Paul has already explained the impact Christ will have on our character. Now, in 3:18-4:1, he deals with the impact Christ will have on our relationships.

What he and all the rest of the New Testament writers have to say about relationships is, from our perspective, profoundly counter-cultural. The New Testament's emphasis is seriously at odds with the way we view things today both in the wider culture of the secular world and in the narrower culture of the evangelical church.

It runs into conflict with the culture of the Western world because that world is based on the philosophy of individualism. The primary social unit today is the person. We live in the world of 'I', 'me', 'mine', 'myself'. We see ourselves as unique and we are acutely aware of the boundaries between ourselves and others. We do not define ourselves essentially as someone else's son or someone else's mother. We define ourselves as discrete individuals who are conscious of inner emotions, feelings and drives. We seek to understand ourselves, our personalities and our make-up primarily through the discipline of psychology. We prize the values of self-reliance and educate people to make their own decisions. Taken to an extreme it leads people to experience difficulty in entering into relationships, experiencing intimacy and, particularly, in maintaining their obligations in relationships they have entered. People, even Christian people, have certainly said to me, 'Pastor, I need to leave my wife and my children in order to find myself.' The social commitment they have made in marriage and the parental responsibility they assumed in parenting children comes lower down their list of priorities than realising the potential of 'the self.'[2]

This way of understanding ourselves would all have seemed very strange to people in the world of the New Testament. In that world they perceived themselves chiefly as people in relationships. They gained their identity from where they came from, from their parents, group, tribe, clan or city. Although they spoke of 'I' they were acutely conscious of how other people saw them and what others thought of them. They found their meaning in life through fulfilling their social obligations.

Given this, it is not surprising that so much of the teaching of the New Testament deals with relationships. Of course, it would be possible to dismiss much of its teaching in this area by saying that it related to a different time and a different culture and that today we need not be bound by that but need to work things out in a different way for our more individualistic culture. But it is not, I believe, merely a matter of cultural difference. We are dealing here not just with a change of culture but with a change in our understanding of who God made us to be.

God declared everything in his creation to be good until the point when he observed Adam's loneliness. That was the first thing he judged to be 'not good'.[3] His way of making it good was to provide a companion for Adam, since he designed human beings to be persons made for relationships. Indeed, the ability to relate, as male and female, is, according to Genesis 1:27, at the heart of what it means to be made in God's image. He made us, it says, in his image to be male and female. What this means is that as in the Trinity, where the persons of the Trinity are distinct yet live in community, we are made to enjoy our distinctiveness and yet we are equally made to live in community. It's part of our constitution that we're made to connect with others and we become more fully human and more complete through our relationships.

Sadly, the fall ruptured the perfect relationship Adam had with Eve and introduced elements of alienation, of jealously, suspicion and power into it. Ever since that time people have been alienated in their relationships with one another and struggled with those same dehumanising forces in their lives. Since Christ came to reverse the effect of the fall, it is not surprising that one of the key marks of God's redemptive work in our lives is that we sort out our relationships, know a measure of healing in them and bring them all under his Lordship.

So we can't dismiss this aspect of the New Testament's teaching on relationships as a matter for their culture then, whilst we need to design a new and individualistic spirituality for our culture now. We need to learn from the wisdom of its teaching, built as it is on principles enshrined in our creation, and ask the Holy Spirit to bring us more and more into conformity with it. A mark of true conversion is that we live no longer for ourselves.[4]

The teaching of this relational ethic challenges the contemporary evangelical church as much as the secular world. It teaches us that the way to test the quality of our spirituality is by examining the quality of the relationships we have, not by measuring the intensity of supernatural experiences, the magnetism of our spiritual power, the frequency of our attendance at meetings, the vigour of our evangelical activism or even the depth of our evangelistic fervour. It teaches us that the real test lies in the realm of the ordinary, the day-to-day, the mundane areas of the family, the work place and the community. It cautions us not to engage in evangelical escapism whereby we run away from the ordinary world into the more exciting world of missions, faith-sharing visits, or, even 'full-time service'.

You can see all this in the response of Jesus to the man out of whom he had just cast a legion of demons. The man wanted to go on the circuit with Jesus, giving his testimony and being held up as a marvellous example of the power of God. Jesus told him to go home and tell them there what great things God had done for him.[5] It would be less exciting, more testing, but also more real. His family relationships needed to be restored and he needed to take his place in the community once more. It was Satan who had destroyed all that, and now it was Jesus who was going to heal it all. The healing in which Jesus was engaged was not just the healing of a possessed spirit and a deranged mind, but the healing of a ruptured family and community. It is a telling incident, since the real challenge for most of us is to demonstrate that 'Christ is our life' in the on-going social structures of which we are a part. We measure spirituality, all too frequently, by a different set of measurements than the New Testament gives us and we need to learn to be more faithful to what it says than what we think it says.

So, what does Paul teach about relationships?

2. Paul's distinctives

The passage from 3:18-4:1 addresses various members of the household and tells them how they are to behave. It is an example of what has become known as a 'household code'. The household was the basic unit in the social structure of Paul's time. It was a large extended family; a much more inclusive unit than the family structure we're used to today. A typical household would include clients, friends, freedmen, slaves and temporary employees as well as members of the extended biological family. They'd all live in the same space, or adjoining space. They might be engaged in a common business and, most likely, they'd be bound together by worshipping a common god. So it was quite a large affair. And at the heart of it stood the all-powerful figure of the father.

To guide the various members of the household about how they were to behave towards one another it was quite common to write down a code of conduct, a 'household code', as it has come to be called, like the one we have here. The New Testament itself contains a number of such codes, all of which are variations on a theme.[6] And scholars have identified numerous examples outside of the New Testament as well. They all acknowledge, generally speaking, the different categories of people found in the household and so give instructions to wives and husbands, children and parents, and slaves and masters.

Since these codes were a common feature of Paul's world, a great deal of discussion has gone on as to whether he has simply borrowed his teaching from elsewhere, whether it was from pagan sources, like Greek philosophy, or from Hellenistic Judaism. But it has not been proved that Paul was dependent on any of the other codes that have been found. What we can say is that, whatever they may have in common, Paul's code is significantly different from others. There are two major factors which make his code distinct. The first is his emphasis on the principle of Christ's Lordship, and the second is his emphasis on mutual responsibilities.

The principle of Christ's Lordship

The household codes of the Stoics were based on the law of nature, but Paul's concern is with the law of our new nature in Christ. Seven times within the space of nine short verses Paul mentions the Lordship of Jesus Christ. Wives are instructed about what is *fitting in the Lord*. Children are told to obey *for this pleases the Lord*. Slaves are to serve out of *reverence for the Lord, as working for the Lord*. They are to remember that they are really serving him, not an earthly master, and they are to serve in the knowledge that one day they *will receive an inheritance from the Lord as a reward*. It is the Lord Christ they are serving. Masters are reminded that they *have a Master in heaven*. Paul's teaching is shot through with references to the Lord.

So, Paul is clearly not advocating a pattern of social behaviour which has its origin in some pagan philosophy class or which has resulted from sociological discussions with civic authorities which were aimed at engineering a convenient pattern for social life. His teaching is not merely a matter of social convention. He is talking about how things should be in Christ and about what impact Christ should have on our relationships. He is talking about what it means to live in the new community under the authority of Jesus as Lord. He places our relationships with one another firmly in the context of our relationship with Jesus Christ himself. Each time he mentions the Lord, he is reminding us that we cannot separate our family, work and community life from our spiritual life.

Some would see his constant reference to the Lord as a veiled threat. From their viewpoint, if Paul says that this is the way the Lord requires us to behave, then we can't argue about it; we've no alternative but to agree. In this way he produces, so it is said, a church of social conformists who accept their lot in life, however unreasonable, without protest and never seek to change it. So, women are kept down and slaves are kept in their place and the patriarchal and hierarchical society of his day is left undisturbed. But this is a gross misunderstanding both of Paul's intention and of what actually happened as a result of the teaching he gives here.

To relate to one another *in the Lord* puts our relationships into an entirely different context than those relationships which exist apart from Christ. If the relationship is *in the Lord* then it means it will be conducted in a way which is consistent with him. It means we shall treat people, whatever their position or status, as human beings made in the image of God and so as having dignity and worth. It means we will not be able to treat people how we like and that there will be no justification for any abuse of power. It means we shall imitate Jesus who came among people not 'to be served, but to serve, and to give his life as a ransom for many.'[7] It means we will recognise that within the Christian fellowship we relate to one another as brothers and sisters and we're all on the same level, standing on the ground of grace at the foot of the cross. It means we won't use people to satisfy our own greed or lust, but we'll love people and put their interests first. It means we won't live life merely on the horizontal level, as if there was not an eternal dimension to take into account. It means that although we may be conscious of having wrongs done to us personally, in the here and now, we can leave God to sort the issues out at the judgment seat when righteousness will triumph at last.[8]

Far from being socially conformist, this ethic was truly revolutionary both in its immediate character, for obvious reasons, and long-term effects. It was this teaching which, when it had permeated beyond the boundaries of the church, eventually undermined the institution of slavery, because it made masters treat their slaves with respect and not just as possessions. Once a Christian master had learned that a person may be his slave in his business life but his brother in church life, it meant he couldn't go on treating him (or perhaps maltreating him) in the same way as once he had. It altered the relationship fundamentally. So slavery was undermined from within and far more effectively than ever would have been the case if Paul had tried to mount an outright assault on it in the context of the non-democratic government of Imperial Rome. What was true of slavery was also true of the family and the status of women and children. It was this teaching of being *in the Lord* which led to a much higher evaluation eventually being given to the worth of women and children and to family life than was previously the case in the Roman empire. After his apparent conversion to Christianity in 312, the Emperor Constantine passed a range of legislation designed to improve the lot of the slave and his family, offer children some protection and secure the improvement of family life. So, far from encouraging the status quo, the early Christians adopted rules of social behaviour which eventually were to have radically reforming effects in society as a whole. Where Christ really is recognised as Lord there is an improvement in the way we relate to one another.

The principle of mutual relationships

There is another major difference between what Paul writes in his 'household code' and that which can be found in those outside the New Testament. The household codes of the New Testament involve the principle of mutuality. Other household codes uniformly stress the power of the father and write from the perspective of the one who was dominant in the hierarchy. Thus, they write about the duties of the wife but, by contrast, the superiority of the husband, the obligations of the children but the rights of the father, the responsibilities of the slave but the authority of the master. The code addressed to the wife, the child and the slave is all about responsibilities while the code for the husband, father and master is all about privileges. These codes are one-sided. But in the New Testament both partners in the relationship have their responsibilities pointed out to them. Here both wife and husband, child and father, slave and master are reminded of their duties and obligations to one another. After reviewing the evidence, the New Testament scholar Ben Witherington concludes that he can find nothing similar in the ancient world.[9] The element of mutual obligation is lacking elsewhere and that puts Paul's advice in a category of its own.

The theme of mutuality is not something which is unique to Colossians. The household code included in Ephesians begins, at 5:21, with the words, 'Submit to one another out of reverence for Christ.' Having established the principle of mutual submission Paul then goes on to spell out in more detail what form that submission will take, first for the wife ('submit to your husbands'), then for the husband ('love your wives, just as Christ loved the church and gave himself up for her'). Most English translations of this passage have done us a disservice by splitting the paragraph in the wrong place and inserting a heading (which is not part of the inspired text!) above verse 22 rather than putting it above verse 21. But Paul clearly intends for the whole household code in Ephesians to be read in the context of the principle of mutual submission which he enunciates.

Similarly, writing to the Corinthians on marriage, Paul says, 'The husband should fulfil his marital duty to his wife, and likewise the wife to her husband. The wife's body does not belong to her alone but also to her husband. In the same way, the husband's body does not belong to him alone but also to his wife.'[10] This is revolutionary. It overthrows any idea that the wife is a mere chattel or plaything of the husband, present merely to gratify his desires and pleasures. It treats the wife as a person in her own right and imposes obligations and restraints on the husband, not just the wife. It makes a genuine and equal partnership possible in a way which was unknown in the ancient world.

This principle of mutuality, which extends beyond husbands and wives to parents and children and masters and slaves, was the logical conclusion of being *in the Lord*. If believers were all equally brothers and sisters in Christ, whatever their gender, age or social status, then it meant that there was no room, in any set of Christian relationships, whether in the church or the home, for a hierarchical system where one strata had all the rights and the other all the responsibilities. Every member was called to be a servant and all were called to serve one another.

Undoubtedly, Paul reflects something of the social context of his day in his writing. It is obvious that he does mirror the fact that his society, in general, was patriarchal. But the twin principles of being *in the Lord* and of being in mutual, not one-sided, relationships are genuinely revolutionary. What he writes is a distinctive Christian ethic and it is only once we have grasped that fact that we are in a position to understand the details of his teaching.

2. Paul's directives (verses 18-21)

With that necessary background we turn now to look at the particular directives Paul gives to Christians in the fellowship at Colosse. In this section we shall limit ourselves to relationships which belong to the immediate family. In applying his words to our society, with its different social structure, it makes sense to separate the immediate family relationships from the work relationships even though, given the shape of the ancient household, it would have made no sense in his day. It means that each can be explored more thoroughly. The first group to be addressed are the wives.

Wives: submission (v. 18)

Wives, submit to your husbands, as is fitting in the Lord. Those words have been the subject of so much misunderstanding over the years and the cause of much unwarranted, arrogant behaviour on the part of men and much grief and suffering on the part of women. We need to read them with care.

The first thing to notice is that this is addressed to Christian wives, not women in general. Here is a directive which has to do specifically with the Christian marriage relationship and how the Christian home should be run, not with the role of women in society generally. Within any family the relationship between the husband and the wife is pivotal. Their relationship is the key to everything else in family life. It was then and it is now. And that is Paul's particular concern. So it is quite wrong to construct a wider theology about the position of women on the basis of this verse.

The second thing is to explore what is meant by the word *submit*. The word did not carry the overtones of subjugation and inferiority that have become attached to it today. We can easily show that it has nothing to do with the idea of the wife's inferiority and the husband's superiority since the same word is used of Christ submitting himself to God the Father[11] and there is no sense in which Jesus is inferior to the Father or less than God. Indeed, the word is used widely to describe how Christians, both men and women, should behave and not just of relationships between a wife and her husband. Every member of the congregation is told to submit to others, as, in particular, are those with prophetic gifts. Christian citizens are told to submit to the governing authorities and members of the church are to submit to church leaders.[12] None of these carry the implication that the one who is doing the submitting is second best or of lesser value.

In all these cases submission means to humbly serve and take the lower place in the relationship. To submit is to be opposed to self-assertion and the insistence on one's rights. The word, which is connected with the mathematical idea of order, implies standing in a right relationship to others. It is to accept one's place rather than to get out of line by striving for more position or more power. It may include the idea of obedience, but it is not synonymous with it. Submission is a broader term than obedience. It is to give yourself to another and to follow the example of Jesus who, though equal with God did not cling to his divine honours, but willingly humbled himself and became a human being who surrendered himself even to death on a cross.[13] The verb is in the middle voice, which indicates that Paul is inviting wives to voluntarily submit themselves to their husbands, just as Christ voluntarily gave himself for us. That is why submission is *fitting in the Lord*. It is consistent with the pattern he set.

It is more than likely that the advice to submit was particularly pertinent to wives in the early church. The gospel had resulted in women discovering a status and liberty which was denied them in Judaism as well as elsewhere in the ancient world. They were full members of the Christian community with roles and responsibilities alongside men which exceeded anything they had known before. But the New Testament hints that, as with so many new experiences, things had got a little out of balance and some women could not handle their new-found liberty wisely, went to excess, and overthrew any sense of decorum or restraint in their relationships with their husbands. Far from commending the gospel to those outside the church, such autonomous behaviour would have scandalised pagan society. Paul here, in Corinthians, and even more in the Pastoral Letters, needs to bring them back in line and, without detriment to their worth and freedom, remind them of their duties and obligations.

It is abundantly clear that the word 'submission' does not mean that the one to whom it is offered has any right to behave in a domineering way, to exact unreasonable obedience or to demean, degrade, abuse and humiliate the one who is submissive. The behaviour of the person who receives submission is limited and governed by being *in the Lord*, just as the incentive for the submissive one is that it is *fitting in the Lord*. Richard Foster pointed out that submission has its limits. 'The limits of the discipline of submission are at the points at which it becomes destructive. It then becomes a denial of the law of love as taught by Jesus and is an affront to genuine biblical submission.'[14] He went on to point out that the disciples were not very submissive to the religious authorities of their day, as, for example, in Acts 4:10-20, because 'they simply understood that submission reaches the end of its tether when it becomes destructive.'[15]

So there is no basis here for encouraging mindless and unquestioning obedience on the part of the wife, however unreasonable the demands of the husband. It is a false premise that there is some biblical authority structure which puts the husband in a superior position over the wife and permits him to exercise an authoritarian and totalitarian hold over her. This verse provides no justification for chauvinism. Nor does any other verse on the subject in the New Testament. It needs to be remembered that while Paul invites the wife to submit to her husband, he never commands the husband to make his wife submit. It is something she offers to him, not something he is duty bound to extract from her.

Back in the 1980s Musashi Sada, then aged 17, hit the top of the Japanese hit parade with the song entitled 'Your Husband and Master proclaims'. Part of it went like this:

Before you become my bride, hear this
You will not go to bed before I do
You will not get up after I do
Cook nothing but good meals
And always look pretty
Keep quiet and follow behind me.

That song has nothing to do with what Paul meant when he taught that wives should be submissive. Unfortunately some Christians think it does. It sums up the attitude of some Christian men today who, while claiming to be defending 'the biblical pattern of family life', fail to treat their wives as significant and gifted persons in their own right and see no other role for them than to stay at home and look after their needs, never voicing any opinion of their own. But this is a scandalous parody of Paul's teaching. You can only reach such a conclusion from this verse by isolating it from its context and interpreting it in an extremely superficial and woodenly literalist way.

The debate over this issue in some American church circles has become so intense that a rewrite of the old gospel hymn has recently appeared on the internet. Instead of singing 'Blessed assurance, Jesus is mine...' some, it is claimed, are now being taught to sing, 'Gracious submission, this is God's test.' The chorus begins, 'Gracious submission, this is my song; Serving my husband all the day long'. The satirical version includes lines about 'Ladies in shackles,' 'Ladies are mothers, they work in the house, serving their husbands, meek as a mouse,' and, 'Men should be leaders, that is the rule; Ladies should follow, it's so very cool.' But such chauvinism has little to do with Paul's intent here and owes its origin to a distorted macho masculinity which is the result of the fall rather than to our being redeemed in Christ.

The third element of the text to which we should give our attention is the phrase *as is fitting in the Lord*. It primarily refers to the fact that as Christians it is appropriate that these wives follow the example of Christ by humbly serving their husbands. If we are Christ's people it is appropriate that we should relate to others as he did. But there is more to it than that. The phrase reminds us that Paul is talking about how we relate to one another in the new creation community of the church. Being *in the Lord* means we have experienced salvation, that we are redeemed, and that affects the way we relate. At creation God established a social order in which there were gender differences, with men assuming certain roles and responsibilities and women others, like that of child-bearing.

But when the fall occurred, as we have mentioned, those differences became distorted and damaging. They were infected by sin, and elements of power, hierarchy, abuse and pride entered into the relationship between men and women in a way which God never intended. The result was a good deal of enmity, alienation and pain. Now those fallen relationships need to be redeemed in Christ. It is not for the new community to perpetuate the sinful patterns of the fallen world, but to model God's original plan where, although there may be different roles and responsibilities, submission is willingly and voluntarily given, and met with gentleness and love, never being abused.

The phrase *fitting in the Lord* reminds us further of Christ's attitude towards women. Nowhere do we see him commanding women to do anything unreasonable. Rather we see him reaching out to them to bring healing and liberty, embracing them as significant members of his itinerant band of disciples, and trusting them with the message of the resurrection. What is *fitting in the Lord* means what is appropriate to those who claim to be disciples of Jesus, and that brings an entirely different complexion to the command to submit than is popularly assumed.

Finally, in trying to understand this verse we might remind ourselves that the best commentary on Scripture is Scripture itself. When Paul wrote similar words in his letter to the Ephesians he introduced them, as we have seen, by saying, 'Submit to one another out of reverence for Christ.'[16] According to that verse, submission is not a one-way street. It is to be a mutual act. The wife submits to the husband and, equally, the husband submits to the wife. In fact, given the frequency with which the command to submit is mentioned in the New Testament, submission is what should characterise all our relationships in the church. The women are not especially picked out as needing to do it more than the men.

Mutual submission leads us down the path of glorious freedom.

It frees us from the need to assert ourselves, to prove ourselves, to be in the right, to defend our corner, to hold on to resentments, to demand vengeance when we've been wronged. It leads us to offering ourselves fully and humbly to be of service to others, which means, we offer our gifts, knowledge and skills as well as offering the more menial aspects of being a servant. Submission builds strong and healthy family lives and strong and healthy churches. It is the refusal to submit that divides and destroys. 'Do you not know,' asks Richard Foster, 'what a liberation it is to give up your rights?'[17]

The way of submission, then, does not lead to abject slavery, but to true fulfilment in Christ.

Husbands: love (v. 19)

The command to wives to submit to their husbands is matched by the equally demanding command to husbands *to love your wives and do not be harsh with them*. The particular word chosen for 'love' is the most exacting word for love in the Greek language. It is the word *agapao*. Again, the best commentary on this is to be found in the parallel passage in Ephesians where Paul spells out his meaning in greater detail. There, the command to love your wife is amplified like this: 'just as Christ loved the church and gave himself up for her...'[18] In other words, this love is love of an ultimate kind. It is much deeper than mere affection, goes well beyond friendship and isn't defined purely in terms of sexual instincts or romantic feelings.[19] All those elements may be a part of it. But this love is defined by the way in which Christ voluntarily gave up his own rights and status and offered himself as a humble servant and a willing sacrifice on our behalf. The husband is called to love in this unreasonable kind of way. He is to forego his own rights and status and sacrifice himself – not just his money and occasionally his time – to serve his wife. Her interests are the ones which are to come first.

The use of the word *agapao* highlights the fact that Paul is writing a specifically Christian code of conduct for the household. Although the word was used by others in the ancient world, no other set of household rules uses it to describe the responsibility of the husband towards his wife.[20] Paul uses a word which brings a distinctive Christian meaning to bear and directly connects the behaviour of the husband to the example of his Lord.

So, husbands, no less than wives, are called to know the freedom which is gained through giving up their rights. In fact, what is required of husbands is a far more demanding obligation than that being required of wives. If we think otherwise, if we think that what is required of the wife is unreasonable while what is required of the husband is easy, it only goes to show we have not understood what is being said. What is required is a love that leads to Calvary; always remembering that Calvary leads beyond death to resurrection life. Here, then, is the way to know true and joyful life in our relationships – to love as he loved us.

Paul puts a practical spin on his command when he adds the words *and do not be harsh with them*. In a way he's simply saying negatively what he has already said positively. Husbands may have had the right in the ancient world to treat their wives as they liked. The husband was a powerful figure. But the Christian husband was to restrain his exercise of power. Husbands were not permitted to act in such a way that their wives became embittered, nor to treat them harshly, as if they were mere property. They were not to be overbearing in their manner and there was no room for petty tyranny. Instead, husbands were to demonstrate care, love, patience, forgiveness and affection for them. The husband was to make it easy for the wife so that she would want to submit to him.

These words, it should be said, may still smack of patriarchy, but, as Margaret MacDonald has pointed out, if they do they actually reflect an ethos of 'love-patriarchy'.[21] And the presence of love in the equation between husbands and wives makes all the difference in the world between these Christian household codes and those to be found elsewhere.

Children: obedience (v. 20)

Turning next to the relationships between parents and children, Paul first addresses the children. The command to them is to *obey your parents in everything, for this pleases the Lord*. It is significant that children are addressed at all in this section. The children in view are obviously those who are younger and still very much in the process of growing up. And yet, they are addressed as full and responsible members of the church, worthy of receiving instruction, and not simply ignored. Having said that, the reality of their place as minors is fully recognised in what is said to them.

Whereas the word to the wives invites them to voluntarily submit themselves to their husband, the command to the children is both expressed more strongly and more specifically. It is an unequivocal, active and absolute command which is given to them. They are to *obey*; not offer a general submission, but an unquestioning obedience. In case there should be any doubt about the limits of their obedience, Paul amplifies his command with the words *in all things*. It is not for the child to negotiate the reasonableness of what the parent is asking of them. That responsibility belongs to the parent and presumably Paul has confidence that, since he is writing to Christian families and since he is going to balance what he says to the children with words to the father, the demands made on children will not be unreasonable or contrary to Christian teaching.

Again, the command is supplemented by a gracious explanation. The reason for obeying one's parents is that *this pleases the Lord*. It pleases the Lord first because it is consistent with what God has invariably revealed about his will for the relationship between children and their parents. The tenor of much of the law and wisdom literature was to enjoin children to honour their parents, respect their guidance, follow their advice and obey their commands.[22] Christians stand in continuity with that teaching and must enrich their understanding of what these New Testament commands mean by setting them in the context of the whole sweep of God's revelation in the Old Testament as well as the New. God hasn't changed his mind. He's still pleased when people behave in the family according to the positive principles set out in the Old Testament.

Then, we know it *pleases the Lord* because we find that Jesus, the perfect Son, obeyed his Father.[23] He freely spoke of himself as one who 'obeyed my Father's commands'.[24] Hebrews speaks of him as learning obedience.[25] Obedience marked his life as a Son. It did not cramp his style or stunt his growth. In fact, obedience was the key to him being the most perfect, most complete and most fulfilled human being there ever was. So, when children obey they are following in the footsteps of Jesus and bringing their lives into contact and conformity with his.

Again, the words may smack to us of belonging to a past age. Modern society, having discovered the child, has become child-centred in its approach to education and family-life. Gone are the days when children were 'to be seen and not heard'. They are often today 'heard and not seen', or so it seems. The role of the parent is perceived in different terms. The key, it is said, (and here I caricature) is not to treat the child as some barbarian invader of society who needs to be socialised and brought into conformity so that they can take their place in the wider society, but to treat the children as persons in their own right who are encouraged to discover for themselves, rather than be taught, and encouraged to unlock all the potential that is already within them.

As Christians, we should have no truck with the authoritarian parental regimes which bred inhibited and stunted children and which either denied them an emotionally warm environment in which to grow or treated them as things to be used or abused. But perhaps there is a need for balance in our society and certainly within Christian homes. Scripture is quite clear that God has given parents responsibilities and put them in a position over children to train and discipline them and to teach them to love God with all their might. The child needs some input as well as being allowed to express his or her own output. If all we do is let children express themselves, we shall soon find that what is expressed can be very ugly and unworthy. There are signs that our society has begun to realise that and, having seen some of its results, is drawing back from some of the excesses of an over-emphasis on a child-centred approach to education.

Whatever happens in wider society, as Christian families we should seek to shape our lives by Scripture and therefore encourage children to follow the pattern of Jesus and be obedient.

Fathers: encouragement (v. 21)

The command to children to obey must not be divorced from the command given to their fathers: *Do not embitter your children, or they will become discouraged.* As Tom Wright pointedly says, 'Children need discipline, so do parents.'[26]

This command is addressed to fathers, rather than both parents, because of the place the father had in the ancient family. In our society the command embraces both fathers and mothers. But in Paul's day the father was a very powerful figure in 'an almost omnipotent position'.[27] The father had the right of life and death over his children and continued to exercise authority over his children even when they had grown up and married. Although it could be relinquished voluntarily at an earlier time, his jurisdiction did not legally end until the father died. The father controlled financial affairs and determined who the child should marry and could even dissolve a son's marriage if he so chose. It would have been a frightening situation unless it had been mellowed by the understanding that the bond between the father and the child should be one of 'reciprocal, dutiful affection'.[28]

Paul amplifies the initial command he gives as his directive to Christian fathers by adding an explanation. They are not, he says, to provoke, irritate or exasperate their children, nor to make them angry. The reason he gives is interesting. If they wield their power in that way, he points out, the children will become discouraged. But that is a fairly tame translation for the word he uses which means something more like 'they will be deprived of spirit'. It is not just that they would become emotionally depressed but that they would become nonentities, nonpersons. And the Christian father will not wish to be responsible for that. The Christian father will long to see his child growing to his or her full potential in Christ. He will long to see all the God-given personality and gifts which are locked up within the tiny child gradually being released until it flourishes in full bloom. He would do anything rather than damage the wonder of what God has created.

So parents are not to behave as Regimental Sergeant Majors to their children, never allowing them an opinion or a voice. Children are not to be treated as property or things, but as people with personality and feelings in their own right. Children are not to be treated as inconvenient interruptions to a parent's career prospects or busy social life, but as a precious gift from God. They are to be cared for in an atmosphere of affection, positive love and encouragement. Where necessary that will include wise and consistent discipline. It means that parents and children will have time and fun together. It means the child will hear their parents express positive approval, see them express affection and know they enjoy their parents' trust. The aim will be to create a home where children are not cramped in their emotional and spiritual growth, where they are able to learn to develop healthy relationships, where they grow to become emotionally and spiritually secure persons, and where they know they are of value and worth.

In other words, just as the husband should so love his wife that she finds it easy to submit to him, so parents should so treat their children that they find it easy to obey them. That makes a high demand on parents. Bill Clinton was right when he said, 'The most difficult job in the world is not being President. It's being a parent.'[29] But God gives grace to those who seek it.

If any single line of this household code is taken out of context it could be destructive. But this is no tyrant's charter nor a manifesto for those who delight in having an inferiority complex. Every element of it is intended to be held together as one element checks and balances another. If wives submit and husbands love; if children obey and fathers do not provoke, and if it is all done in the context of the Lordship of Christ, here is a recipe for the creation of a united, harmonious and attractive Christian home. It will lead to the formation of quality relationships which render the gender divides and generation gaps irrelevant. It will create a family life which is envied by many and where each member will fulfil their potential. But, remember, here is not a formula which can be imposed on others outside of Christ. However much natural wisdom these verses contain, so making them applicable to all, here is a way of living that only ultimately makes sense to those who have subjected themselves to the law of Christ. And here is a way of life which is only possible as his Holy Spirit renews us in the image of Christ.

9

In the Community

Colossians 3:22-4:6

[22]Slaves, obey your earthly masters in everything; and do it, not only when their eye is on you and to win their favor, but with sincerity of heart and reverence for the Lord. [23]Whatever you do, work at it with all your heart, as working for the Lord, not for men, [24]since you know that you will receive an inheritance from the Lord as a reward. It is the Lord Christ you are serving. [25]Anyone who does wrong will be repaid for his wrong, and there is no favoritism.

[1]Masters, provide your slaves with what is right and fair, because you know that you also have a Master in heaven.

[2]Devote yourselves to prayer, being watchful and thankful. [3]And pray for us, too, that God may open a door for our message, so that we may proclaim the mystery of Christ, for which I am in chains. [4]Pray that I may proclaim it clearly, as I should. [5]Be wise in the way you act toward outsiders; make the most of every opportunity. [6]Let your conversation be always full of grace, seasoned with salt, so that you may know how to answer everyone.

1. In the working world (3:22-4:1)

> Slaves (3:22-25)
> > Work is worship (vv. 22-23)
> > Work is rewarding (vv. 24-25)
> > Work is dignifying (v. 24)
>
> Masters (4:1)
> > The question of justice
> > The question of judgment

2. In the wider world (4:2-6)

> The importance of prayer (vv. 2-4)
> The importance of wisdom (vv. 5-6)

My colleague, Mark Greene, has recently undertaken some research into what congregations think of their preachers. While the majority who responded were complimentary about the quality and general helpfulness of the sermons they heard, an interesting fact emerged. The sermons were judged to be far more helpful when dealing with church and personal issues than those to do with home or work. In fact, 50% said they had never heard a sermon on work. And 47% said that the preaching was marked by a lack of relevance, depth and challenge. Mark commented, 'This reflects a pietistic, church-centred preaching emphasis – the further Christians get from the church building the less likely they are to have an adequate base of teaching to lead their lives in a godly manner.'[1]

How different are the letters of Paul. The early church had not yet fallen into the trap of ghettoization. The early Christians lived their lives as part of the wider community, even though they formed a distinct and close community as Christians too. They couldn't avoid contact with others even if they had wanted to. On the contrary, they seem to have rejoiced in engaging with those who didn't share their Christian faith and they used their social life, their involvement in the market-place and workaday world as a primary channel for evangelism. Not surprisingly, then, when the early Christian leaders wrote to the young churches they wrote about issues to do with real life, with money, status, family, work and slavery. The early Christians wanted to know how to behave as Christians both at work and in the world.

Some of Paul's typical teaching on these subjects is be found in this passage (3:22-4:6). It deals first with relationships in the world of work (3:22-4:1) and then in the world of the wider community beyond the church (4:2-6). Admittedly, dividing Paul's letter in this way is somewhat false. The 'household code' we studied in the last chapter is strictly a unit which stretches from 3:18-4:1 and the question of employment is all of a piece with the discussion of relationships within the family. That's because in those days the household was the base both for the family and for work. The question of wider relationships with the world is then a separate one on the agenda. But from our viewpoint, because of the way we live today, it makes sense to split the agenda between the family item and the work item. So, we now turn to what Paul has to say to slaves and their masters and then to the general comments he makes about how Christians should conduct themselves in the world.

1. In the working world (3:22-4:1)

Slaves (vv. 22-25)

At first sight, Paul's comments belong to a different era and have little to say to ours. Although slavery still exists in our world, it doesn't characterise the employment situation most of us know, even though we may sometimes joke about our bosses as slave-drivers and wanting 'slave-labour'. But before we dismiss this passage as irrelevant to our world we need to take time to understand what the institution of slavery was like in Paul's day.

Slavery was a widespread and commonly accepted feature of the social fabric and economic system of the Roman world. In earlier days many had become slaves because they had fallen into debt, but by Paul's time most were either those who had been born into it or were prisoners of war. It is estimated that over 85% of the population of Rome and Italy were slaves in the first century AD. Slavery certainly did have its dark side. Aristotle called slaves 'human tools'.[2] In 61 AD, the Roman prefect, Pedanius Secundus, was murdered. The law said that if a slave did not prevent the murder of his master, he would be put to death. Pedanius Secundus owned four hundred slaves, and hardliners in Rome exacted the letter of the law as a reprisal. All four hundred of his slaves were executed.

But there is another side to the story. For the most part the life of slaves was not intolerant. Some masters were quite indulgent towards their slaves and during the first century, the above incident notwithstanding, more and more humanitarian legislation was passed in their favour. Slaves could accumulate wealth and buy their freedom or start their own business. Whilst some were involved in menial tasks as labourers, many others became craftsmen or were engaged as architects, estate managers, tutors, scholars, physicians and administrators. Some have argued that slaves had certain advantages over freed men since they had a financial security the freed person lacked. Most slaves were set free by the time they were thirty and probably only served a maximum of seven years in servitude.

Although on moral grounds slavery may never be justified, one can understand why the historian R. H. Barrow concludes, 'slavery comes nearest to its justification in the early Roman Empire: for a man from a "backward" race might be brought within the pale of civilisation, educated, trained in a craft or profession and turned into a useful member of society.'[3] All this puts the slavery to which Paul is referring in Colossians in a different light from the cruel sort of eighteenth-century slavery we're used to seeing portrayed in modern Hollywood epics. It makes it more probable that his words have something to say to our contemporary, but very different, employment situation today.

One further comment is in order before we look at Paul's instructions to slaves. As before, we must bear in mind that Paul is not writing a general social ethic (even though what he writes has wider implications), but a set of instructions as to how Christians should relate to one another. The early church had a good number of slaves among its members[4] and a few who were slave owners. Through their conversion to Christ they faced an unprecedented situation. Slaves and owners alike were recipients of the grace of God. Neither had a prior claim on Christ or a superior basis for relating to him. Through Christ they had become brothers. How was that to affect the way they related to each other in their work situation? Some undoubtedly thought that their level standing in Christ had revolutionary implications for their relationship at work and sought to overthrow any idea that one had to submit to the authority of the other. Some slaves presumably would have been happy to take advantage of the situation and presume on their Christian masters, assuming that they would be forgiven if they failed to do the work required to the standard expected. Equally, masters could have taken advantage of their Christian slaves and assumed they would do more than was required and not ask for any reward.

Paul's approach was to encourage them to transform the nature of this relationship from within rather than to overthrow it altogether. The point is illustrated not only by the instructions he issues here, but by his handling of a specific situation we know about which had arisen at Colosse. Onesimus was a runaway slave. He was owned by Philemon who was one of the hosts of the church at Colosse. Onesimus had been converted in Rome under Paul's ministry[5] and had become closely associated with Paul's work and had proved very useful to him. Paul refers to him as 'my son' and as 'no longer a slave, but better than a slave, as a dear fellow believer'.[6] And yet, he still sends him back to his owner, recognising that Onesimus's conversion has not wiped out the fact that he is still Philemon's property. He asks Philemon to welcome Onesimus home, but not for cheap grace. Paul also recognises that a penalty for Onesimus's wrongdoing might be justly required. If so, he offers to pay it himself rather than for it to be exacted from Onesimus. In other words, whilst the outward form of the master-slave relationship is genuinely maintained (Onesimus is still a slave who is required to be obedient to his master), the inner heart of the relationship is transformed (they are 'fellow believers in the Lord'). The latter cannot do away with the former, but it can change it.

So, what did Paul teach slaves and what, through them, would he teach us about work today? Three significant issues emerge.

Work is worship (vv. 22-23)

Paul is realistic in his understanding of work. It is obviously demanding and may well be mundane. There will be times when it is difficult and totally devoid of excitement. That's life. Consequently, the slave is likely to cut the corner wherever he can. Truth to tell, there is a natural tendency in most of us to try to get away with the minimum and only to work harder when we are being watched by someone in authority. But Paul elevates work above the level of it being a necessity, an inescapable chore, or, merely a way to earn a living. Work is a spiritual issue. It is an act of worship, an offering to God of one's total life. So, slaves are to obey their masters, not just to win favour from them *but with sincerity of heart and reverence for the Lord. Whatever you do*, Paul tells them, *work at it with all your heart, as working to the Lord, not for human masters...* . Work is not a separate compartment from faith. It is one way in which faith will work itself out in life.

Paul wrote in this way about work because he had a firm grasp of the Old Testament's teaching about it. He knew that God designed human beings to work. It was part of his creation plan for us. We were never meant to be idle or enjoy uninterrupted leisure. True fulfilment as human beings would come about not by escaping work but accepting it. From the start Adam was told both in a general way to rule over creation and be fruitful and multiply and also was specifically given the task of working in the Garden of Eden and taking care of it.[7] So we must disabuse ourselves of any idea that work was a consequence of the fall. It was part of God's design for us before then. It was the gift of a wise Creator. And it still is.

The fall, of course, corrupted it. Part of the curse was that from that point on, the work in the garden was to be 'painful toil'. The ground was to 'produce thorns and thistles' and producing food came to require hard labour and sweat.[8] Adverse elements were to enter our world and taint our experience of work. So, while we remain a part of this fallen world our experience of work will inevitably continue to carry the scars of God's curse. For some it is drudgery, for some monotonous, for some alienating, for some a strict taskmaster. For others it is creative, enjoyable and fulfilling but, even for the most enthusiastic, it is never perfect. There are always alienating elements to it.

As Christians we live within the reality of the fallen world, with all the implications that has for our attitude to work, and yet, at the same time, we are called to redeem work and to offer it as an act of worship to God. Worship is not something we only do on a Sunday, at 11 am or 6.30 pm, when we gather together to sing a few hymns or songs, say a few prayers and listen to a sermon. It's what we do with the rest of our lives as well. It's what we offer to God whole time, not part time. So it has as much to do with 11 am on Monday, on Tuesday, and on Wednesday... as on Sundays. The Christian has seen, in Mark Greene's words, that, 'work is not an intermission from the main action, something we do so that we can then do other things, it is an integral part of the main action, an intrinsic part of our walk with God.'[9]

Paul flags this up by telling the slaves that they are to work *with sincerity of heart and reverence for the Lord...as working for the Lord and not for human masters.* He is the one whom we should always seek to please in the way we work. Understanding work as worship will affect the quality of our work and the integrity of our attitude. Since we're *working for the Lord*, we shall want to do the very best job possible. We won't be content with shoddy workmanship. We shall seek to imitate the standard of excellence we see in his workmanship even though we shall not always achieve it. And we will be people of integrity. We won't lay it on when we have to, just because some inspector is looking at us. That's no big deal. The Lord is always looking at us. No, we'll do good quality work all the time, whether we're being watched or not, because it's in our nature to do so; it's what our hearts are like.

The way we answer the phone, wash the dishes, teach the class, operate the machine, turn in an essay, advise our boss or do our deals, as well as preach our sermons, should all be an offering to God. To help us make them worthy sacrifices we need to learn to practise the presence of God, as Brother Lawrence put it. Lawrence was a clumsy seventeenth century monk who worked in the kitchens in his French monastery. From his own experience he taught the following principles:

1. The most holy practice, the nearest to daily life, and the most essential for the spiritual life, is the practice of the presence of God, that is to find joy in his divine company and to make it a habit of life, speaking humbly and conversing lovingly with him at all times, every moment, without rule or restriction, above all at times of temptation, distress, dryness, and revulsion and even faithlessness and sin.

2. We should apply ourselves continually, so that, without exception, all our actions become small occasions of fellowship with God, yet artlessly, but just as it arises from the purity and the simplicity of heart.

3. We must do all that we do with thoughtfulness and consideration, without impetuosity or haste, both of which show an undisciplined spirit; we must work quietly, placidly and lovingly before God, and pray to him to approve our toil, and by this continual attention to God we shall break the Demon's head, and make his weapons fall from his hands.[10]

David Prior, the Director of the Centre for Marketplace Theology, has recently pointed out how part of our difficulty in practising the presence of God at work is that we make a simple but important mistake in our thinking. We think about taking God to work with us whereas in fact he is already there.[11] We feel that he depends on us for an introduction to the workplace whereas the truth is he is the one who sends us into the workplace and will meet us there when we arrive. He quotes one city gent who has the right perspective. As he arrives at his office every morning and the doors slide open before him he says, 'Good morning, Lord.' It's that attitude which Paul is commending to the Christian slaves at Colosse and would commend as well to the Christian workers in the modern world. It's what turns work into worship. And it's what leads the slaves to *obey* their masters not just when they feel like it but *in everything*.

Work is rewarding (v. 24)
Again we are confronted by Paul's realism. One of the reasons we work is to get paid for it; to earn a reward. Money is still a powerful incentive to work even if it is not our ultimate motivation for doing so. And there's nothing wrong with that. The Bible is far less sheepish in talking about rewards than we are. We sometimes fall into a superspirituality which stresses that our salvation is by grace alone and not works to such an extent that we rule out the place of works and the rewards they bring altogether.

The situation Paul is addressing here is one where the workers might not get the rewards they justly deserve. What then? Should they protest, down tools and go on strike? There may be times in our more impersonal industrialised world where such action is necessary in the cause of justice, especially justice for the sake of others. But Paul's answer to Christians in the more personal world of the ancient household is 'no'. He advises, rather, that they place their experience in a larger frame of reference. *You know*, he says, *that you will receive an inheritance from the Lord as a reward.* As slaves they were not permitted to own property or receive an inheritance. That may be unjust. But God is a God of justice and one day will serve as the final arbiter in their affairs. Then they will discover that what was denied to them on earth is granted to them in heaven. They will be heirs of God's kingdom and receive an inheritance which outshines any they might have received down here. They will experience through Christ a true reversal of their fortunes.

So they are encouraged to look to the future and leave any injustices they suffer to God to sort out on their behalf.

Work is dignifying (v. 24)

Work is a dignifying activity, not a degrading activity. The apostle Paul was happy to make tents and earn his own keep by manual labour. In fact, he preferred to support himself this way rather than charge his hearers for the privilege of preaching the gospel to them.[12] This was in part because Paul was trained as a Jewish Rabbi and to them manual labour was never despised but seen instead as an honourable course to take. They did not adopt, to any significant degree, the ambitious mentality that is common among us which devalues manual labour and leads us to think that you work in a factory, or serve as a hospital porter, or stack shelves in a supermarket only just as long as you have to or until you can escape to a more satisfying occupation. Behind this attitude lay a good understanding of the doctrine of creation. God's creation of the world was seen by them as a manual task and that lent dignity to all human labour, however menial.

But there is another reason why Paul tells the slaves that doing their job well is dignifying. He reminds them that at the end of the day they are not serving a human master at all. Rather, it is the Lord Christ you are serving. It is unusual for him to use this particular title for Jesus Christ. It is as if he puts Lord and Christ together deliberately to emphasise the majesty and honour of the person whose slaves they really are. He's telling them that, no matter how humble the job they have to do, doing it for Jesus transforms it into something special. We can readily understand that on an ordinary human level, can't we? We may only be the cleaner, or the one who opens the post.... but if the person whose office we clean or whose post we open is Lord So-and-So, or Prince This, or, Managing Director That, then the job is elevated in status and we are elevated with it. It's no longer a menial task. Who we work for, who the master is, makes it worthwhile, and worthwhile doing with all our might.

I shall never forget listening to the testimony of a nurse at an evangelistic meeting, years ago. She was describing some of the less pleasant aspects of the task of nursing; talking about the frequency with which she had to empty bed pans and visit the sluice to clean up a patient's vomit. But as she spoke of it she radiated joy and love, not because she was a masochist, but because she was alight with the fact that in serving her patients well she was serving Jesus. His presence made her have a different approach to her work than that which could be found among her fellow nurses. Strange as it may seem, it was one of the most winsome and persuasive evangelistic addresses I have ever heard. She understood that serving the Lord Christ made even the smelliest and dirtiest task she had not only an act of spiritual worship but an act which dignified her as a human being. How powerful our witness would be if we could grasp this vision. Instead of enduring work, escaping from it as soon as we could and seeing it as a necessary evil, we would be transformed. Others would notice and ask us what was going on and we'd have a great opportunity of talking about the one whom we're really serving.

Masters (v. 1)

Looking at the number of words Paul uses, he seems, at first glance, to be grossly biased in favour of the slave masters. Four verses give some detailed instructions to the slaves, whereas he says all he wants to say to their masters in one brief verse. But it's the content not the amount of what he says which matters. The masters would probably have been few in number in the church. What he tells them may not be much, but its dynamite. He tells them that as Christian masters they must bear two things in mind in their treatment of slaves. First, they must behave with justice and, secondly, they must remember the judgment. The talk of justice and judgment was sufficient to revolutionise the attitude of any master towards his slaves.

The question of justice

Masters are commanded: *provide your slaves with what is right and fair*. What is right has to do with the abstract principle of justice. What is fair has to do with the concrete practice of justice. Literally it calls for even-handed treatment; for acts of fairness in the management of the slaves. Although Paul does not directly challenge the institution of slavery, such a call would do much to improve their treatment and conditions of work. Their lot would be considerably eased. It's even been suggested that the call for fairness was a call to provide them with an honest wage for their work rather than using them as cheap labour.[13]

Others, besides Paul, were concerned about the humane treatment of slaves. Plato, Aristotle and Seneca had all advocated it.[14] It was a live issue. But Paul is doing more than adding his voice in support of some of the Roman and Greek intellectuals who were his contemporaries. His advice draws on the call for justice found in the Old Testament, where the treatment of aliens, strangers and slaves is a major theme. The Jews were forbidden to exploit the weak and commanded to exercise special care of those who might be vulnerable. The sabbath commandment, for example, was originally intended to ensure that even servants got a day off and weren't kept working non-stop day after day.[15] In part it was given to protect the weak. Israel was regularly reminded that they once had been subject to injustice in Egypt and that their experience of slavery should be enough to prevent them from inflicting such injustice on others. So, they were told, 'When an alien lives with you in your land, do not ill-treat him. The alien living with you must be treated as one of your native-born. Love him as yourself, for you were aliens in Egypt. I am the LORD your God.'[16] The God of Israel has revealed himself to be a God who is passionately committed to justice. The evidence of the New Testament is that God has not changed his mind but continues to show concern for questions of human rights. So, in giving this command, Paul is not mirroring the secular humanism of his day but the true humanism which arises from the nature of God himself. Of all people, Christians should be genuine humanists and passionate about human rights.

The question of judgment

A second reason for saying that Paul is not parroting the voice of others is that he introduces into the command the question of judgment. His words might well have disturbed some of the slave owners and would probably have been humbling to them all. He reminds them that they are not autonomous individuals who have the last word, being answerable to no one. Rather they *also have a Master in heaven*. And, just as their slaves are accountable to them and subject to judgment by them, so the masters are accountable to God and subject to his inspection and judgment. He has the last word and if they have lived unjust lives and treated their slaves harshly they cannot expect to be treated kindly by God. Some who read this letter might have recalled Jesus' parable of the unjust steward with its clear teaching that the way we treat others will determine how God treats us.[17] The reality of future judgment is a powerful incentive to ensure that we live in the present world with compassion and humility.

Paul, then, may not say much to slave owners, but what he does say is sufficient to restrain evil behaviour and transform the relationship they have with their slaves. It leads them to treat their slaves as dignified human beings, not mere tools to be used; as people made in the image of God, just as they themselves were.

Crossing over the centuries, these words still have relevance to our very different economic system. Everyone of us who is a worker is called to work for the Lord and so to work with integrity and care; producing work which is marked by quality and trustworthiness. Every employer is called to manage with integrity and justice; treating their staff as people, paying an honest wage for their work, looking to ensure that they offer fair conditions of service and showing uprightness in all their dealings with those they employ. If not, one day they will be answerable for it.

2. In the wider world (4:2-6)

Paul now leaves the question of relationships in the household and addresses the broader question of how Christians should relate to the wider community. As is often the case when he draws his letters to a close, a number of short, almost abrupt, commands pour forth from his pen. The two themes which emerge from these verses concern the importance of prayer and the importance of wisdom.

The importance of prayer (vv. 2-4)

He begins by asking the Colossians to pray generally (v. 2) and then specifically for him (vv. 3-4). We know that the New Testament church prayed for governments, for general social issues and for the conversion of people outside of the church, believing it to be pleasing to God to do so.[18] Prayer was not just for the needs of those in the fellowship. So, here, Paul exhorts the Colossians to *devote (them)selves to prayer* and he uses the most inclusive word for prayer he can find. He's encouraging them to engage in every kind of prayer: in thanksgiving, in adoration, in petition, in intercession (that is, requests for others) and in supplication (that is, requests for yourself).

This in itself is significant. I've sat through many services when little, if any, praying for the world is done. It has usually been in a church which is a lovely, warm and supportive fellowship but one which has become quite introverted. They pray fervently for one another and about the most trivial of their concerns, but the immense needs of the wider world are neglected.

The letter began with Paul praying for the Colossians (1:9-14). Now he turns the tables on them and asks them to pray for him. Prayer is one of those ministries where our dependence on each other in the body of Christ is most apparent and our faith in God is revealed most clearly. It is a ministry everyone of us can engage in on behalf of others. Thank God for those elderly, often house-bound, believers I have known who have devoted themselves to prayer. I am sure that we shall discover in heaven just how vital the hidden prayer of multitudes of unknown saints has been in making the 'upfront' ministry of others effective. I shall never forget visiting one of my elderly church members one day, who seemed to be more excited than usual. So I asked her why. She was excited, she said, because the next Sunday we had a guest missionary preacher at the church whom she had never met but had prayed for for the past twenty-five years on a daily basis. Now I don't wish to detract from his gifts, which were many, when I say that I suspect that much of his effectiveness in ministry was due to her. And they had never met! She was a woman who did what Paul commanded and devoted herself to prayer.

What Paul asks them to pray for is no less interesting. We would be tempted to pray that Paul might be kept safe, or set free from the prison where he was and vindicated. He asks that they might pray that he might have further opportunities to proclaim Christ, whether from the prison cell or through being released, and that he might do so with a clarity which was persuasive. However experienced Paul might have been as a preacher, he does not presume that speaking the gospel is going to come easily to him. There are spiritual dynamics involved. The opposition of Satan needed to be overcome and doors needed to be opened.[19] The anointing of the Spirit was needed so that what was a mystery might be revealed to people.[20] And those spiritual forces, both bad and good, were only engaged through prayer. Prayer was not therefore an added extra for Paul's ministry, but the essential fuel which mobilised it.

The tone of Paul's language is also noteworthy. He seems acutely conscious of the opposition of Satan in this area. Prayer is not something which just happens, but something the Colossians must devote themselves to. It's going to require determination and persistence. Most of us know how true to life that is. How easily we're sidetracked from prayer. The least little thing and prayer gets interrupted. We can't manage it for a day or two and before long we find we're not doing it at all. We meet for prayer in our housegroups and spend our time chatting so that we only have a few moments left at the end to actually talk with God. We find it easier to do almost anything else other than pray. Even last century, Bishop J. C. Ryle said that he had 'come to the conclusion that the great majority of professing Christians do not pray at all'.[21] And it must be worse today. Prayer is a battle. Satan will do anything to keep us from it and employ any strategy to prevent us doing it. Human weakness and lethargy have to be overcome. Prayer doesn't just happen. We pray when we consciously set aside time, fence it around and commit ourselves to it.

The urgency of resisting the temptation to prayerlessness is underlined when Paul adds the phrase *being watchful*. It's a term that comes from guard duty! It's a word which recalls the Garden of Gethsemane where the disciples failed to keep awake with Jesus. The Colossians were under threat from false teaching and prayer was going to be a vital weapon in combating it. It was vital that they kept their eyes open to what was going on and their senses alert. It reminds us that there is an enemy out there waiting to seize his moment and trip us up; so we must keep alert or else we'll fall too.

Later in the chapter, when Paul speaks about Epaphras (v. 12), he returns to the theme of prayer as something which requires hard work and alert discipline. Epaphras, he says, *is always wrestling in prayer for you*. Clearly prayer is not always going to be a picnic. Often it's sheer hard work. Sometimes it's warfare. But it is a key weapon in our spiritual battle, so we dare not neglect it. Writing about the spiritual armour described in Ephesians 6,

Clinton Arnold describes prayer as the bottom line of our spiritual armour and concludes:

> Prayer is at the heart of spiritual warfare. Prayer is so vital because it is the means of intimacy and communion with the almighty Lord. Prayer is also an expression of faith. The very act of prayer is an admission that 'there is someone greater than I' and that 'I am not able,' ... Part of spiritual warfare is the recognition that you are not able in your own strength; you need God to hold you by the hand and fight on your behalf.[22]

These are passionate words Paul writes about prayer. Prayer is vital, as well as difficult. But it's important to keep it in perspective, which Paul does by telling the Colossians not only to be *watchful* but also to be *thankful*. As they engage in the contest with Satan, using prayer as their weapon, they are not to do so with fear and trepidation, as if they might lose, but rather 'with the confidence and assurance that their resources in Christ are more than equal to the potential challenges'.[23] So, for all the difficulties, there is every reason to be thankful.

The importance of wisdom (vv. 5-6)

Our relationship with God should be characterised by prayer. Our relationship with those outside of the church should be characterised by wisdom. Three things are uppermost in Paul's mind as he instructs the Colossians and, through them, us, about how to behave wisely in the wider world. Wisdom will mean that we shall be sensible in our actions, alert to our opportunities and gracious in our speech. These three aspects of wise Christian living all relate to our witness for Christ. They govern how effective, or ineffective, we are in our evangelism. Looking at the current state of affairs in the church it seems as if his words of advice are as necessary now as when he first penned them to the Colossians.

The theme of wisdom has threaded itself through this letter. Paul began by praying that the Colossians would be filled with spiritual wisdom (1:9); he characterised his own ministry as one of teaching with wisdom (1:28); he spoke of Christ as the fulfilment of wisdom (2:3); he warned that some wisdom, the wisdom of the false teachers, was a sham (2:23); and he encouraged Christians to admonish one another with wisdom in their worship services (3:16). The wisdom he has in mind here is the practical type of wisdom that we read about in the book of Proverbs, which leads to people living sensible lives, free from folly and stupidity. To be wise like this is more than being intelligent or clever. It begins with a deep respect for God, develops in the person who has a teachable spirit and leads to the growth of a person who is morally and spiritually mature. The wise person is one who makes doing right attractive and delightful and who demonstrates the obvious advantages of living in a godly way. It's about God's truth brought down to earth and being practised in the ordinariness of everyday life. If we want to win *outsiders* to Christ then we must behave with wisdom.[24]

It's amazing how some of the early Christians frequently lacked such wisdom. We do not know if Paul had a particular reason for mentioning this to the Colossians, but we know that there was a fair degree of folly to be found among other early Christians as they continued to live in ways which owed more to their preconversion days than to the fact that they were new creatures in Christ. The divisions, sexual immorality and spiritual excesses which were found at Corinth, for example, were hardly likely to commend the gospel to unbelievers. Paul had to write to the Thessalonians to instruct them to control their sexual passions and not to break up marriages and families because of lust.[25] Drunkenness, and a general lack of self-discipline, seems to have been a problem at Thessalonica.[26] At Ephesus they may well have faced that problem alongside a whole range of other ungodly behaviour, including lying, anger, filthy talk, stealing and sexual immorality. Paul's exhortation to them to put away pre-Christian behaviour concludes with words reminiscent of Colossians. He writes, 'Be careful, then, how you live – not as unwise but as wise...'.[27]

The simple point is this. How on earth did these early Christians think they were commending their gospel to an unbelieving world if they carried on living in the same stupid way they did before they became Christians? Who would be attracted by a message which was so patently ineffective? Was it not obvious to them that their actions were in flat contradiction to their words? It was to others who, consequently, would not bother to consider the claims of the gospel further.

Would that this was a problem which was to be found only in the early church. Sadly, the present day church betrays signs of still lacking basic wisdom. Unfaithfulness in marriage, premarital sex, abuse, gossip, greed and legal battles are all common among us. We still behave before a watching world with folly and then wonder why our evangelism makes so little impact. If we want to win outsiders for Christ, the church has to show a much greater concern to behave wisely than it often does.

The second aspect of wisdom is that of seizing the opportunity for witnessing to Christ when it is presented to us. We are to *make the most of every opportunity* just as we would snap up the bargains at a sale. The opportunity to witness will not always be there, any more than the bargain will always be available in a sale (although, admittedly, some shops seem to have permanent sales these days!). If we flunk the opportunity it may never return.

I have a painful memory of at least one failed opportunity. I was involved in a difficult pastoral situation where it was necessary to persuade a disturbed young lady of her need to get into an ambulance and enter a psychiatric unit for a few days. The professionals had been there for some time but had failed to persuade her and, short of using force which they were rightly unwilling to do, the situation seemed hopeless. At that point the family called in the pastor. When I arrived and spoke gently to her it was obvious that I was not going to succeed where others had not. There was only one thing to do and that was to pray. I prayed, silently but urgently, and prayer worked. Before long, and in front of open-mouthed paramedics, the girl meekly got up and walked with me into the ambulance. As they closed the ambulance doors they asked me what my secret was. Why had I succeeded where they failed? But then I enacted a greater failure. Instead of telling them that I had a powerful God and that prayer worked, I passed the question off, mumbled something stupid, and took some of the glory to myself. The opportunity was gone, never to return. We can never count on getting a second chance to share the gospel. So we must use the opportunities when they arise.

So far, we have applied Paul's words on a personal level. But he might well have had a more social and political application in mind when he told the Colossians to seize their opportunities. Persecution against the early Christians was spasmodic. But there were periods when it was widespread and severe. During such intense times it was difficult, but never impossible, to commend the gospel. Paul tells them they should evangelise while they had the freedom to do so. For all our Christian heritage in the Western world, it would be foolish for us to think that we will always have the opportunity to preach Christ. Already, in Great Britain, their are signs that the nation's commitment to pluralism and its unwillingness to offend those from other faith backgrounds, is curtailing our freedom to celebrate Christian festivals and speak Christian truth. A family in Lincoln were told recently that they could not put a cross on the grave of their seven-year-old daughter. The local authority pointed out a rule to them which stated that, 'Crosses are discouraged, as excessive use of the supreme Christian symbol is undesirable.'[28] Instead, they were given permission to erect a headstone featuring Mickey Mouse. We dare not presume that opportunity will always be there. So, to quote John Keating, the exhilarating English teacher in the film 'Dead Poet's Society', we must 'Seize the Day'.

The third aspect of wisdom in relation to those outside has to do with our choice of words. Our words need to be courteous, not arrogant (*always full of grace*); interesting, not bland (*seasoned with salt*); and thoughtful, not superficial (*so that you may know how to answer everyone*). Again, this is an area in which evangelical Christians often fail. We are often so anxious to see someone converted and so sure of what God has done for us that we come across as superior, boring and unable to listen. On numerous occasions I have watched enthusiastic Christians trying to witness to their friends and doing more harm than good by every word they spoke.

An MP told me recently that the Speaker of the House of Commons had attended a National Prayer Breakfast. As she was being escorted around the tables and being introduced to the guests, an inept Christian asked her in superior tones, 'And when did you last meet with the Lord?' I guess it is difficult to faze the Speaker. She must be used to far more unruly behaviour in the House than that. But it lacked courtesy. Quick as anything she replied, 'I meet with him at prayers in the House of Commons every day.' But she was not amused by such an ungracious and condescending question. Haughty speech of the 'we've got the answers and are safely on our way to heaven; you, poor fool, haven't and are on your way to be damned' variety does nothing to commend a loving and gracious Saviour. Nor does speech that does not engage with the real world, listen to the real aches of people and struggle with the real questions which they have. Paul says, 'In witnessing, be gracious, stimulating and deep.' People will listen to speech like that.

So, Paul presents us with the way in which Christ makes a difference to another set of relationships, those which are to do with work and the world.

At work,

- as employees, we must work with integrity and for Christ
- as bosses, we must manage with justice and in humility

In the world,

- we must commit ourselves to prayer
- we must relate to people with wisdom

All the research done into why people get converted shows that the overwhelming reason is not that they are attracted by clever arguments, but that they are attracted by winsome people. To allow Christ to transform our attitude to work and our relationships at work will, then, prove to be a powerful means of evangelism – far more powerful than having learned the pat answers to questions we think people are asking. To let Christ mould us until we show wisdom in our relations with friends, relatives, work colleagues and acquaintances is again a far more significant issue in reaching unbelievers for Christ than is adopting the techniques of the latest fashionable evangelistic strategy. Evangelism is about people and people are made for relationships. So, naturally, love is going to be the key.

And it all needs to be fuelled by prayer. Witnessing takes us into the realm not of human recruitment, but of spiritual warfare. Without prayer, nothing will be effective. With prayer, doors of opportunity will be opened, and the outsiders will walk through and become insiders in the community of God's grace.

10

In the Church
Colossians 4:7-18

[7]Tychicus will tell you all the news about me. He is a dear brother, a faithful minister and fellow servant in the Lord. [8]I am sending him to you for the express purpose that you may know about our circumstances and that he may encourage your hearts. [9]He is coming with Onesimus, our faithful and dear brother, who is one of you. They will tell you everything that is happening here.

[10]My fellow prisoner Aristarchus sends you his greetings, as does Mark, the cousin of Barnabas. (You have received instructions about him; if he comes to you, welcome him.) [11]Jesus, who is called Justus, also sends greetings. These are the only Jews among my fellow workers for the kingdom of God, and they have proved a comfort to me. [12]Epaphras, who is one of you and a servant of Christ Jesus, sends greetings. He is always wrestling in prayer for you, that you may stand firm in all the will of God, mature and fully assured. [13]I vouch for him that he is working hard for you and for those at Laodicea and Hierapolis. [14]Our dear friend Luke, the doctor, and Demas send greetings. [15]Give my greetings to the brothers at Laodicea, and to Nympha and the church in her house.

[16]After this letter has been read to you, see that it is also read in the church of the Laodiceans and that you in turn read the letter from Laodicea.

[17]Tell Archippus: 'See to it that you complete the work you have received in the Lord.'

[18]I, Paul, write this greeting in my own hand. Remember my chains. Grace be with you.

---

1. Those who took greetings (verses 7-9)

    Tychicus: a fellow-servant (vv. 7-8)
    Onesimus: a dear brother (v. 9)

2. Those who sent greetings (verses 10-14)

    Aristarchus: a fellow prisoner (v. 10)
    Mark: a restored failure (v. 10)
    Jesus: a co-worker (v. 11)
    Epaphras: a hard worker (vv. 12-13)
    Luke: a dear friend (v. 14)
    Demas: a future liability (v. 14)

3. Those who received greetings (verses 15-17)

    The Laodiceans: the church's family (vv. 15-16)
    Nympha: the church's hostess (v. 15)
    Archippus: the church's pastor (v. 17)

4. The final greeting (verse 18)

Lists can be boring. Every September a list of three hundred or so names arrives on my desk. Many of them mean very little to me. In fact, I receive not one list but several. They contain the names of those who will be studying with us during the year. So, the Registrar helpfully organises the same names in all sorts of ways. They're listed according to their surnames, their study groups, their accommodation, their personal tutors, their nationalities and their denominations. To begin with, they are just names. Reading through them is almost as unexciting as reading through the London telephone directory. But I know that before long I will read the list with entirely different eyes. Mere names quickly become real people. Each person named on the list has a story to tell of how they became disciples of Jesus Christ, how he's led them to Bible College, the gifts he's placed in their lives and what they want to go on and do in the future. In some cases the story is amazing. The stories are full of miracles, of daring exploits for God, or of costly sacrifice. In some cases they are harrowing, as some come from a part of the world which has suffered much. In other cases they're quite ordinary, but just as valuable. As time goes by, every person listed becomes so much more than a name. They become friends, fellow-travellers with Christ, people we get to know, love and respect. When that happens the list becomes exciting, it comes alive.

We're tempted to pass over the lists of names in the Bible quickly. They're dull, or so we think, with little of spiritual worth to teach us. We read through them hurriedly, if we read them at all. The worst ones may be in the Old Testament, not least because most of the names there are unpronounceable. But even those lists of names which occur at the end of some of Paul's letters, which usually have a bit more meat on them, are not lists we take too seriously. Yet, they're the names of real people, each with a story to tell. They're names from which we can learn quite a bit about the early church and our own spiritual development.

That's certainly so with the list at the end of Colossians. Ten individuals are named as having some significant role, with one other person, Barnabas, being mentioned in passing. They fall into three groups. First, there are the people who were to take

Paul's letter to Colosse. Next come those who were to stay with him but wanted to send greetings to Colosse. And thirdly, there are those who are especially named among the church at Colosse to receive special greetings. And what a mixed bunch they were.

1. Those who took greetings (verses 7-9)

Paul has arranged for two very different individuals to act as his postmen and take the letter he has written to Colosse and also to tell them a lot more personal news which isn't contained in the letter. One is Tychicus and the other Onesimus. One was a *faithful minister*, the other an unfaithful slave. But both now were useful to Paul and useful in the cause of the gospel.

Tychicus: a fellow servant (vv. 7-8)

Tychicus hailed from Asia[1] and very probably from the area of Colosse itself. He seems to have joined Paul's travelling band in Greece, gone on with him to Troas and then up to Jerusalem at the end of Paul's third missionary journey. Most likely he was sent as a delegate by the Asian churches to join Paul and to take their financial contribution to the church at Jerusalem.[2] That part of the story is explained in 2 Corinthians 8 and 9. After that he stayed with Paul and was used by him on a number of missions including being sent to Ephesus[3] and, on another occasion, to deliver letters; one to the Ephesians[4] and, of course, this one to the Colossians.

Tychicus stayed with Paul during some difficult times towards the end of his ministry and seems to have become very close to him. The way Paul speaks of him shows something of the deep relationship they had. He was a *dear brother* to Paul. Paul had, no doubt, come to depend on him and value his willingness to serve. When Paul was unable to travel himself, he could trust Tychicus not only to deliver his messages but amplify them without distorting them. Paul knew he could depend on him. It's his reliability which is picked up next as Paul goes on to call him a *faithful minister*. He served the church with loyalty.

Paul also speaks of him as *a fellow-servant in the Lord*. For

Paul, the bottom line is that Tychicus, like himself, is nothing more than a slave (which is the word used) of Jesus Christ. That's what really mattered. The possibility of becoming a slave was something which horrified every Jew and Paul, being by nature a proud Jew, would not have found it easy to refer to himself and others as slaves of Jesus Christ. Yet, the wonder of God's transforming grace in his life was such that again and again he boasts of being a slave of Christ Jesus.[5] He possesses no greater title than that. In our day we go in for inflated titles to boost our egos. People are Directors, Senior Managers, Presidents, Right Reverends. Even our Bible translations want to soften the blow and avoid calling Paul a slave and use the word 'servant' instead. But the truth is that the leader of the most successful missionary band that there ever was was content with the title 'slave of Christ Jesus'. It meant he never lost his focus (Jesus was his Lord) and that he always kept himself in perspective (his task was to be obedient). It's an honour, then, that Paul refers to Tychicus as *a fellow-servant*.

Tychicus shines as a trustworthy servant, in relation to Paul personally, the church generally and the Lord particularly. The trustworthiness we see in him is a quality which is all too often missing in Christian circles today. People do things when they feel like it just for a week or two and then give up. Steady reliability is a quality worth cultivating.

Onesimus: a dear brother (v. 9)

When you know his background the reference to Onesimus is a bit of a shock. Onesimus, as we mentioned in the last chapter, had been a runaway slave. We do not know the circumstances which caused him to abscond, but we know that one day he took flight from Philemon, his owner, and made his way to Rome. There he was converted. So, in the past, Onesimus had been anything but reliable. He had proved extremely untrustworthy. What is more, a common slave like Onesimus would have been a person of no real consequence in the ancient world outside the church. But what a difference Christ makes. Paul now describes him as *our faithful and dear brother*; terms which are very similar to those he used of Tychicus. Conversion had brought about a radical change of life for Onesimus. Reliability had replaced unfaithfulness and the slave had become a close member of the family.

Paul was not just making these nice things up about Onesimus. He's careful in what he says by way of a recommendation. We see this in the way that he uses two phrases very like those he used of Tychicus but does not overstep the mark by using the third. He does not call Onesimus *a faithful minister*, as he had Tychicus, for that would be untrue. What is more, Paul had evidence for the claims he was making. Following his conversion, Onesimus had stayed with Paul in prison and had become useful to him.[6] Ironically, Onesimus, which was a common slave name, means 'useful'. Paul is saying that through his conversion he now is able to live up to his name.

The introduction Paul gave Onesimus here, together with the personal letter he wrote to Philemon, should have ensured that Onesimus was greeted with a genuine warmth when he ventured into the church at Colosse and not with any degree of suspicion, whether openly expressed, quietly murmured or silently felt. The early Christians really believed that if anyone, no matter what their background, became a Christian, then the power of the gospel was such that they became a new creation.[7] The gospel genuinely made them into different persons and gave them new starts. In the early church they lived by that belief.

Do we today? The way I've seen some converts treated makes me doubt it. Rather than believing that the gospel can radically change people and release them from their past, many in the contemporary church seem to believe that 'a leopard can't change his spots'. So they go on being suspicious of people because of their past way of life. In this suspicion they are betraying that they do not truly believe any longer in the gospel as the power of God.

When Onesimus returned to Colosse he still had to face the music from Philemon. He was, after all, a runaway slave as far as the law of the land was concerned and there were severe penalties for that. Paul pleads with Philemon that the music be played in gentle tones rather than harsh ones. We don't know what happened. Philemon probably took Paul's advice and forgave Onesimus. But whatever happened between Philemon and Onesimus we know that the runaway slave went back to Colosse as a person with dignity, status and usefulness in the family of God.

Two very different people, then, were to carry the letter to the Colossian church. But through Christ they had both become trustworthy and useful servants.

2. Those who sent greetings (verses 10-14)

Paul was writing this letter in prison, as verse 18 makes clear. The prison was probably in Rome, although some have suggested alternative locations. With him there in prison were a number of companions and he now mentions six who are going to stay with him while Tychicus and Onesimus go off to Colosse. The thing that strikes one immediately is that three (Aristarchus, Mark and Jesus Justus) are Jews, while the other three (Epaphras, Luke and Demas) are Gentiles. If the gospel was powerfully demonstrated in the life of an individual like Onesimus, it was equally powerfully demonstrated in the collective life of the group who gathered around Paul. The great gulf between Jew and Gentile really had been bridged, and Jew and Gentile had been brought into the same family and now worked hard, side by side, for the same Lord. It was just as Paul had claimed it should be earlier in his letter.[8] The gospel actually worked!

Aristarchus: a fellow prisoner (v. 10)

Aristarchus was a common name. This one is likely to be the one who came from Thessalonica[9] and he had probably been converted under Paul's ministry there.[10] He had been with Paul during the riot at Ephesus[11] before accompanying him to Jerusalem and then travelling on to Rome.

We know little of him except one intriguing thing. Paul describes him as *my fellow-prisoner*. What's curious is that Paul does not use the obvious word for prisoner but a word that emphasises that he was a prisoner of war. Most commentators believe that this means that, unlike the others who are mentioned, Aristarchus was actually remanded in prison with Paul rather than free to come and go as they were. Either he was there under investigation himself and facing similar charges to Paul or, as others suggest, he had voluntarily asked to share the regime of Paul's imprisonment with him. If so, it would have been more than a gesture of solidarity, it would have been real solidarity. When we want to express solidarity with the homeless or political prisoners we sometimes make a gesture of sleeping rough for a couple of hours or being locked in a cage for a time. But we know it's not going to last long and that we shall soon be out, tucked up in our own warm beds or at liberty again. For Aristarchus, there would have been no such guarantee.

James Dunn[12] reminds us that the culture in which they were living was one which revolved around the values of honour and shame. In such a society it would have been a remarkable expression of loyalty and commitment to Paul for Aristarchus to voluntarily share in his imprisonment. But such is sometimes the call of love. If our love for one another is to be patterned on the love of Christ, who left his secure place in heaven to submit himself not only to our human condition but to death on a cross, then to share in someone's imprisonment when you don't have to is not such a far fetched thing to do.

Mark: a restored failure (v. 10)

How good it is to see Mark listed here. Paul and Mark had a 'history' which meant that they might well not have been on speaking terms. Mark came from a prominent Christian family. His cousin was Barnabas, one of the most attractive characters in the early church, whose ministry was to encourage others. Barnabas had been a close companion of Paul's on the first missionary journey and Mark had gone with them. He journeyed with them through Cyprus and sailed on to Perga. But Mark was perhaps more idealistic than realistic, a young man full of enthusiasm but without the stamina needed for this itinerant life.

The prospect of going further into the interior seems to have been too much for him, so he left Paul and Barnabas and set sail for Jerusalem.[13]

Some time later Paul proposed to Barnabas that they revisit the churches where they had preached. Barnabas was keen to do so but wanted to take John Mark with him. Paul was hesitant and had clearly not forgotten being let down by Mark before. He wasn't prepared to let it happen again. Hard as it is to believe, Luke tells us that Paul and Barnabas had 'a sharp disagreement' about the matter. How could anyone fall out with lovely, gentle, encouraging Barnabas? Yet, Paul, pioneering go-getter, Type A personality *extraordinaire*, managed to do so! As a result Paul went one way and Barnabas another, taking Mark with him.[14]

By the time Colossians was written, whatever bad blood there had been between them then had been sorted out, and Mark is numbered among the close companions of Paul. He had been a failure, perhaps out of naive and overzealous youthfulness. But he had now matured, probably due in part to Barnabas' careful mentoring. Whatever failings there had been were a thing of the past. Paul tells the Colossians, *if he comes to you, welcome him*. It sounds as if some of them might have heard that he had proved unreliable and weren't sure how they should react to him. But Paul had sent instructions on ahead to make sure that he would be welcomed without any cloud of suspicion hanging over him.

The last glimpses we get of Mark occur in the later New Testament letters. In the Second Letter to Timothy the aged Paul longs to see him 'because he is helpful to me in my ministry'.[15] Obviously, full reconciliation had taken place between them and there was a great respect and affection between them. Then, in 1 Peter 5:13, Peter describes him as, 'my son Mark'. Obviously Mark had become a companion not just of Paul in his old age but of Peter too. In fact, there is a tradition, stemming from the early church bishop of Hierapolis, Papias, that Peter passed on his memories of Jesus to Mark, who then composed his Gospel using them as the raw material.

F. F. Bruce commented that, 'Mark may have been the kind of person who always works best in association with a senior partner.'[16] If so, it's important to note just how great the contribution Mark made in this secondary role. Ideally placed, because of his background, to be a bridge between Jews and Gentiles, Mark became a reliable assistant to both Paul and Peter and, in addition, wrote one of the most graphic accounts of the ministry of Jesus Christ. No mean accomplishment for a second fiddle.

But what is most encouraging to me about Mark is simply this: he's a reminder that you can make mistakes and recover from them. The failures, especially of youth, don't rule you out of ministry forever. The bad decisions of the past can be overcome. The foolish claims we make, especially when young, when our tongues outdistance our abilities, do not have to handicap us permanently. Mark recovered, Mark learned, Mark matured and Mark became useful. And, if you're in that position, so too can you. But you might be wise to look for a Barnabas figure for yourself who, when you make mistakes, can set you on your feet, give you renewed confidence in Christ and wise practical guidance to help you mature in your gifts.

Jesus: a co-worker (v. 11)

Jesus Justus is the one man of whom we know nothing else. Jesus was a common name and it was just as common to distinguish one Jesus from another by adding a Roman surname to it. He joins Aristarchus and Mark, fellow Jews, in sending greetings. It would be nice to say more about this co-worker of Paul but there is nothing further which can be said.

Epaphras: a hard worker (vv. 12-13)

Epaphras receives more space than anyone else in this list of greetings. It is probably explained by the fact that he was well-known at Colosse since he belonged to them and was the founder of their church.[17] It may be that some were suspicious of him and that is why Paul takes time to commend him at length. Why they were doubtful about him, if they were, is not stated. It has been suggested that he had tried to uphold the true position of Christ in the face of the false teachers but that when he did not seem to be winning the argument, he left to go and seek Paul's advice about the matter. A less charitable interpretation is that when he failed to win the debate against the false teachers, his competence was called into question and he ran away to shelter behind Paul, just as a younger brother who is being bullied at school hides from his attackers behind his big brother. But all this is speculation. It may be that there is nothing more in it than the need for Paul to combat the general rumours about leaders that all too quickly spread in churches and cause unrest. After combating the false teachers for so long it would be understandable if Epaphras was exhausted and needed to get away and rest, though doubtless some would have been unsympathetic to this quite reasonable action and accuse him of desertion. Whatever the reason, Paul gives Epaphras a glowing reference. *I vouch for him*, he says, *that he is working hard for you and for those at Laodicea and Hierapolis.*

It's likely that Paul is alluding to something of the battle situation in which Epaphras has found himself with the false teachers, for the word he uses for 'hard work' is one which stresses the idea of strenuous toil, hard labour, and the struggle associated with warfare. Obviously, Christian leadership was taxing. It was demanding to find oneself seeking to stand for truth and correct error. It is quite wide of the mark to see leadership in the church as easy, full of privileges and making little demands on those who exercise it. It requires the skill and stamina of a general in a prolonged battle situation. Satan sees to it that it is so. Unfortunately, Satan, in fulfilling his strategy, all too often has church members as his allies. Those who should be fighting with Christian leaders against unbelievers, fight instead against Christian leaders by rumour, accusation, innuendo, suspicion and by opening the door to false teaching.

In this situation Epaphras had clearly distinguished himself. In addition to commending him for his hard work, Paul awards him four other accolades in his letters. Twice in Colossians he refers to him as a fellow slave of Jesus Christ.[18] Being a slave of Jesus was, as we have seen, Paul's favourite way of describing himself.

So to describe Epaphras in the same way indicated just how much Paul thought of him. He is described as *a faithful minister of Christ*.[19] Far from running away or misleading the congregation in his teaching, the pastoral leadership exercised by Epaphras was characterised by faithful and steady reliability. He, and his teaching, were trustworthy. Then in Philemon Paul speaks of him as a fellow prisoner. He was willing to share the hardship and shame of Paul's imprisonment. He was the sort of minister who would move beyond his own comfort zones. The quality of his character was seen in the way he made sacrifices and paid the cost of ministry. Finally, in the verses before us now, Paul speaks of him as a prayer warrior.[20] What a seasoned, well-rounded and committed Christian worker Epaphras was. What a model he should be to those of us who aspire to Christian leadership today.

What Paul writes about Epaphras as an intercessor is worth exploring. For a second time Paul uses battle language; this time to describe his friend's practice in prayer. *He is always wrestling in prayer for you.* As in his general ministry of leadership, so in his particular ministry of intercession he found that being a Christian was no picnic. Prayer was a struggle, a striving, an agony. His experience of prayer was like Jacob wrestling with God[21] or Jesus in the Garden of Gethsemane.[22] Prayer was no breeze. It was hard work. It required commitment. It took effort. St Benedict said that 'to work is to pray'. Paul said of Epaphras that 'to pray is to work'. How rare it is for people to grasp this. In a busy action-centred ministry all too often people require immediate access to their pastors. When I was in local church ministry I sometimes speculated on the reaction I would receive if I had told my church members that I couldn't see them when they wanted me to because I was too busy praying. Would they have thought, 'Oh, the pastor is working!' Or would they have thought, 'Oh, the pastor's skiving again!' Charles Bridges, a godly Anglican clergyman of the nineteenth century, wisely observed that, 'we shall find that our most successful efforts for our people were the hours – not when we were speaking to them from God, but when we were speaking for them to God'.[23] Epaphras knew that. Perhaps we would be more successful servants of Christ if we knew it too.

The burden of Epaphras' prayer for the Colossians is threefold. He prays, first, that they might persevere (*that you may stand firm*). They had an urgent need to remain faithful to Christ who, as the supreme centre of creation and of salvation, was more than sufficient for their needs. Epaphras defines what they are to be dogmatic about. They were not to take their stand on the false teaching or the trivial speculations of philosophers. But they were to stand firm *in all the will of God*. He prays, secondly, that they might be *mature*. Maturity would prevent them from being seduced by nonsense and sidetracked by ill-founded excitement. They would be able to assess what was right, good, deep and true, and distinguish it from what was wrong, bad, superficial and false. They would be able to live with reality without sacrificing the ideal. They would be able to find their way through the tension of the 'already' but 'not yet' aspects of salvation. Maturity would mean they weren't going to go off course or get knocked sideways. His third prayer is that they might be *fully assured*. His desire was to see them become people of settled convictions. Most of all, these were to be settled convictions about Christ. His concern was not that they might be able to repeat, parrot fashion, some answers against the false teachers, without really being persuaded themselves of the answers or without understanding what they were saying. His concern was that they should be deeply persuaded for themselves that Jesus Christ was the pre-eminent one and that they should be captivated by him, and him alone.

Colosse was fortunate to have a pastor like Epaphras, although they didn't appreciate him. From a human viewpoint, his deep spirituality, evidenced in prayer, and his deep commitment to the work of the gospel, evidenced in hard work, should have been more than enough ordinarily to build up the church at Colosse and protect it from false teaching. That it appears not to have been so is a reminder of the intensity of the spiritual battle we're in, and a reminder that leaders are at the sharp end of it.

Luke: a dear friend (v. 14)

Luke is best known to us as the writer of the Gospel which bears his name and the Acts of the Apostles. He comes down to us as a man who combined accurate historical research with unsurpassed artistry in story telling to write two books introducing us to the story of Jesus and his followers. But to Paul, he was something different. He was *a dear friend*.

Although this is one of only three explicit references to him in the New Testament[24] we can build up a fairly accurate picture of Luke. He was a Gentile, most likely born in Antioch of Syria. He was a medical doctor, hence, perhaps, his eye for detail. And he was skilled in writing the Greek language. One early edition of his Gospel tells us in the prologue that he was single, which might well explain why he was free to travel so much, capturing the events of the early church and occasionally joining Paul on his missions.

One speculative suggestion is that Luke and Paul studied together at the University of Tarsus. But this is pure speculation. However it was that Paul and Luke met in the first instance,[25] by the end of Paul's ministry Luke had become a very dear friend to Paul. At a later date, when Paul was forced to be less active in his travels, he writes somewhat plaintively to Timothy that 'only Luke is with me'. It seems that Luke was the one companion whom he'd come to depend on above all others and who never deserted him. Paul writes of him with real affection.

It's a very human picture. Paul was the great leader, the pioneering evangelist. He was always forging ahead into new territory and, as we've seen in his handling of John Mark, he was perhaps not always as sympathetic to those who couldn't keep up the pace as he should have been. Yet, for all that, he was still a man with a need for friendship and companionship. It gives us a glimpse of a man who was not emotionally self-sufficient, always on top and never dependent on others. Rather, Paul comes over as a sensitive and vulnerable man, just like the rest of us after all.

Leadership is often lonely. Perhaps inescapably so. At the end of the day the leader has to take the decisions, stand by them and take the responsibility for them, no matter how they turn out. At the end of the day the leader has to listen to all and not over-identify with any one group or faction in his team. At the end of his life, the Christian leader stands before God, alone, to give an account of his leadership. It's the very loneliness of leadership which means leaders need friends. The old advice that pastors should not develop friendships within their congregations because it could jeopardise their ability to minister to all was, I think, well-meaning but fundamentally flawed. Discretion is needed. The ability to listen even-handedly to all is certainly necessary, and tact is essential if one develops friendships within one's congregation. Friendships outside of the congregation may be ideal but are likely to be more distant and not to be as close by definition. We need friends. We were made for friendships. So why should pastors or leaders be denied them, if they observe the safeguards, among those whom they lead? To be a friend to a leader is a wonderful ministry. To listen to them, encourage them, distract them by enjoying some leisure activity together, joke with them, make them feel ordinary, bolster them and never threaten them or seek to invade their territory, is to be a wonderful provision of grace to a leader. Leaders need friends.

So, thank God for Luke the writer. Thank God for Luke the doctor. Thank God for Luke the fellow-worker. But, above all, thank God for Luke the friend.

Demas: a future liability (v. 14)

It is ironic that the Bible mentions Luke's name alongside that of Demas twice, but that the two occasions are so different. Here Demas, of whom we know very little, is mentioned as one of Paul's companions who sends greetings to the church at Ephesus. The next time we read of him we read that, 'Demas, because he loved this world, has deserted me and has gone to Thessalonica.'[26] While Luke remained loyal and available, Demas let Paul down and left him in the lurch. There is more than a hint that his reason for doing so was that some material interest assumed greater importance in his life than the work of the gospel.

It has been pointed out that the greeting from Demas to the Colossians is in sharp contrast to the more fulsome and affectionate greetings which have been sent by others. The mention of Demas is 'brief, almost curt'.[27] Perhaps Paul already had an inkling of the way things would develop. Perhaps Demas was already sending out signals of not being really committed. Perhaps they already knew that he was developing into a liability rather than an asset.

It is a sad but instructive case. Demas had the special privilege of working alongside one of the greatest evangelists, foremost theological thinkers, most excellently skilled pastors and strategic missionary leaders the church has ever known. Yet, he still gave up. Perhaps Demas had become over-reliant on Paul and his team and had not developed his own life of discipleship. So when a knock came and disappointment reared its head he had nothing to sustain him. It was his own decision to leave and his, and no one else's, responsibility. He couldn't pass the blame on to Paul for it. So, sadly, his name comes down to us today sullied as a deserter who, to our knowledge, never came back.

Being in the right circle of influence guarantees nothing. Church history and recent experience both testify to those who were once active for Christ and keen in their discipleship and then gave up. Other interests take over, casting a shadow over the authenticity of what they had done for Christ until then. None of us can rely on being under a good ministry, being associated with some work for Christ, or being friends of some spiritual leader as a means of ensuring our continuing discipleship. That's a matter of personal responsibility. Let's avoid adding our name to the list headed by the name of Demas.

3. Those who received greetings (verses 15-17)

The Laodiceans: the church's family (vv. 15-16)

The name of the church at Laodicea is forever tainted by the letter in the Book of Revelation which describes them as lukewarm in their commitment to Christ.[28] They prided themselves so much on their wealth and self-sufficiency that they did not see that they

were 'wretched, pitiful, poor, blind and naked'. Christ urged them
to learn from his rebuke and repent, not only so that they might
avoid the terrible judgment of being spat out of his mouth, but so
that they could have the joy of his presence among them restored.
But when Paul wrote to the Colossians, that was still to come.

At the time of his writing this letter, the Laodiceans were a
church down the road, ten miles away, with whom the Colossians
were in fellowship. John Donne famously said, 'No man is an
Island, entire of itself; every man is a piece of a Continent, a part
of the main.'[29] He might have equally said, 'No church is an island,
entire of itself, every church is a piece of a Continent, a part of the
main.' Some churches pride themselves on their doctrinal purity
and separation from any potential source of contamination. But in
doing so they are liable to fall into other temptations: those of
arrogance, self-sufficiency and pride. It is obvious that there is no
such thing as denominations in the New Testament. But it is just
as evident that each New Testament church formed close
relationships with others and was engaged in mutual
encouragement and support, often looking to those outside of
themselves for apostolic direction. The collection for the poor
church in Jerusalem mentioned in 2 Corinthians 8 and 9 gives us
an insight into that, as do these verses about the relationship
between Colosse and Laodicea. They recognised each other as
brothers and sisters in Christ and were to swap the letters they had
received and to read them publicly in their meetings.

The reference to the letter *from Laodicea* is an intriguing one.
Paul writes of a letter *from* the Laodiceans. Some say that means
it is a letter written by the Laodiceans. But it is far more natural to
read it as a letter written by Paul to the Laodiceans which was to
be passed on from them to the Colossians. If so, what was this
letter? J. B. Lightfoot,[30] a famous New Testament scholar of the
last century, set out the case for it being the letter which we know
as the Letter to the Ephesians, and argued that it was designed to
be a circular letter, to be passed from church to church. He built
his case on the fact that, with the exception of the address, there
are no specific references to the Ephesian church in the rest of the
letter. He believed that Tychicus would have dropped a copy of

the letter off at Laodicea on his way to Colosse to deliver their letter, the one we have been studying. That idea commended itself quite widely for some time, but although some modern commentators still consider it a possibility,[31] many no longer do so, mainly because they think that Ephesians was probably written after Colossians.[32] The truth is that we can only speculate about what this letter actually was. It is just as likely that the letter was lost at some stage and is unknown to us. The important point to draw is that already Paul's letters were being circulated and read in the house churches and given serious attention alongside other Scriptures. In Peter's second letter he refers to the way some people distorted Paul's letters and added the significant phrase 'as they do the other Scriptures'.[33] It seems they already carried the weight of apostolic authority and were recognised as foundation documents of the Christian church. That's a very good reason for giving them serious consideration now and not dismissing bits of them, as some do, merely as Paul's personal opinion.

So, from this reference to the Laodiceans, three significant issues emerge. First, a church can be doing well spiritually at one time but then, within a short space of time, run into spiritual difficulty, as the history of Laodicea, subsequent to this reference, shows. No church can afford to believe itself secure. We need to keep on our toes spiritually. Secondly, no church ought to function in isolation from others. Any local church is part of a wider family and can benefit from support and help from others as well as having support to offer others. If churches seek to function according to a biblical pattern they ought not to be independent but interdependent. Thirdly, Paul's letters were received and welcomed as the inspired writings of an apostle whose words were to be read and whose message was to be studied within the fellowship.

Nympha: the church's hostess (v. 15)

Paul also sends his greetings to *Nympha and the church in her house*. It has to be said that there is some uncertainty about the name. It comes in both a masculine and a feminine form although, to my mind, the weight of the evidence is to interpret it, as the

NIV does, as a woman's name. The church, we are told, met in her house. The early church had no buildings of its own for a couple of centuries and made use of the houses belonging to the wealthier members of their congregations as meeting places. In a place like Rome or Corinth there might well have been several such house churches meeting, perhaps occasionally coming together for a larger gathering.[34] One of the larger houses could hold thirty people, or if very large, maybe up to fifty for such worship and fellowship gatherings.

There is nothing improbable about a woman acting as the hostess of the church. Women played quite a prominent role in the leadership of the early church as the list in Romans 16 and the incident at Philippi, in Acts 16:11-15, shows. A number of women in the ancient world are known to have been quite wealthy business people who managed households, slaves and estates in their own right. There would be nothing remarkable about a woman doing so if she were either single or widowed. So, it seems natural to assume that Nympha would have been such a woman who after her conversion opened her home for the church. It also seems unlikely, as Robert Banks has stated, that she 'would take an insignificant part in the proceedings in favour of socially inferior male members who were present. To do that would be socially unacceptable...'.[35] Just because she was a woman did not mean that she would be relegated to the kitchen to serve tea and cakes (or the ancient equivalent). Her role as hostess would be much more substantial than that.

So much seems clear. But there is an intriguing question which arises from this reference to *Nympha and the church in her house*. Why is she mentioned and not Philemon? We know that Philemon lived in Colosse and had a church which met in his house.[36] Why isn't he mentioned here whilst Nympha is? Some resolve the puzzle by saying that Nympha was actually the hostess in the church at Laodicea rather than Colosse since she's greeted in the same breath, as it were, in which the Laodiceans are mentioned. Perhaps. It does make sense of verse 15. But there is no reason why there may not have been more than one house church in Colosse. Moreover, since Paul is going to write a personal note to Philemon and greet him much more fully there than anything he could have included in a more general letter, there is no real reason to greet Philemon here. Perhaps it was that Nympha needed special encouragement and recognition at this time. There is probably a very ordinary explanation to the conundrum which escapes us but which would have been perfectly plain to those who originally received the letter.

Archippus: the church's pastor (v. 17)

The last person mentioned is Archippus. He seems to have served as a pastor to the church, or at least one of the house churches, in Colosse. Paul's concern for him has to do with his work of service which he has *received in the Lord*. From Philemon,[37] where Paul describes him as a 'fellow-soldier', we know that he was committed to the work of the gospel. The same text might also suggest that he was a member of Philemon's household and may even have been Philemon's son.

Paul sends him a very clear, very direct message and asks the church to pass it on. It reads a bit more like a public rebuke than a gentle encouragement. *See to it that you complete the work you have received in the Lord.* With the passing of time and the lack of further information about Archippus we don't know what that work was. But it would have been clear to Archippus and presumably to those in the church too. It sounds as if he was in danger of failing to fulfil the commission he had received from the Lord himself. Was he weary? Was he in danger of giving up? Was he getting too discouraged to go on bothering? Was he getting side-tracked by some of the false teaching? Was he in danger of drifting? Had he already gone away? After all, Paul asks them to pass on the message, so it doesn't sound as if Archippus was around or else Paul might have addressed him directly.

Even though we do not know what precisely provoked Paul to make this remark, it is a challenge which is applicable to all the Lord's servants. If God is genuinely the source of our ministry he will also be our supply. All our service, from the beginning, through the continuation of it, right to its completion, is *in the Lord*. The

Lord 'is his sufficiency – his full supply for all its demands, and
for every occasion'.[38] Archippus, then, need not fear that he will
have insufficient resources to complete what he has begun. And
he has no excuse for giving up until the Lord relieves him of his
commission just as surely as the Lord gave it to him in the first
place. The temptation to coast in Christian ministry, if not actually
to give up, is strong. But every servant of Christ needs to complete,
not half-complete, the work the Lord has committed to them.

With these words to Archippus the list of greetings comes to
an end. The journey through the list has been like a walk around a
well-stocked portrait gallery. Here are real men and women who
made up the early church. Some were Jews and some Gentiles.
Most were men but one a woman. Some were free and some were
prisoners. Some were successes and some failures. Some were
well-known and some relatively unknown. Some were leaders and
some followers. Some were rich and some were slaves. Some were
zealous and some were struggling. Some began well but were
faltering, one began poorly but was now doing well. But they all
made up the church and together they give us an insight into its
early life and witness. The church today is just as varied. How
rich the family of God is because of its diversity – a diversity
which is brought into harmony because of faith in one supreme
Lord, Jesus Christ, who is the pre-eminent one in our universe.

4. The final greeting (verse 18)

The final greeting is brief. Timothy may actually have written the
rest of the letter, but Paul signs it off in his own hand – a hand, as
he reminds his readers, which is chained. The one who has written
these marvellous words about Jesus is not free to roam around the
world, nor to preach wherever he likes. His circumstances are far
from enviable. His liberty curtailed. But from that prison cell he
speaks an eloquent message concerning the one in whom all reality
is found – a message which still reverberates around the world
today because it is true.

His last word of greeting brings the letter full circle. *Grace be
with you*. It began with grace and it ends with grace. Grace is the

rock-bottom reality on which we all depend before the majestic King of the universe who reigns above every other authority or power we could encounter. Grace is what enables us to continue to live in Christ. Grace is what flows from Calvary where our enemies have been disarmed and shamed. Grace is what is needed for us to live a life where we set our hearts and minds on things above. Grace is what is needed in our relationships. Grace is what is needed to live responsibly before a watching world. And grace is what we find in Christ, who is our life. Reality is found in him.

References

Chapter 1

1. Paul Heelas, *The New Age Movement* (Oxford: Blackwell, 1996), pp. 2 and 15.
2. George Veith, *A Guide to Contemporary Culture* (Leicester: Crossway Books 1994), p.211.
3. Most standard commentaries will outline the options. But see especially John Barclay, *Colossians and Philemon*, New Testament Guides (Sheffield: Sheffield Academic Press, 1960), ch. 3.
4. Clinton Arnold, *The Colossian Syncretism: The interface between Christianity and Folk Belief at Colosse* (Tubingen: Mohr, 1995).
5. Acts 9:1-19.
6. Galatians 1:11-12.
7. 1 Timothy 1:2.
8. 1:2, 14, 16, 17, 19, 28; 2:3, 9, 11, 12, 15.
9. Romans 3:23-24.
10. Philip Yancey *What's So Amazing About Grace?* (Grand Rapids: Zondervan, 1997), p.64.
11. *ibid.*, p.15.
12. In 1 and 2 Timothy he adds mercy to the greeting alongside grace and peace.
13. Luke 6:44.
14. John 13:34.
15. Jurgen Moltmann, *Theology of Hope* (London: SCM, 1967), p.20.
16. Colorado Springs: NavPress, 1993.
17. John 1:14.
18. *Quadrant*, March 1997 (Christian Research Association).
19. Martin Robinson and David Spriggs, *Church Planting: The Training Manual* (Oxford: Lynx, 1995), p. 9.
20. Patrick Johnstone, *The Church is Bigger Than You Think* (Fearn: Christian Focus & Bulstrode: WEC, 1998).
21. John R W Stott, *Your Mind Matters: The Place of the Mind in the Christian Life* (London: IVP, 1972), p.23f. He is referring to Paul's use of these words in Ephesians 1:17-19; 3:14-19; Philippians 1:9-11 and Colossians 1:9, 10.
22. D A Carson, *A Call to Spiritual Reformation: Priorities from Paul and his Prayers* (Leicester: IVP, 1992), p.101.
23. *ibid.*, p.102.
24. Romans 12:1-2.
25. J. I. Packer, *A Passion for Holiness* (Cambridge: Crossway Books, 1992), p.31.
26. Matthew 5:1-7:29.
27. Genesis 1:28.
28. John 15:5.
29. *Op. cit.*, p.109.
30. George Ritzer, *The MacDonaldization of Society* (Thousand Oaks, Ca: Pine Forge Press, 1996). Ritzer traces the way in which the production of fast food both mirrors and shapes the values of contemporary societies.

Chapter 2

1. J. D. G. Dunn, *The Epistle to the Colossians and Philemon*, NIGNT (Carlisle: Paternoster, 1996), p.91.
2. Dermot McDonald, *Commentary on Colossians and Philemon* (Waco: Word Books, 1980), p.44.

3. Peter Lewis, *The Glory of Christ* (London: Hodder & Stoughton, 1992), p.239.
4. John 1:18.
5. Genesis 1:27.
6. John 1:1-2.
7. See, for example, Genesis 27 and 1 Chronicles 5:1.
8. Lewis, *op. cit.*, p.240.
9. *ibid.*
10. John 1:3.
11. Lewis, *op. cit.*, p.108.
12. Stephen W Hawking, *A Brief History of Time* (London: Bantam Press, 1988), p.127.
13. John 5:17.
14. Acts 17:28.
15. J B Lightfoot, *Saint Paul's Epistles to the Colossians and Philemon* (Grand Rapids: Zondervan, 1959), p.156.
16. Richard Bauckham, 'First Steps to a Theology of Nature', *Evangelical Quarterly* 58.3 (1986), p.239.
17. Available from EEN, 10 E. Lancaster Avenue, Wynnewood, PA 19096-3495, USA.
18. Psalm 24:1.
19. Ephesians 1:4.
20. Michael Griffiths, *Cinderella with Amnesia: A Practical Discussion of the Relevance of the Church* (London: IVP, 1975), p.54.
21. P. T. O'Brien, *Colossians, Philemon*, Word Biblical Commentary (Waco: Word Books, 1982), p.50.
22. Colossians 3:1.
23. Lewis, *op. cit.*, p.247.
24. F. F. Bruce, *Commentary on the Epistles to the Ephesians and Colossians*, NICNT (Grand Rapids: Eerdmans, 1957), p.207.
25. H. D. McDonald, *Jesus – Human and Divine* (London: Pickering & Inglis, 1968) p.140.
26. Genesis 3:14-19.
27. John Milton, *Paradise Lost*, Book X, 668-671.
28. Romans 8:20, 22.
29. Bruce, *op. cit.*, p. 210.
30. Richard Bauckham, *op. cit.*, p.240.
31. Colossians 2:13-15.
32. Romans 8:22.
33. Lewis, *op. cit.*, p.251.
34. *Authentic Christianity from the Writings of John Stott*, Chosen and introduced by Timothy Dudley-Smith (Leicester: IVP, 1995), p.471.

Chapter 3
1. Romans 1:21-25.
2. John Stott, *The Cross of Christ* (Leicester: IVP, 1986), p.192.
3. Don Richardson, *Peace Child* (Ventura, Ca: Regal, 1974).
4. See, for example, Leviticus 4:20, 26, 31 and 35.
5. Leviticus 1:3, 10; 3:1, 6; 4:3, 23, 26, 32 etc.
6. Hebrews 4:15.
7. Romans 12:1, 2.
8. Thomas Oden, *After Modernity .... What? Agenda for Theology* (Grand Rapids: Zondervan 1990). p.22.
9. See Acts 16:25; Philippians 1:29, 30; 1 Thessalonians 1:6.

10. The commentaries of J. D. G. Dunn, *The Epistle to the Colossians and Philemon*, NIGNT (Carlisle: Paternoster, 1996) and N. T. Wright, *Colossians and Philemon*, TNTC (Leicester: IVP, 1986) are particularly helpful in explaining these ideas.

11. See A. McGrath, *The Enigma of the Cross* (London: Hodder & Stoughton, 1996), p.165. The Luther quotation is from his *Sermon on the Cross and Suffering*.

12. *op. cit.*, p.116.

13. Ephesians 5:25.

14. Acts 10:9-23.

15. Acts 9:1-19.

16. Gregory of Nazianzus, *In Defence of his Flight to Pontus: Oration 11* 19, NP-NF, Second Series, VII, (Grand Rapids: Eerdmans, 1993), p.209.

17. In 1 Thessalonians 5:14 we have another example of Paul encouraging pastors to use a variety of approaches according to individual needs rather than mass producing.

18. See also 1 Corinthians 4:14; Colossians 3:16; 1 Thessalonians 5:12 and Titus 3:10.

19. There would be the need, for example, to look at his use of encouragement (*parakaleo*) and other strategies for an exhaustive list. See Derek J. Tidball, *Skilful Shepherds: Explorations in Pastoral Theology* (Leicester: IVP, 1997) for a fuller discussion of such matters.

20. Acts 20:28.

21. See, for example, Michael Jacobs, *Towards the Fulness of Christ: Pastoral Care and Christian Maturity* (London: SPCK, 1988).

22. 2 Corinthians 5:1-15 and 1 Corinthians 9:24-27 are two examples where this future orientation of ministry is expounded further.

23. Bruce Hindmarsh, *John Newton and the English Evangelical Tradition between the Conversions of Wesley and Wilberforce* (Oxford: Clarendon Press, 1996), p.114.

24. *ibid*.

25. Quoted in Peter L Berger, *A Rumour of Angels: Modern Society and the Rediscovery of the Supernatural* (Harmondsworth: Penguin, 1979) p.98.

26. Galatians 1:7.

27. Jude 3.

Chapter 4

1. Romans 10:9 and 1 Corinthians 12:3 both demonstrate how fundamental the confession of Christ as Lord was in the early church.

2. John Finney, *Finding Faith Today* (Swindon: Bible Society, 1994), pp.23-31.

3. The same word is used by Paul in 1 Corinthians 11:23 about the Lord's supper.

4. 1:12; 2:7; 3:15, 16, 17, and 4:2.

5. E.g. Numbers 11:4-20.

6. Acts 17:21.

7. Jonathan Sacks, *The Politics of Hope* (London: Jonathan Cape, 1997), p.209.

8. *ibid*, p.132.

9. Grace Davie, *Believing without Belonging: Religion in Britain since 1945* (Oxford: Blackwell, 1994), p.79.

10. A full discussion can be found in Clinton Arnold, *The Colossians Syncretism: The interface between Christianity and Folk Religion at Colosse* (Tubingen: Mohr, 1995) p.158-194, and in most of the commentaries.

11. Nigel Wright, *The Fair Face of Evil* (London: Marshall Pickering, 1989) p.143. This quotation, in fact, summarises the view of Walter Wink in *Naming the Powers* (Philadelphia: Fortress Press, 1984). Wright shares Wink's view at this particular point but not at all points.

12. H. C. G. Moule, *Colossian and Philemon Studies: Lessons in Faith and Holiness* (London: Pickering & Inglis, n.d.), p.144.

13. E. Peterson, *The Message*, (Colorado Springs, Co: NavPress, 1993).

14. H Dermot MacDonald, *Commentary on Colossians and Philemon* (Waco: Word, 1980), p.78.

15. Gregory of Nazianzus, *Letter to Cledonius the Priest against Appollinarius*, NP-NF, Second Series, VII, (Edinburgh: T & T Clark, 1989), p.440.

16. Galatians 5:24 and 6:15.

17. 1 Corinthians 15:3-4.

18. See Romans 4:15; 5:20 and Galatians 3:19-20.

19. Exodus 32:32.

20. Matthew 27:37; Mark 15:26; Luke 23:38 and John 19:19.

21. Martin Luther, 'Lectures on Galatians, 1535', *Luther's Works* Vol. 26, ed. Jaroslav Pelikan (St. Louis: Concordia, 1963), pp. 284 and 292.

22. Isaiah 43:25.

23. Isaiah 44:22.

24. Jeremiah 31:34.

25. The final words of this verse could either mean 'through him', that is through Christ or 'through it', that is, the cross. If God is the subject of the verse, as seems preferable, then either reading is permissible. If Christ is its subject, as some would argue, then the final words would necessarily be 'by the cross' as in the NIV.

26. N. T. Wright, *Colossians and Philemon*, TNTC (Leicester: IVP, 1986), p.116.

27. *ibid.*

28. J. D. G. Dunn, *The Epistles to the Colossians and to Philemon*, NIGNT (Carlisle: Paternoster Press, 1996), p.170.

29. Gustav Aulen, *Christus Victor* (London: SPCK, 1931), p.87.

30. Galatians 5:1.

Chapter 5

1. Peter L Berger, Bridgette Berger & Hansfried Kellner, *The Homeless Mind* (Harmondsworth: Penguin, 1974).

2. Clinton Arnold, *The Colossian Syncretism: The interface between Christianity and Folk Belief at Colosse* (Tubingen: Mohr, 1995), especially Part II, on which much of this chapter is dependent.

3. Acts 15:1-35.

4. 1 Timothy 4:3.

5. Proverbs 23:19-21; 28:7; Ephesians 5:5; Philippians 3:19.

6. 1 Timothy 4:3-4.

7. Romans 14:20.

8. 1 Chronicles 23:31; Ezekiel 45:17 and Hosea 2:11 for example.

9. Matthew 4:2; Mark 9:29 (mg); Acts 13:2 and 14:23.

10. Quoted in H. D. MacDonald, *Commentary on Colossians and Philemon* (Waco: Word, 1980), p.96.

11. Erica Heftmann, *Dark Side of the Moonies* (Harmondsworth: Penguin, 1982), p.117f.

12. It is possible to translate *the worship of angels* as meaning the worship practised by angels rather than the worship offered to them. But since the latter makes more sense in the context, and since we know that worship was offered to angels, that seems to be the preferred meaning.

13. Arnold, *op. cit.*, p.242.

14. 1 Timothy 2:5.

15. Mark 7:15.

16. It is a theme he develops most fully in Galatians. See especially 3:1–4:7 and 5:1-15.

17. Ronald M. Enroth, *Churches that Abuse* (Grand Rapids: Zondervan, 1992), p.144.

18. Hebrews 8:5 and 10:1.

19. Heftmann, *op. cit.*, p.282.

20. 2 Corinthians 12:1-10.

21. Galatians 5:22-23.

22. John 1:14.

23. Hebrews 12:26-27.

24. Romans 1:19-20.

25. Romans 1:25.

26. Romans 1:25; Ephesians 4:17-18.

27. John 14:8-10.

28. Roger Hargreaves, *Mr. Clever* (Handforth: World International, 1978).

29. Quoted by Martin Luther in 'Lectures on Galatians, 1535', *Luther's Works*, Vol 26, ed. Jaroslav Pelikan (St. Louis: Concordia, 1963), p.68f.

30. Heftmann, *op. cit.*, p.1.

Chapter 6

1. John Stott, *Focus on Christ* (Eastbourne: Kingsway, 1985), p.14.

2. *ibid*.

3. 1:8, 9-12, 29; 2:5; 3:15-16.

4. John 16:14.

5. *op. cit.*, p.10.

6. 2:20.

7. Romans 6:4-5, 8, 11.

8. H. G. C. Moule quoted by Dermot McDonald, *Commentary on Colossians and Philemon* (Waco: Word Books, 1980), p.103.

9. Titus 2:13.

10. Philippians 2:11.

11. Romans 8:18-21.

12. H. G. C. Moule, *Colossians and Philemon Studies* (London: Pickering & Inglis, n.d.), p.194.

13. See further, Ralph P. Martin, *Colossians: The Church's Lord and the Christian's Liberty* (Exeter: Paternoster, 1972), p.110f.

14. McDonald, *op. cit.* p.106.

15. NEB uses this word.

16. I owe this explanation to J. D. G. Dunn, *The Epistle to the Colossians and Philemon*, NIGNT (Carlisle: Paternoster, 1996), p.216.

17. James 1:19-20.

18. Murray J. Harris, *Colossians and Philemon. An exegetical Guide to the Greek New Testament* (Grand Rapids: Eerdmans, 1991), p.149.

19. N. T. Wright, *Colossians and Philemon*, TNTC (Leicester: IVP, 1986), p.137.

20. Hebrews 9:27.

21. Michael Griffiths, *Cinderella with Amnesia. A Practical Discussion of the Relevance of the Church* (London: IVP, 1975), p.78.

22. Mark 8:35.

23. 2 Corinthians 3:18 (NRSV).

24. Philippians 1:6.

25. Philippians 2:12, 13.

26. Genesis 2:9.

27. Wright. *op. cit.*, p.139.

28. For example in Galatians 3:28. On this occasion Paul mentions the gender divide as well.

Chapter 7

1. Quoted in Philip Yancey, *What's So Amazing about Grace?* (Grand Rapids, Mi, Zondervan, 1997), p.31.
2. David F. Wells, *Losing our Virtue: Why the Church Must Recover Its Moral Vision* (Leicester: IVP, 1998) p.97.
3. *ibid*, p.100.
4. Gertrude Himmelfarb, *The De-moralization of Society: From Victorian Virtues to Modern Values* (London: IEA Health and Welfare Unit, 1995), p.11.
5. *ibid*, p.11f.
6. Matthew 9:36; 14:14; 15:32; 20:34; Mark 1:41 and Luke 7:13.
7. Luke 10:33.
8. Luke 15:20.
9. Donald Messer, *Contemporary Images of Christian Ministry* (Nashville: Abington, 1989), p.85.
10. God the Father in Titus 3:4 and Christ in Ephesians 2:7.
11. Romans 12:3.
12. James Houston, *The Transforming Friendship* (Tring: Lion, 1989), p.20.
13. Romans 12:16.
14. Galatians 5:23; Ephesians 4:2; 1 Timothy 6:11; 1 Peter 3:15.
15. Numbers 12:3, RSV. NIV uses 'humble' but 'meek' is preferable.
16. Philip Yancey, *What's So Amazing About Grace?* (Grand Rapids: Zondervan, 1997), p.87.
17. 1 John 4:16.
18. 1 John 3:16.
19. They are well set out in Peter T. O'Brien, *Colossians, Philemon*, Word Biblical Commentary (Waco: Word Books, 1982) p. 203f., and Murray J. Harris, *Colossians & Philemon: Exegetical Guide to the Greek New Testament* (Grand Rapids: Eerdmans, 1991) p.164.
20. Philip Yancey, *The Jesus I Never Knew* (London: Marshall Pickering, 1995), p.21.
21. Colossians 1:18.
22. Matthew Henry, *Commentary on the Whole Bible*, VI (London: Marshall, Morgan and Scott, 1953 edn), p.764.
23. Leroy Eims, *Be The Leader You Were Meant To Be* (Wheaton, II: Victor Books, 1975), p.19.
24. Acts 17:11.
25. 1 Corinthians 14:26-33.
26. The phrase comes from Gordon Fee, *God's Empowering Presence* (Peabody: Hendrickson, 1994), p. 653. He has a particularly good discussion of the meaning of this verse, pp. 648-657.
27. 1 Corinthians 3:21.
28. David Coffey, *Build that Bridge: Conflict and Reconciliation in the Church* (Eastbourne Kingsway, 1986), p.98f.
29. Herbert M. Carson, *The Epistles of Paul to the Colossians and Philemon* TNTC (London: Tyndale Press, 1960), p.89.
30. John Barclay, *Colossians and Philemon*, New Testament Guides (Sheffield: Sheffield Academic Press, 1996) p.88.

Chapter 8

1. *Supporting Families: A Consultation Document* (London: Home Office, 1998), p.4.
2. For the biblical background to this argument see, Bruce Malina, *The New Testament World: Insights from Cultural Anthropology* (London: SCM, 1981), pp. 51-70. For a

contemporary application, see Jonathan Sacks, *The Politics of Hope* (London: Jonathan Cape, 1997), and p.90f. where individualism was discussed.

3. Genesis 2:18.

4. 2 Corinthians 5:15.

5. Mark 5:19.

6. Ephesians 5:22-33; 1 Timothy 2:1-15; 5:1-2; 6:1-2. 17-19; Titus 2:1–3:8 and 1 Peter 2:13–3:7.

7. Mark 10:45.

8. Romans 12:19.

9. Ben Witherington III, *Women in the Earliest Churches*, SNTS Monograph 59 (Cambridge: Cambridge University Press, 1988), pp. 42-47.

10. 1 Corinthians 7:3, 4.

11. 1 Corinthians 15:28.

12. 1 Corinthians 16:16; Ephesians 5:21; Romans 13:1; 1 Peter 2:13 and Hebrews 13:17.

13. Philippians 2:6-11.

14. Richard Foster, *Celebration of Discipline* (London: Hodder & Stoughton, 1980), p.195.

15. *ibid.*

16. Ephesians 5:21.

17. *op. cit.*, p.98.

18. Ephesians 5:25.

19. The Greek words for love were 'orge' (affection), 'philia' (friendship), 'eros' (sexual love) and 'agape' (self-giving love).

20. P. T. O'Brien, *Colossians, Philemon*, Word Biblical Commentary (Waco: Word, 1982), p.223.

21. Margaret Y. MacDonald, *The Pauline Churches: A Socio-historical Study of Institutionalisation in the Pauline and Deutero-Pauline Writings*, SNTS Monograph 60 (Cambridge: Cambridge University Press, 1988) pp.102-104.

22. See Exodus 20:12; Deuteronomy 6:4-9; Proverbs 1–7.

23. The Father referred to here is his heavenly Father. We know little about his relationship with Joseph, his earthly father, but a case can be made out that his relationship with Joseph would have mirrored that of his relationship with God the father, and *vice versa*. For a recent discussion see, Jack Dominian, *One Like Us: A Psychological Interpretation of Jesus* (London: Darton, Longman and Todd, 1998), pp.71-83.

24. John 15:10.

25. Hebrews 5:8.

26. N. T. Wright, *Colossians and Philemon* TNTC (Leicester: IVP, 1986), p.148.

27. Eva Lassen, 'The Roman Family: Ideal and Metaphor' in *Constructing Early Christian Families* ed. Halvor Moxnes (London and New York: Routledge, 1997), p.105.

28. *ibid.* p.107.

29. Quoted in *The Observer*, 25th October 1998, p.18.

Chapter 9

1. Mark Greene, 'Is Anybody Listening?' *Anvil* 14, 4 (1997), p.286. To help preachers improve in this area Mark has developed a tool entitled *The Three Eared Preacher*, which is available from the Open Learning Department, London Bible College, Green Lane, Northwood, Middx, HA6 2UW.

2. Quoted in A. A. Rupprecht, 'Slave, Slavery', *Dictionary of Paul and his Letters*, ed. Gerald F. Hawthorne and Ralph P. Martin (Leicester: IVP, 1993), p.881.

3. R. H. Barrow, *The Romans* (Harmondsworth: Penguin, 1949), pp. 99f.

4. 1 Corinthians 1:26.

5. Philemon 10.
6. Philemon 16.
7. Genesis 1:26-28 and 2:15.
8. Genesis 3:17-19.
9. Mark Greene, *Thank God it's Monday* (London: Scripture Union, 1997 edn), p.33.
10. Brother Lawrence, *The Practice of the Presence of God*, trans. E M Blaiklock (London: Hodder & Stoughton, 1981) pp.68f.
11. He made this comment in a recently produced video called *God & work* (Northwood: LBC, 1998). See further his *Practising God's Presence at Work* (New Malden: CMT, n.d.).
12. 1 Corinthians 9:1-18 and 1 Thessalonians 2:6-9.
13. P. T. O'Brien, *Colossians, Philemon*, Word Biblical Commentary (Waco: Word Books, 1982), p.232.
14. *ibid.*
15. Deuteronomy 5:12-15.
16. Leviticus 19:33-34; see also, Deuteronomy 15:12-15; 24:17-22.
17. Matthew 18:21-35.
18. 1 Timothy 2:1-4.
19. 1 Corinthians 16:9.
20. 2 Corinthians 4:1-6.
21. J. C. Ryle, *Practical Religion* (London: James Clarke & Co., 1959 edn), p.50.
22. Clinton Arnold, *3 Crucial Questions about Spiritual Warfare* (Grand Rapids: Baker, 1997), p.43.
23. J. D. G. Dunn, *The Epistle to the Colossians and to Philemon* NIGTC (Carlisle: Paternoster, 1996), p.262.
24. See Daniel Estes, *Hear, My Son: Teaching and Learning in Proverbs 1-9* (Leicester: Apollos, 1997), p.75.
25. 1 Thessalonians 4:1-8.
26. 1 Thessalonians 5:6-8.
27. Ephesians 4:25-18.
28. *The Times*, 6 June, 1998.

Chapter 10
1. Acts 20:4.
2. F F Bruce, *The Pauline Circle* (Exeter: Paternoster Press, 1985), p.87.
3. 2 Timothy 4:12. See also Titus 2:12.
4. Ephesians 6:21.
5. Romans 1:1; 2 Corinthians 4:5; Galatians 1:10; Titus 1:1.
6. Philemon 10.
7. 2 Corinthians 5:17.
8. Colossians 3:11.
9. Acts 20:4; 27:2.
10. Acts 17:1-9.
11. Acts 19:29.
12. J. D. G. Dunn, *The Epistle to the Colossians and Philemon* NIGNT (Carlisle: Paternoster, 1996), p.276.
13. Acts 13:13. The reference there is to John. Mark had two names: John was his Hebrew name and Mark his Greek one.
14. Acts 15:36-41.
15. 2 Timothy 4:11.
16. *op. cit.*, p.75.

17. Colossians 1:7.

18. Colossians 1:7 and 4:12.

19. Colossians 1:7.

20. Verse 23.

21. Genesis 32:22-32.

22. Luke 22:39-46.

23. Charles Bridges, *The Christian Ministry* (London: Banner of Truth, 1958. First published 1849), p.149.

24. The others are in 2 Timothy 4:11 and Philemon 24. For further details see Bruce, *op. cit.*, pp.35-43.

25. 2 Timothy 4:10.

26. 2 Timothy 4:10.

27. Dunn, *op. cit.*, p.283.

28. Revelation 3:14-22.

29. *Devotions*, XII.

30. J. B. Lightfoot, *Saint Paul's Epistles to the Colossians and Philemon* (Grand Rapids, Mi, Zondervan, 1959 reprint of 1879 edition). pp.33, 243f. and 274-300.

31. For example, N. T. Wright, *Colossians and Philemon* TNTC (Leicester: IVP, 1986), pp.160f.

32. See P. T. O'Brien, *Colossians, Philemon*, Word Biblical Commentary (Waco: Word, 1982), pp.25f.

33. See 2 Peter 3:15-16.

34. Some see 1 Corinthians 14:23 as an example of this wider gathering.

35. R Banks, *Paul's Idea of Community* (Exeter: Paternoster, 1980), p.127.

36. Philemon 1, 2.

37. Philemon 2.

38. Dermot McDonald, *Commentary on Colossians and Philemon* (Waco: Word Books) pp.145f.